A MEMOIR

ONE-MISSION MAN

An American POW's Struggle to Survive Hitler's Nazi Prison Camp

DAVID RIRIE
with
ROGER W. NIELSEN
and
CAROLYN RIRIE NIELSEN

TETON CREST

ONE-MISSION MAN
An American POW's Struggle to Survive Hitler's Nazi Prison Camp

COPYRIGHT © 2012 Teton Crest Publishing

All rights reserved. Except as permitted under the United States Copyright Act of 1976, no part of this book may be reproduced or transmitted in any form or by any means, electronic or mechanical, including photocopying, recording or by any information storage or retrieval system, without prior permission in writing from the publisher, Teton Crest Publishing. Scanning, uploading and distributing this book via the Internet or via any other means without permission of the publisher is illegal and punishable by law.

All rights reserved including the right of reproduction in whole or in any part or form. Unless otherwise noted, all photos are courtesy of the David and Jody Ririe family, Max and Mar Dean Ririe, the David and Leah Ann Ririe family, and the National Archives.

Library of Congress Cataloging in Publication Data:

Ririe, David, 1921-; Nielsen, Roger W., 1948; Nielsen, Carolyn Ririe, 1949.
    One-Mission Man : a memoir/David Ririe with Roger W. Nielsen and Carolyn Ririe Nielsen,
    Includes references and index
    ISBN 978-0-9820355-9-7 (perfect bound)
    1. Ririe, David, 1921 –. 2. World War II – Germany – Memoir
    3. Prisoner of War – Germany – Memoir 4. Mormons – United States – Memoir
    I. Nielsen, Carolyn Ririe, 1949 –; Nielsen, Roger W., 1948 – II. Title

---

Cover design: Ethan Nielsen Arts, Gainesville, Florida

Published by

TETON CREST PUBLISHING
Idaho Falls, Idaho

Visit us at tetoncrest.com

A MEMOIR

ONE-MISSION MAN

An American POW's Struggle to Survive Hitler's Nazi Prison Camp

DAVID RIRIE

with
ROGER W. NIELSEN
and
CAROLYN RIRIE NIELSEN

TETON CREST

CONTENTS

Dedication/Acknowledgements		iv
Preface		v
Chapter 1	The Mission to Poland	1
Chapter 2	Snake River Country	9
Chapter 3	Heeding the Call	19
Chapter 4	Cadet Ririe	25
Chapter 5	Aptitude Determinates	34
Chapter 6	Bombing Basics	47
Chapter 7	Wings and a Commission	57
Chapter 8	Days of Tedium	66
Chapter 9	Flying High	73
Chapter 10	Numbered Days	82
Chapter 11	Dulag Luft	90
Chapter 12	Stalag Luft 1	99
Chapter 13	Unrelenting Boredom	107
Chapter 14	Tunneling Out	117
Chapter 15	Fighting Chance	137
Chapter 16	Turning Point	144
Chapter 17	Chaos Reigns	151

Chapter 18	Disquiet in Camp	160
Chapter 19	Final Days	168
Chapter 20	Camp Lucky Strike	174
Chapter 21	Days of Frustration	184
Chapter 22	Over the Ocean Blue	193
Chapter 23	Overland Trek	199
Chapter 24	Citizen Ririe	211
Afterword		218
Photographs/Illustrations		126
Source Notes		219
Bibliography		230
Index		233
About the Authors		240

DEDICATION

This book is dedicated to my fellow prisoners of war who were with me in Stalag Luft 1 during World War II.

ACKNOWLEDGEMENTS

I acknowledge the assistance of the following members of my family: My wife Joanne whose undying encouragement has been omnipresent during sixty-five years of my life. I also give thanks to my daughter Nancy Ririe Simkins who assisted in the preparation of the manuscript.

PREFACE

Part of this narrative I draw from daily entries that I wrote in my journal in May 1945 after my liberation by the Russians from Stalag Luft 1. I would have written a diary while I was in prison, but most of the time I didn't have paper to write on. Moreover, if the Germans discovered I had a diary, they would have confiscated it. Needless to say, most of my days in the camp were very boring anyway.

Within these pages I refer often to food and how much the lack thereof consumed my mind. Of course, the famine I experienced was relatively minor, especially in comparison to the hungry people of the world. Yet, the days in the stalag when food was scarce and my body and mind were weak from lack of nutrition, food in any form was a constant concern for me. Changing my focus required a concerted effort. Even now, many decades after the March famine in Stalag Luft 1, I often wake up in the night and feel hungry. Thankfully, we have a full refrigerator.

I still shudder when I remember shivering in the snow as we stood to be counted, dressing in all of my extra clothes before hitting the sack, and trying to sleep on a canvas cot with a single blanket as temperatures dropped into the teens while rain and wind beat against a leaky tent at Camp Lucky Strike. These were difficult times for me and other prisoners of war (POWs). Incidentally, I sleep with my socks on.

Gratefully, my suffering was minimal compared to airmen held in Japanese prisons, who were unmercifully tortured. Or the men in other stalags the Germans force-marched across Germany in winter and the spring of 1945. Russians in the east were about to overrun the stalag camps and the Germans obliged the POWs to hike westward. Among that group were my crew members John Russell and Vincent Muffoletto. At the time John was ill and Vincent prodded him on by saying, "Come on John, we can make it." At times Vincent carried John. They did make it and they smile today when they talk about it.

For a while after the war I felt animosity toward the German and Japanese people, but that had nothing to do with race. After all, they were enemies. I can truthfully say that attitude has been set aside. The meritorious service of the Japanese Americans who fought in battles against the Germans have my heartfelt gratitude and admiration.

In these pages I write about numerous breaches of military discipline, especially in the first few days after our liberation when Colonel Hubert "Hub" Zemke, the Senior Allied Officer, and his staff were trying to establish control. I hope the readers of this account won't judge me or the other absent-without-leave (AWOL) ex-POWs too harshly for our behavior.

I believe part of the reason for our carelessness was that Army Air Corps members were less disciplined to military "spit and polish" than our colleagues in the Coast Guard, Navy, the land-based Army, and especially the Marines. We were cocky and probably a pain in the neck to other service branches and our superior officers. Even our jaunty salutes attested to our aversion to discipline.

Yet, when we were in the air formation, we were extremely disciplined. Our very lives depended on our exactness, our skills, our obedience to orders, and our full cooperation within the squadron. One didn't become a pilot or a navigator, a radio operator, a flight engineer, a gunner, or — as in my case — a bombardier without discipline. With that in mind I hope our unruly behavior in the days immediately following our liberation will not tarnish our legacy.

Regretfully, my journal writing is not always complimentary to our senior officers, or "wheels," as we designated them. In the heat of those moments, I did not stop to think of the pressure those men were under. The war in Europe was over, but the work wasn't done by any means. Added to the challenge of mop-up operations, removal of booby traps, providing for the occupying forces, punishment of men responsible for war crimes—all of whom were making themselves scarce—was the responsibility of coordinating affairs with allies and giving aid to our starving defeated enemies.

Furthermore, they had to worry about transferring men and resources to the Pacific Theatre. On top of it all came increasingly impatient ex-POWs demanding to quickly go home to the United States. The magnitude of the problems these leaders solved was remarkable. They deserve medals for their service.

The entertainment amenities the Army provided for us at Camp Lucky Strike were outstanding. Motion pictures and live performances by talented performers entertaining the troops did wonders to improve our morale in a trying situation. I am grateful to those entertainers for their contributions, for making me feel appreciated and for providing fun-filled hours during a very boring time. Their support of the military was unsurpassed. Some, like band leader Glenn Miller, lost their lives while striving to keep our morale high. Others gave freely of their talents, but in my opinion, none matched Bob Hope in the generosity of his contributions to the troops.

I also pay grateful respect to the Red Cross and the YMCA. The largesse of these two organizations not only helped us survive our incarceration, but thanks to the food, books, sports equipment, and other materials, it made our lives as POWs tolerable.

—DAVID RIRIE
Salinas, California

CHAPTER 1

The Mission to Poland

Before dawn on April 11, 1944, my B-17 flight crew gathered in the briefing room of the 388th Bomber Group of the U.S. Eighth Air Force in the small town of Knettishall, Suffolk, England. A major explained that the purpose of our mission, the first for us with our shiny new B-17 Flying Fortress bomber, was to bomb an aircraft plant in Posen, Poland, and the headquarters of Germany's 21st Military Region (Wehrkreise). The flight was lengthy, 675 miles (1,086.5 kilometers) one way. In fact, the map on the wall of the briefing room didn't display the entire route. Moreover, we were informed that the weather might be bad and were assigned secondary targets of opportunity in case we couldn't see our target at Posen.

Our pilot, Second Lieutenant Edmund J. Ely; the copilot, Second Lieutenant Frederick H. Pratt; the navigator, Second Lieutenant William L. Ellis; and I, the bombardier, Second Lieutenant David Ririe, had been awakened at 4:00 a.m. by a staff sergeant at our Nissan hut, a corrugated metal building with round roof. The remaining six members of our ten-man crew were enlisted men, and they slept in another area. After showering and dressing, we walked in darkness to the mess hall for breakfast. All lights were off to protect the base from a night raid by the German air force, the notorious Luftwaffe.

At 5:15 a.m. the briefing for the 388th's ninety-second mission began. We were in the left wing position of element one of A Group, the lead squadron for the 45th Combat Wing, flying in a composite pairing with the 96th Bomber Group. Together we made up Combat Wings Three and Four of the Third Air Division. Our Wing was to follow Wing Four to Posen.

By 5:30 a.m. we were on our feet shaking hands with the other flight crews wishing each other good luck and a safe journey. All of us were confident and eager to prove ourselves in combat. A truck carried us to a supply shed to pick up parachutes and gear before being shuttled to the plane where Ely had already started the four powerful Pratt and Whitney engines. The propellers' strong backwash pressed the hatch door against our bodies as I held it open for Ellis. He grasped the door frame with his hands, tossed his legs above his head and entered the plane feet first like an acrobat returning from a swing on a high wire. I followed him a moment later as the rest of the crew boarded through doors closer to their stations in the plane. As the crew checked equipment, Ely maneuvered the mammoth B-17 into the A Group lineup awaiting takeoff. By 7:13 a.m. all aircraft on the mission were airborne.

Around us dozens of planes slipped into formations, assembling in groups of eighteen to form a combat wing. Once formed, combat wings joined with other combat wings to make up a strike force. As soon as a formation was ready, three spare planes that had taken off as standbys turned around and flew back to base as planned. One B-17 aborted with mechanical problems.

Over 900 B-17s and B-24s from the Eighth Air Force left England that morning with the goal to destroy Focke-Wulf and Junkers aircraft production centers in Eastern Germany. We were given only six P-51 and four P-38 fighter groups as escort, which was highly inadequate with the bombers so widely dispersed. As one of 274 B-17s from the Third Bombardment Division forming the strike force we headed east over the North Sea and tested our guns. When we fired together the whole plane shook. The noise was deafening, the odor of cordite, a smokeless explosive powder developed by the British to replace gunpowder, was overwhelming.

Our spirits were high as adrenaline surged through us. In our pockets we each had a small escape kit containing folding money, a first aid kit, a waterproof map, a small compass and a few rations. We wore heavy leather coats to keep us warm at 35,000 feet, inflatable Mae West life jackets, and a parachute harness with its assorted straps and hooks ever prepared for an instantaneous exit. Every crewman had a parachute, but not everybody's was close at hand. The ball turret gunner's parachute hung from a hook beside the escape hatch at the tail end of the plane's waist.

When we reached the Danish Peninsula our P-51 fighter escort returned to base, their fuel supplies diminished. Not long after the fighters departed we saw for the first time ominous black puffs of smoke bursting from *ack-ack* or anti-aircraft guns. The enemy guns missed us by a mile, but we were so nervous one of the crewmen involuntarily hit the deck. Someone yelled at him to get up, and he sheepishly replied, "I didn't want to see what was happening."

At 11:49 a.m., we reached the Baltic seacoast and were turning to a more direct course toward Posen when twenty-five German Me 109 twin-engine fighter planes attacked us, flying up from behind, shooting terrifying rockets at our formation. Our guns were hopeless as the fighters' range exceeded ours, until one of the planes ventured too close and our engineer gunner, Staff Sergeant Leo K. Kornoely, shot it when it came into range. The fighter fell to the earth in a ball of flames.

As the formation reached the coastline near Stettin, it became apparent the cloud shield would prevent us from bombing Posen, because to drop our payload accurately, we needed to see the target visually. Ely radioed for instructions and listened, aghast, as wing leaders quarreled over which secondary target to bomb. It was an embarrassing, difficult moment. I felt my face turning red, my heart pounding in my chest. Finally, the radio crackled, "Rostock," a seaport in North Germany on the Baltic Sea.

As we approached Rostock we saw the city in the distance clearly through a cloudless sky—just as clearly as its anti-aircraft batteries saw us. Uncomfortably accurate ack-ack filled the air. Using a tracing configuration in which four shots in a straight line followed each other in rapid succession, the Germans lined us up in their sights and fired. Two shots exploded in front of us in billowy clouds of black smoke and I held my breath in anticipation of shots three and four. The third shot hit with a jolt. The impact lifted the tail of the plane and tossed us forward in our seats. Metal fragments pierced the thin aluminum skin covering the fuselage, sounding like gravel thrown on a tin roof. Sergeant Thomas Neill, the tail gunner, yelled that the tail was riddled with gaping holes but he was uninjured.

Ely fought to keep the plane level. Minutes later we lost an engine, making it difficult for us to maintain our place in the formation, but Ely held the plane stable until we reached the target. With a sigh of relief, at 1:15 in the afternoon, we dropped the payload from an altitude of 15,700 feet. The tension eased considerably as Ely turned the plane for home, heading out over the Baltic Sea. Suddenly Ellis jubilantly announced that our escort was approaching. Our ecstasy died instantly as ten or twelve German FW 190 fighter planes, flying four abreast, attacked the squadron, shooting away a large section of the vertical stabilizer of the plane next to us, *Shoo Shoo Baby*. As Baby fell smoking into the sea, five parachutes drifted down to the cold waters, but the men were never recovered and were assumed to have drowned.

An FW 190 suddenly flew up from below our plane and fired. Tracer bullets streamed straight at us, but our belly turret gunner, Sergeant Vincent J. Muffoletto, the only one who could have fired, didn't see the attacker until it was too late. Incendiary bullets splattered the plane, starting a fire in the radio room. Sergeant Kornoely grabbed the extinguisher and sprayed the flames, but it was a hopeless effort. When the flames engulfed the entire back end of the plane behind the radio compartment, Ely commanded us to bail out. Sergeant Kornoely and the radio operator, Staff Sergeant John M. Russell, jumped out the bomb bay opening while the waist gunners, Sergeants Harvey L. Ringer, Constantine

G. Scourbys and Muffoletto, jumped from the aft escape hatch. Neill escaped through the access door at the back of the plane.

In the nose Ellis and I moved to make our escape through the hatch under the cockpit, but a tracer bullet had damaged the door and we couldn't open it. "We can't get out," we frantically yelled at Ely. "Hang on, we're going in," he replied. In desperation he dived the plane toward land, some twenty miles distant. We dropped fast and, luckily, the wind doused the flames, trailing billows of black smoke behind us.

As we flew over the coastline, German gunners took aim and fired at us with small arms. Shells spattered the nose and the plane began burning again. In response I gave the Germans a burst from the nose machine gun. When we reached a low altitude Ely leveled the plane and the escape hatch door suddenly fell open, too late for us to bail out. Ellis and I were still trying to extinguish the fire when Ely brought the plane down hard in a belly landing on an open field.

We hit the earth with a heavy thud. The plane shook uncontrollably as it slid on its belly over the rough ground. Inside the nose, Ellis and I bounced around like rubber balls, knocking against walls, guns, and seats. My feet held firm against the floor until the plane came to an abrupt stop. The force yanked me out of both flight boots and flung me into Ellis as searing pain shot up from my feet and ankles.

Meanwhile, Ellis, in confused terror, trying to regain his footing, kicked and stomped on the object that lay beneath him—me. His panic deepened when the nose gun handles fell against his neck, pinning him down and increasing his claustrophobic desperation. When the plane finally came to a halt both of us were bruised and scratched. A cut on Ellis's forehead bled profusely.

For a moment we lay dazed in the shambles. The plane was heavily damaged. Doors were missing and windows, including the Plexiglas nose, were shattered and gone. A few yards away sat a smoking engine fully detached from the plane. To our surprise and relief, Pratt was unhurt and quickly extricated us from the debris.

Pratt half carried us, one under each arm, away from the smoldering plane, when we heard Ely call for help. Pratt dropped us a safe distance from the wreckage and rushed back to Ely, pulling him through a window in the cockpit. As they hobbled over to join us one of them whispered hoarsely, "We have company," pointing to a troop of German soldiers running toward us shouting, with guns drawn. Ironically, we had crash-landed on the grounds of the Anti Aircraft Gunner Training School, Defense Unit Two military reservation, located two kilometers northeast of Bad Doberan, near Rerik in Mecklenburg, Germany.

As the Germans surrounded us Ellis, enraged, yelled as loudly as our captors, "Damn you bastards." Frantically we shouted at him to shut up and stop cursing before he got all of us shot. He quickly calmed down. Suddenly, a great burst of flame enveloped the plane in a fiery ball. As we stared at the burning wreckage I remembered the Norden bombsight, the army's top-secret analog computer for calculating precision bomb drops, which I had vowed to demolish if I was ever shot down. "I forgot to destroy the bombsight," I gasped. "Don't worry," Ely whispered. "The fire will destroy it."

Encircling us with guns pointed, the German soldiers gestured wildly, but we didn't understand what they wanted us to do. Finally, one of them approached me cautiously, pushed me in the chest hard with both hands and knocked me over. I lay on my back, expecting to be beaten or killed, but the German unlaced my shoes and roughly jerked them off my feet. Intense pain swiftly rushed over me, but I was relieved that he didn't kill me. The soldiers promptly stripped us of clothing and confiscated our belongings. After appropriating our watches, escape supplies, and Ely's fancy Western 38 mm pistols, they tossed our clothes back to us and allowed us to dress. (They later gave me a receipt for my watch, bless their little hearts.)

At 1:30 p.m. the four of us stood shaking in a dazed condition until our captors loaded us into a Ford truck and drove into town. The soldiers lodged Ely, Pratt, and me in an uncomfortable jail for the night, but they conveyed Ellis, who was still bleeding from the gash on the forehead, to an infirmary where an army doctor roughly sewed up the cut using an oversized needle and no anesthesia.

My cell was stark. A solid wood plank without springs or mattress, with a raised board at one end instead of a pillow, served as my bed. A folded blanket lay neatly at one end. Despite its lack of comforts, after the door clicked behind me I climbed up on the bed, slid under the blanket and immediately dropped to sleep.

In the middle of the night I awoke and in the dark I assessed my situation. The shock of what had happened enveloped me in a gloomy cloud. Physically, I was in fairly good condition. My clothes were tattered and torn; an unknown sharp object had sliced through my shoe leather, but thankfully, hadn't cut my foot. Still, I could hardly walk. My sprained, swollen ankles smarted intensely. My abrasions, scratches, and bruises also hurt. Worst of all, I felt hopeless.

The melancholy I felt is difficult to describe. I felt terrified, a feeling that had not really come to me until that moment, and I felt miserable because I was out of the war after my first mission and no longer able to contribute to eventual victory. I felt awful about losing the new plane, which we had named *The Expectant Father* in honor of Ely whose wife was soon to have a baby. I realized part of the reason we were attacked was because our new airplane was bright silver, signaling to the enemy we were an inexperienced crew, a proverbial sitting duck. Why wasn't our plane camouflaged? I wondered.

The cold quiet darkness augmented my depression. I pulled the blanket tightly around my neck and stared blankly into the nothingness. I began to remember the movies I had seen depicting German cruelty. Terror struck my mind as I realized I had a Jewish first name and a Roman nose. Fear overwhelmed me. I fully expected the Germans would persecute, torture, or kill me the next morning. In panic I leaped from the bed and searched frantically for a window. High on the wall I found one, securely fastened, with a wooden shutter drawn tight over it on the outside. Disappointed, I peered through the cracks in the shutter. I could neither see nor hear anything. Absolute black. Tomb-like silence. Defeated, I returned to my bed.

I lay in misery, pondering my situation, praying earnestly that when my parents and family received the "Missing in Action" notice announcing my disappearance, they, in some way, would know I was alive and well. Tears welled in my eyes and slowly rolled down my cheeks. Unexpectedly, the words of a blessing I received before I left home forcefully entered my mind. "You will return home rejoicing," I had been promised. Immediately the words comforted and strengthened me. I no longer felt worried. With my mind at ease I drifted into a restful sleep.

CHAPTER 2

Snake River Country

In accordance with Scottish family tradition, I was named after my grandfather who was named after his grandfather, David Ririe. In 1847 my great-grandfather, James, a factory laborer, joined the Church of Jesus Christ of Latter-day Saints in Edinburgh, Scotland, set sail for America in 1853, and eventually settled on a farm in Ogden, Utah, where he flourished and acquired large landholdings. His marriage to Ann Boyack in 1855 produced twelve children including my grandfather, David, born in 1860.

After leaving home at age sixteen to raise sheep in the desert with his brother James, David homesteaded a 120 acre farm in Jefferson County in southeastern Idaho. In 1893, at the age of 33, he married sixteen-year-old Leah Ann Lovell, the slim, spirited daughter of his Scottish next-door neighbors, Joseph H. and Ellen Radford Lovell, who bore him eight children, including my father, James Edmond.

A prudent, strait-laced Mormon with rugged good looks, Grandfather was of ordinary height, with broad shoulders, piercing brown eyes, short brown hair, bushy eyebrows, high forehead and cheekbones, and a shaggy mustache covering a firm mouth. Known as a progressive farmer, he was an avid leader in attracting industry to the area and a key figure in constructing the valley's irrigation canal system. In 1914 he petitioned the Oregon Short Line Railroad Company to build a spur to service the outlaying communities north of Idaho Falls and helped obtain right of ways for the railroad. While David secured a route and land for the line his wife Leah Ann cooked daily meals for nine months for the seventeen-man crew constructing the depot and spur. Railroad executives were so grateful they dubbed the new depot "Ririe." The same year David donated twenty acres of land to the community, platted a township in its center, and actively sought neighbors. Once the name Ririe adorned the new rail depot residents readily accepted it as the name of the town and in 1915 the city council signed incorporation papers.

Although today scarcely more than a crossroads, Ririe was then a center of commerce in the sagebrush-studded country 200 miles north of Salt Lake City, Utah. Still a barren frontier when grandfather arrived, civilization had taken only a tenuous hold. The thick wooded hills on both sides of the fertile valley teamed with game – deer, elk, moose, bear, cottontail and jackrabbits – and cutthroat and rainbow trout swam in such abundance in the wild Snake River fishermen seldom returned home empty handed. Most inhabitants made a comfortable living raising livestock and growing potatoes, hay and other irrigated crops in the valley but also growing grain crops on un-irrigated land on the high plateau fields in the hills which they called dry farming.

Grandfather's business ventures exposed his family to the prosperous side of life. Before his death in 1919, he had become vice president of the First National Bank of Ririe and owned stock in the Ririe Mill and Elevator Company, the Ririe Garage, the Ucon gristmill, the Farmers Equity Elevator Company, and served as president and water master of the Farmers Friend Canal Company. After he died at the age of 59 while undergoing radium treatments for cancer in his jaw, conditions changed for my grandmother. The night before grandfather's funeral a fire broke out in Ririe that burned the east side of Main Street to the ground and completely destroyed several businesses. A severe depression brought on by a floundering post-World War I market followed the fire and strangled the economy. Despite her efforts grandmother lost all her husband's financial interests except the 140 acre farm.

ONE-MISSION MAN

By 1921, when my father married my mother, Verna Fanny Perry, Ririe had acquired the amenities of a small town—sawmills, gristmills, a grocery store, a hotel, a few bars plus a schoolhouse and a church. The following year I was born in my grandmother's two-story, 14 room stone house grandfather built in 1906. My official Idaho birth certificate shows my birthday as March 19, 1922, but my mother insisted that my birth occurred on March 20th, claiming the attending physician, a Dr. Price, submitted an incorrect date of birth. I am sure that my mother, who possessed a wonderful memory, would not confuse the date of her first painful birthing event.

Prior to my birth my parents lived with Grandmother. As soon as Dad could arrange finances, he had a small two-room house built for our family on the western edge of the farm he shared with his mother and brothers, one-half mile west of Ririe. Besides our in-town farm Dad owned a 1,000 acre dry farm at Granite Creek, twenty-miles to the east on the rolling hills known as Antelope Flats.

Adjoining our dry farm, in the hills above Conant Valley (pronounced Coonard), my father leased land from the government for grazing cattle. In this secluded canyon on the south fork of the Snake River, early summer brought a carpet of emerald grass around a string of small silver lakes. Along the east side, the river meandered like an enormous snake and, chameleon-like, displayed varying shades of color depending on the time of day. Each fall the valley decor changed to intense colors ranging from the deep red of the chokecherry to mottled brown, orange, and yellow of the many species of grass. Evergreen pines and the shaking golden leaves hanging from the white branches of quaking aspens along Gordon Creek added to the Lord's decorative scheme.

On weekdays during the summer we lived in a humble cottage at the dry farm and raised wheat and barley. Dad awoke before daylight to corral, feed, and harness the horses. After breakfast Mother joined Dad, each driving their own team of horses to plow, harrow, rod-weed, or plant the fields. At night, silence reined, much deeper than at our house in Ririe. Only the mournful howl of coyotes or the hooting of owls occasionally broke the quiet of the night. During the day we dealt with dust, grasshoppers, and ground squirrels, but the cool mountain air made our summers at the dry farm captivating.

At age three I caught pneumonia, which almost took my life. My parents admitted me to the Idaho Falls hospital, 19 miles to the southwest, where I recuperated for nearly two months. One morning the physician who operated on me, Dr. West, came into my room and showed me a vial full of pus he had drained from my lungs. The surgery left a scar on my back that in later life I often jokingly referred to as a wartime gunshot wound, until I discovered that my children believed me and were boasting their heroic dad had been wounded in action.

My sweet mother cared for me tenderly as I recuperated. Dr. West recommended that I walk with my arms stretched around a broomstick held horizontally across my back and underneath both armpits to pull my shoulders back. Firmly believing that this therapy would straighten my weakened back and slumping shoulders, Mother religiously insisted that I walk that way for a period each day. In this awkward, uncomfortable therapy, I felt like a little scarecrow.

Soon after my release from the hospital, my two-year-old brother Max Henry, who was my best friend, accidentally hit me on the foot with an axe, sending me back to the hospital for a brief stay.

Max and I had very few toys, but we devised endless entertainment from available materials. Despite occasional arguments and scraps, we cooperated to create a magnificent make-believe farm we operated with cogwheel tractors pulling imaginary plows in the form of mother's tablespoons.

One morning when I was about five years old Dad went to work and left a saddled horse in the corral. I climbed up into the saddle, untied the horse from the post, and kicked the beast in the side, starting my ride of the century. After circling the house several times, the horse ran under the clothesline. The line caught me under the chin and pulled me over backwards until I thought my head would be severed from my torso. Finally, I jerked the line off, freeing the horse, which set off at a full gallop, running up and down the hills with me hanging on for dear life. Just when I decided I would be thrown off the horse or die from fright, Dad, who was working at the far end of the farm, came running over the hill. Somehow, he grabbed the rope hanging around the horse's neck and rescued me.

My brother Clive Perry joined the family in April of 1927; I was five years old, and Max was three and a half.

In our community parents enrolled their children in the public school when they reached six years of age. When the time arrived for me to start school, wheat harvest was in full swing, so my parents, who were needed on the dry farm at Granite, placed me under my Grandmother Ririe's care for the first weeks of school. I felt excited about going to school, but I was also afraid. The teacher arranged our classroom with six rows of desks and five desks in each row. Geniuses sat in rows one and two. Slow students sat in rows five and six. Pupils in rows three and four were neither bright nor dull in the teacher's opinion. The teacher spent most of her time with the more forward pupils, less time with the middle row students and those in the dumb section. I don't know the criteria the teacher followed to designate smart or dumb students, but I ended up in the second desk on row six. I didn't mind that we spent less time with the teacher than the other groups, but I did mind being in the slow group.

From the beginning the teacher acted impatient with me. I couldn't remember the difference between a "b" and a "d." When I misspelled a word in our lessons, she made me stay after school and write the words one hundred times on the blackboard. I not only learned to spell by this tortuous, repetitive method that made my arm ache, but I also improved my penmanship. These and other oft-repeated errors soon convinced me I was in the right desk.

Perhaps I wasn't listening or was too bashful to ask the location of the bathrooms my first day and I was in woeful distress when the teacher dismissed the class for recess. Outside, I scanned the playground for an outhouse. I spotted swings, a baseball diamond, and a slippery slide in full use, but no toilet stood on the horizon. At length I wandered to the far side of the school grounds, entered an empty woodshed, and I relieved myself.

I visited the woodshed regularly until one day, to my horror, as I pulled up my pants, the little fat girl who occupied desk four in our dumb row stood in the doorway. Apparently, we had been sharing the same toilet. The following day she wet her pants and the teacher scolded her. From then on I just held everything until I returned home. After several agonizing days I became ill, and my parents admitted me to the hospital. The doctor diagnosed "inflammation of the bladder" as the cause of my illness. Back at school I finally inquired about the bathroom.

My second year at school was as miserable as the year before. Furthermore, my schoolmates and I contracted every disease that came along that year, including chicken pox. The epidemic almost closed the school when all of the first graders caught the disease after thoroughly examining a mysterious scab on Max's head. Later, diphtheria passed through the community, followed by measles, quarantine signs decorating our front yards.

On July 12, 1929, my sister, Anne, was born and passed away three days later. Mother had stepped on a slick pile of dandelion stems Max and I had left on the steps. She slipped and fell, probably causing her to deliver the baby prematurely.

My parents were upstanding, clean living, honest, neighborly, responsible, and one hundred percent true to the Church of Jesus Christ of Latter-day Saints. So when the Church called Dad to serve a six-month proselyting mission in Trenton, New Jersey, and Allentown, Pennsylvania, soon after my sister's death, Dad accepted the call. It made for a long winter for all of us.

The summer after Dad's return, on July 5, 1930, I was baptized in a ditch flowing from the Farmer's Friend Canal and my father confirmed me a member of the Church. At the time, the Ririe Ward congregation contained 719 members, of which 196 were children.

In the spring of 1932, the third year of the Great Depression soon after my tenth birthday, one of our neighbors, Andrew Young, ran out of feed and persuaded Dad to buy his 100 head ewe flock. Dad sent Max and me, with our shy horse Banjo, to care for these sheep, plus 24 ewes belonging to another neighbor, Hyrum T. Moss, who was also our bishop at church.

Max and I lived with the hired man and his wife at the dry farm during the week and Mother brought us home on Saturday night so we could have a bath and go to church with the family on Sunday. Day after day we herded the sheep to the creek for a drink, into the mountain pastures to graze, back to the creek, then to the corral, morning and afternoon. While the sheep grazed we wandered through the rolling hills, exploring and playing.

Mother often came to visit and read to us from *The Children's Friend*, the church's magazine for children. Once in a while the hired man cared for the sheep so Mother could take us to town. One afternoon on an outing, we were sitting in the car when two little boys passed by, cursing terribly. Mother looked at us and remarked, "I'm glad my boys don't swear like that." We had gotten into a bad habit of swearing, partly in anger at the sheep, and partly in imitation of the hired man. We decided to mend our ways.

As there was always a possibility that one of us could get too close to a rattlesnake in our wanderings, Mother and Dad coached us in snakebite first aid. One afternoon as Max and I rested near a road cut, a rattlesnake tumbled over the ledge and landed on the road uncomfortably close to us. We quickly dispatched the big snake, and cut off his rattles for a souvenir. We were wrapping the rattles in a piece of cloth, when we thought we heard another snake in the bushes. Grabbing our sticks we proceeded to search the brush.

After a while we gave up searching and were heading back to work, when I discovered my leg was bleeding from a painful puncture wound. With snakes on our minds, we decided I had been bitten. Following Dad's instructions, Max took a razor blade out of our snakebite kit, placed a tourniquet on my leg and prepared to cut my leg so he could suck the poison out. Just as he prepared to make the incision, he noticed to my great relief that there were no fang marks on my leg. Max didn't operate and my scratch quickly healed over.

At the end of summer we corralled the sheep and Dad had them sheared, barely clearing enough on the wool to pay for the shearing. Then Dad shipped the sheep back to the valley, where we sold them at a loss. Bishop Moss paid Max and me $21 each for caring for his sheep, our first real earnings.

While we were wandering after sheep at Granite, the Ririe school board came to the startling discovery that they had more students enrolled for the third grade class than they had classroom space. By general acclimation, they announced to the parents they had decided to promote six or seven of the most mature third grade students into the fourth grade in September. One morning before school started my parents called me aside and revealed that Max and I would now be in the same grade. I was furious. "I don't want that little snot-nosed kid in my class," I wailed, stamping my foot. But it was to no avail. Soon after we arrived at school Max was integrated into the fourth grade class with little fanfare and we continued as classmates through our tenure at Ricks College.

Besides managing the farm, Dad was a whirlwind of energy in the community. He served on school boards, committees, and fair boards. He became the first president of the Ririe Lions Club, the chairman of the Ririe Grain Growers, and president of the Potato Cooperative, a grower's marketing group that shipped produce under its own brand to Boston, Chicago, and New York markets. While Lions Club president, Dad started the Jefferson County Fair at Ririe, an annual event that included displays, patriotic meetings, baseball games, a carnival, dancing, and in later years a rodeo held in an arena that he and I helped build. Later, Dad introduced a car-parking contest to the fair, awarding people prizes if they could make the best time at parallel parking.

Community activities such as these involved our entire family. The fair sponsored an old time parade that Max and I entered and won several times. For one parade during our teenage years we borrowed the banner from the church's youth program, the Mutual Improvement Association (MIA), tacked it to the side of the wagon and won first place. The MIA's leaders tried to persuade us to donate the cash prize to the organization, but we kept it. No doubt the banner might have influenced the judges, but we reasoned that since we had done the work the money was ours.

One year the rodeo committee of Clark, Idaho, asked Dad to loan his large white Holstein bull to the bull riding event in the town's Fourth of July celebration. Max and I were very pleased and wagered that no one would be able to ride our ferocious bull. When the other fellows saw the bull's enormous size they agreed and for a couple of days the committee had difficulty finding a rider. Finally, a rough young men in our town, whose drunken condition had also been responsible for his entering the women's lavatory by mistake, volunteered. As he mounted the bull, a hush fell over the crowd. The chute opened and our gigantic bull sauntered slowly out into the ring and stopped. The young man kicked him in the ribs but our bull just stood there. Everyone laughed heartily as the young man dismounted in disgust. Our ferocious bull turned out to be a Ferdinand.

When I turned twelve years of age I was ordained a deacon in the Aaronic Priesthood of the Church. A short while thereafter, Bishop Moss called me to be president of the Deacon's Quorum. At that time the quorum included men who were twenty, thirty, and possibly even fifty years old. I felt inadequate, but honored to be chosen as president.

With the depression in full swing, the U.S. Government initiated a Public Works Administration (PWA) project in our community to erect a meeting hall, using native pine logs. For some reason the project fell by the wayside and lay half completed in the center of town. Dad and his older brother, Joseph, both on the school board, proposed that the school district pass a bond issue to finish the building as a gymnasium and auditorium for the school. The proposal caused a commotion, mainly among town members who did not have children in school.

Before the proposition came to a vote, rigorous and heated campaigns raged on both sides of the issue. On Election Day both Dad and Uncle Joe shuttled voters to and from the polls, and they mustered school children, including those of the opposition, and marched them through town behind a banner, which read, "We Want Our Gym." Dad and Uncle Joe won the battle and a short while later the city completed the building, which eventually became a civic center.

At thirteen and fourteen years of age, Max and I had enrolled in Ririe High School. By now Carma, born May 22, 1931, and Wayne J, born August 1, 1933, had joined our family. Six years after Wayne was born, when I was a senior in high school, my youngest brother James A was born on November 30, 1939.

CHAPTER 3

Heeding the Call

All during our high school years Max and I worked on the farm when we weren't in class. Dad flattered us, saying we were more reliable than any hired men he ever employed. Unfortunately, due to helping Dad with the wheat harvest on the dry farm, Max and I always missed starting high school at the beginning of the fall term. Then, we would only be in class for a week when the district suspended school for the annual two-week sugar beet and potato harvest vacation.

Fanning the flame of our discontent, the summer before we started high school, Dad purchased a herd of cows for us to milk to round out our education. All of the milking at that time we did by hand, so the milker became well acquainted with each cow and her disposition. Max hated cows and I wasn't exactly fond of them, but we grudgingly accepted our lot and worked together to lighten our burden. Since I loved sports more than Max, I suggested he milk at night, and in exchange I would milk in the mornings. In this way I earned the privilege of playing football and basketball after school.

During this time Dad was extremely busy in the Church. He was called as bishop of the Ririe Ward in 1935, when he was about thirty-five years old, and he served faithfully for seven years. As one of his first actions, he persuaded the Church to sponsor a seminary at Ririe High School. Under his leadership the Church moved an old building to a lot adjoining the high school and remodeled it into a very good classroom.

Meanwhile, Dad kept things humming in the ward. He established a building fund and remodeled the chapel, replacing the pews, adding new classrooms and a recreation hall. Dad donated his time and equipment, and his sons to Church projects, and Max and I often found ourselves working on the chapel renovation. I drove a team of horses to scrape out the excavation for the basement of the new addition.

Dad was a serious student of the scriptures and few men were better informed in basic doctrine. I enjoyed listening to him expound gospel principles, because he spoke with enthusiasm, interest, and authority. When the Ward Teaching program, in which all priesthood men visited member families on a monthly basis, languished, he assigned an Aaronic Priesthood boy to be his companion, and together they visited the 200 families in the ward. The next Sunday at priesthood meeting, Dad announced that the ward teaching was 100% completed for the month. Then he asked if the men would accept the challenge to keep it that way. The record improved.

During the Christmas season Dad spent much of the holidays working on the ward's annual financial reports. The reports were cumbersome, because many of the members paid tithing "in kind," donating bushels of wheat or chickens, pigs, or cows, etc., to the Church instead of money. To make matters worse, Dad's spelling was atrocious and his handwriting wasn't the best. He asked me to copy all of his reports in my handwriting, and then he swore me to secrecy regarding the confidential personal financial information I'd become privy to.

Periodically Dad assigned Aaronic Priesthood young men to deliver supplies to the widows of the ward. Grandpa Ririe had died years before Max and I were born, so we often wondered why Grandma never received any assistance. One Saturday afternoon as Max and I distributed a load of firewood to the ward's widows, on our own initiative we delivered the last of our wood to Grandma's door.

"Who sent you with this wood?" she demanded.

"We are delivering it to the ward widows, as Dad assigned us to do in priesthood meeting," we replied.

"Well, you can take this wood back to your Dad and tell him that when I need help from the bishop, I'll let him know."

Mother was a member of the Primary presidency and the ward organist, playing for hundreds of funerals (I believe Dad spoke for an equal number of such occasions). Once Mother came home from a funeral and said with a good-natured grin, "It's been quite a day. Dad spoke at the funeral, I played the organ, and David led the funeral procession with a team of horses and a Hoover wagon." Absentmindedly I had driven a team of horses onto the road in front of the lead car in the funeral procession just as it departed from the church parking lot. I proceeded to the next corner, where I turned down the road towards home and the procession took the other fork towards the cemetery.

In her quiet, patient way Mother looked after things very efficiently at home when Dad's church work, civic duties or business called him away from our home. We were riding home from Sacrament Meeting one Sunday evening when Max asked, "Dad, now that you are bishop, are all of us bishops?" Dad replied, "No son, you're not bishops, just me and your Mother."

Mother and Dad sincerely believed our church to be true and often bore their testimonies to us. Once a panic-stricken family drove into our yard requesting that Dad come quickly. Their little boy had inhaled carbon monoxide while sleeping on the floor of his father's car and had stopped breathing. Mother explained that Dad wasn't at home and sent one of my brothers to our neighbor, Arlo Moss, who returned and gave the boy a priesthood blessing. Within minutes after the blessing the little boy was breathing normally and playing with my brothers and sister. Mother testified to us the Lord brought him back from death by the faith accompanying the blessing.

One Sunday afternoon, Dad took Max and me to the bishop's office in the ward meetinghouse, and Josiah Call, the Rigby Stake patriarch, laid his hands upon our heads and gave us patriarchal blessings. Mine included the phrase, "You shall return home rejoicing."

In 1940 when it came time to enter college, Max and I complied with Mother's wishes and attended Church-sponsored Ricks College in Rexburg, Idaho, where she and Dad had attended when it was still a high school. Hyrum Manwaring, the college president, and Oswald Christensen, a well-known Church scholar still taught at the school when I enrolled and they remembered my parents. When Professor Christensen called Max to be president of the religion class, the elderly pedagogue remembered that he had chosen Dad for the same position twenty-five years earlier. Mother had been vice president of the student body and her brother L. Tom Perry taught at the college for a while.

After one quarter of our freshman year Max left school to help Dad with the farm. Thereafter we alternated attending college and helping Dad. Whoever was in school at the time drove or hitchhiked home each weekend and helped Dad and the at-home brother with Saturday work.

When at school, Max and I lived in the Ricks College dormitory. The dorm was a cooperative affair. Boys lived on the ground floor, while girls occupied the top floor of the two-story building and we shared kitchen and house cleaning duties. Normally the girls washed the dishes and waited on tables while the boys peeled potatoes or washed pots and pans.

Both Max and I started the fall quarter our second year at Ricks and were happily enjoying our education when Dad called me home. He had been filling the loft using his newly purchased hay chopper when the loft collapsed, dumping several tons of chopped alfalfa hay into the milking parlor below. Since Max left school the previous year, Dad asked me to help clean up the mess. We milked in hastily constructed stanchions out of doors, leaving the tons of chopped hay in the barn, while we repaired the damaged hayloft.

I sorely missed the warm barn for milking. Adding insult to injury, Dad decided to re-shingle the barn roof despite the freezing winter temperatures.

Soon after I arrived home I was ordained an elder in the Melchizedek Priesthood and Dad, as bishop of the ward, called me to serve as deacon's quorum instructor to teach the twelve-year-old boys. The assignment was enjoyable but temporary and by Sunday, December 7, 1941, I was back at Ricks when the Japanese bombed Pearl Harbor. The next day the U.S., Great Britain and their allies declared war on Japan.

The fear of a Japanese invasion permeated even our backwater community. Dad immediately volunteered as a civil defense warden. The local National Guard contingent was called to active duty, and I often observed men of the student body board the train on their way to the war as I passed by the Rexburg train station. "For years we have collected our scrap iron and sold it to the Japanese," a man I knew quipped. "Now they are shooting it back at us."

I was nineteen years of age and already registered for the draft. Dad promised he would call me on a mission for the Church when I reached twenty-one years of age. The call never came. In 1942 the Church announced it would call only older men ordained as high priests or seventies on full-time missions for the duration of the war. In September of 1942, my friend Sterling Mason and I drove to Pocatello where we took tests to enter the Army Air Corps. Both of us passed the mental exam, but because of a hernia Sterling flunked the physical and was rejected. I was told to wait for my orders.

The resounding response to the call to arms apparently overwhelmed military training facilities. As a result many volunteers were sent back to college or told to wait until a place opened up for them. Consequently, I again registered at Ricks and attended two quarters before I received my overdue orders.

Ricks College changed that year, mainly due to the preponderance of girls in my classes. For one dance the college asked each boy to take two girls. The boys, including me, happily complied, but I found that not all of the girls were as pleased. Summoning courage, I asked two girls but only one accepted. The other, a cute coed from Ririe, turned me down flat, stating, "Only if you ask me, and me only, will I go with you." Humiliated, I never got the inclination to date her or anyone else at school after that incident.

Since all of the boys had either volunteered for military service and were waiting to be called up, or were waiting to be drafted, it was difficult for us to concentrate on our studies. To compensate I associated myself with the brightest fellows I could find, we reviewed our lessons as a group, and tested each other on the subject matter. The keen competition stimulated us to greater effort.

Back home in Ririe life continued to add complications. Dad accepted a call to serve as a counselor to President George Christensen in the Rigby Stake of the Church. My brother Clive struggled in high school and had a fight with a seminary teacher. Though serious, the altercation likely resulted from the turmoil caused by the war and the attention directed toward those of military age. The boys caught in the excitement of the war but not yet old enough to serve chafed under the restriction.

To demonstrate their patriotism, Clive and my dad's cousin, Cleo Freeman, joined the Navy without telling their parents. When the recruiting officer called Cleo's home to tell him to report for duty, Cleo's mother, Aunt Josephine, answered the telephone and nearly had apoplexy. When she informed the recruiting officer that Cleo and Clive were only 14 years old, the recruiter became distressed. Before my parents knew what had happened, Josephine had extricated both boys from the Navy's clutches and doled out a severe tongue-lashing on poor Cleo and Clive for lying about their ages. Clive, delayed but not dissuaded, joined the Navy as soon as he qualified.

Six months after I volunteered for the Army Air Corps, I received my orders to report to Santa Ana, California, for pre-flight training. Regrettably, I lacked one quarter from graduating with a teaching certificate. The war had already altered my life.

CHAPTER 4

Cadet Ririe

When the quarter ended at Ricks College on March 11, 1943, my father's cousin George Lovell drove his brother Rendon and me from Rexburg to Ririe. I was unloading my possessions from the Lovell vehicle when Mother rushed out of our house holding a letter. The War Department ordered me to report in Salt Lake City on March 18th, just two days shy of my twenty-first birthday, preparatory to going to Santa Ana, California, for pre-flight training.

For six months I had anxiously awaited my orders. Now that they had arrived, I was not so anxious. The letter contained a list of recruits who were to report at the same time, and I was relieved to know I would have company on the trip to California.

My remaining days at home passed quickly. On Saturday night I attended a farewell party for me and another serviceman, Jay Gardner, who was leaving shortly for duty in the Navy. The party included a program and a dance in the high school gymnasium. Everyone was jovial, and I realized that an entire community was behind me, encouraging me to shed my shyness. I danced with several females and girl cousins who wished me well.

Sylvia Reading, my dad's youngest sister, served dinner to my family Sunday afternoon, and we attended Sacrament Meeting together in the evening. The bishop asked me to speak, and in a choked up voice I bore my testimony and asked for the blessings of the Lord upon the congregation and myself.

Ultimately, the morning of my departure arrived. I packed a few clothes, a box of Aunt Sylvia's candy, and a new shaving kit from Uncle Parley in my suitcase. With my family and Grandma Ririe in the car, I drove to the train station in Idaho Falls, feeling a peculiar sensation that it might be a long time before I would drive an automobile again.

When I purchased my ticket from the stationmaster, Dad, Mother, and my three-year-old brother Jimmy decided to ride with me to Pocatello, saying they wanted us to be together for as long as possible. Conductors began calling for passengers to board. Grandma Ririe took a five-dollar bill from her purse, pressed it into my hand, and gave me a kiss on the cheek. On the platform Max, Carma, and Clive wished me luck. Wayne, my little pal, bit his lip to keep from crying.

Dad didn't say much during the trip until we neared Pocatello. Finally, he looked at me and said with a tear in his eye, "I sure hate to see you go, but I would have hated it more if you had been unwilling to go." He then advised me to avoid making mistakes, but not to feel bad if I did, unless I made the same mistake twice.

Reaching Pocatello, I kissed Mother and Jimmy good-bye, shook my father's hand, and watched as they stood next to the tracks and waved their hands in farewell as the train pulled away from the station. Tears clouded my vision as I looked longingly at my mother. Soon my parents faded from sight and I sat there with a tremendous lump in my throat. Maybe I should have waited to be drafted, I thought.

A little boy in a seat in front of me noticed my misery and presented me with an orange. I thanked him, peeled and ate the orange without tasting it. After a few minutes the boy's father sat down beside me and we talked about Star Valley, Wyoming, and the Snake River until we reached Salt Lake City. My first train trip over, I checked into a hotel near the station and fell exhausted into bed. Considering the long emotional day I had just experienced I should have slept soundly, but I tossed and turned all night, worrying that I would sleep in and miss my first appointment with the Army. To be sure, if I had known then about the Army's "hurry up and wait" culture, I would have enjoyed a peaceful slumber.

At 4 a.m. I gave up trying to sleep, dressed and reported to a military policeman sitting at a desk in the train station, who growled at me to wait until time for the troop train to leave. Upset by the testy soldier, I slumped into an open seat next to several forlorn men about my age, all wearing faces suggesting their best girl had just jilted them.

A big bull-headed fellow sat down on a bench opposite me, introduced himself, and began relating uninteresting facts of his life. Within an hour I knew all his accomplishments: a graduate of the University of Utah, he performed wonderfully on the school's football team, was a group major in the Reserve Officer Training Corps (ROTC), and aspired to revolutionize the Santa Ana cadet program upon his arrival in California. In short, I had met my first army braggart.

At six o'clock a porter informed us that the train would probably not leave until eleven o'clock, and in true Army style, he ordered us to stay in the station until departure time. I sought out the cafe and ate a breakfast that on any other morning I would have eagerly devoured, but I was too bewildered to savor the food. My stomach was as restless as the shaker chain in our combine harvester.

After breakfast I managed to elude the long-winded Ute and came across an empty bench. I laid down and promptly fell asleep. At ten o'clock a heavy-set sergeant calling the roll woke me. All conscripts were present except a man named Perkins. In my tired and unsettled state I began to worry about Perkins and ponder what penalty might be imposed upon him for his failure to report. When time arrived for us to board, the conductor ushered us up the steps into the train, and I glanced out a window just in time to see a man break his embrace with an attractive woman and hastily enter the train. Perkins had arrived!

On my way to find a seat, I passed through one of the rail cars and spotted a duffle bag bearing the letters "BYU," which stand for Brigham Young University, a Church school in Utah. The duffle rested against the leg of a tall blond fellow. Approaching an empty chair next to him and a freckle-faced young man, I timidly asked if the chair was taken. The fellow I judged to be from the "Y" answered, "No, go ahead. Sit down." I introduced myself to Newell (Stan) Clark, from Mona, Utah, and Edward Peterson, from Anaconda, Montana. Neither of the men had much to say although I attempted a couple of tries to start a conversation, and I judged that they, like me, had a hollow feeling in their stomachs. Nonetheless, I told myself, I had better stick close to Clark. He can't be bad. He's from BYU.

A few minutes later the train, dubbed *The Challenger*, rolled out of Salt Lake City heading in a southwesterly course for Santa Ana. Shortly, a porter passed through the car announcing the first call for dinner. A couple of the young men in the car and I made our way to the dining car. I was so homesick, the food was a little hard to swallow, but after the meal I felt happier. After dinner the burly sergeant in charge entered our car and ushered us to a Pullman car where he informed us that we would sleep two men in the lower bunk and one in the upper. Clark won the upper bunk in a coin toss, and Peterson and I shared the lower. We immediately "hit the hay" and soon slept, rocked into a deep slumber by the rumbling of the iron horse.

Morning came too soon. The porter's call to breakfast aroused us at sunup. I had my first glimpse of the Mojave Desert with its sagebrush, grease wood, and Joshua trees. As we approached San Bernardino, I overheard the conductor growling at the brakeman for allowing the Santa Fe train to overtake our train. The shouting grew louder and soon the argument rivaled the fury of a thunderstorm. I thought wars and jealousy between railways had subsided with the fading away of cowboys and Indians, but apparently, some old boys weren't about to give up the fight.

Soon, oranges hanging from thousands of trees, closely spaced towns, and large factories replaced the desert as we approached Los Angeles. Regrettably, we didn't see much of the city, because after arriving at the station, the surly sergeant hustled us onto an electric train, our means of conveyance to the Santa Ana Air Corps base. By now I knew my new friends well enough to call them Eddie and Stan. Ironically, while we were getting acquainted, the University of Utah blowhard "polished apple" with the sergeant in charge.

Old Sol burned through a haze and muggy heat greeted us as we filed out of the electric train on the station platform at the neat little city of Santa Ana. I admired its beautiful streets lined with trees and flowering shrubbery. In the cooling shade I sat on my bag waiting for the next mode of transportation, when a depressed GI plopped down next to me and mournfully sang the lyrics to *Don't Get Around Much any More*, a popular song of the day by Duke Ellington and Bob Russell. I admired his voice and sympathized with him—and felt sorry for both of us.

After we sat thirty minutes under the tree, a convoy of trucks lumbered up the street, and eighteen of us climbed into the back of one of them. The sergeant fastened the door while an impatient private raced the motor, ground the gears, and jerked the battle-gray truck forward as motorcycles escorted us the remaining five miles to the base. Disregarding the comfort of his passengers, the driver rounded street corners at a fast clip, throwing us against the sides of the truck with every turn. I had completely lost my sense of direction by the time the corporal at the gate waved us through, not that I needed it very much. From this point on Army personnel told me when and where I needed to be every moment of the day.

A beefy lieutenant took command when we unloaded from the truck, ordering us to pile our bags next to the building and file into the reception room as he called our names. My name comes near the end of the alphabetical list, and the sergeant mispronounced it. By the time I finished filling out questionnaires and emerged from the building, my arms full of mimeographed sheets on military courtesy, discipline, and other air corps expectations, the sky was nearly dark. The weather, mercifully, had turned fair and cool.

The conscripts formed in columns of four and the boastful Ute took over, marching us through the dusk to our quarters. We had learned a valuable truth—a "suck up" gets places fast in the Army. He counted cadence above the catcalls and jeers from the barracks as we passed:

"Don't sign anything or you'll be sorry."

"Don't twist my arm. I'll be a bombardier."

"Get a load of that head of hair!"

"Anyone from Texas?"

"My, what a beautiful suit of clothes."

We grinned and chuckled as we ambled along with a bag swinging from one arm, and the newly acquired papers tucked under the other. When we arrived at the barracks a surly first lieutenant named Heath waited out front and ordered us to lay our possessions down and walk two blocks to a mess hall. Frankly, it was not a puzzle to ascertain why the Army called mealtime "mess," at Santa Ana anyway. We sat at long tables in the order in which we had lined up. If you chanced to end up in the seat at the far end of the table, you learned it was called "starvation corner" for good reason. After listening to a lengthy lecture by Lieutenant Heath concerning the rules of the mess hall, we sat down and ate heartily.

Returning to the barracks we waited in line for about an hour to be issued bedding and a footlocker. I attached myself to Clark and followed his BYU bag to a bunk at the far end of the upper story of Barrack C. I threw my blankets down on the cot and lay down for a much-needed rest following the first of many long days in our new home.

On Saturday, morning, March 20, my true birthday, after a restful night beneath warm blankets, I received my initiation into Army life with 5:30 a.m. reveille. Nonetheless, it was a perfect spring day, the base glorious with spring green, the light sparkling through the windows. To my delight, when I scanned the row of bunks to see whom I was bunking with, I discovered the row was occupied by Mormon boys, who like me, had followed Clark's BYU duffle bag.

After breakfast Heath shuffled us off to the barbershop where ten barbers in a row removed two hundred fleeces in an hour and a half, averaging about one and a half minutes per haircut. Then the barbers complained they had missed their previous record by ten minutes. I measured my longest hair after the butchery and discovered it was all of an inch long. In subsequent haircuts at that base, the clip artists would inquire as I entered the chair, "Do you want your hair washed?" If I answered, "No," because the service was costly and totally unnecessary, the irked barbers administered an unforgettable haircut. This bunch of civilian barbarians should have been employed closer to the front lines where they would have put the combatants in a fiercer fighting mood.

Following our shearing we went to the Post Exchange (PX), where most of us purchased liquid shoe polish because it was on sale, was easier to apply, and polished beautifully. At noon a lieutenant made us throw all of our newly purchased polish in the trash, saying liquid polish causes shoe leather to crack. We suspected collusion between the PX and the lieutenant, who we guessed rifled through the trash and collected the banned polish, then resold it to the PX to foist off on the next batch of rookies. However, we could not prove our allegations. The rest of the day we spent listening to a lecture and practiced drilling. Learning to be a first-rate soldier seemed almost insurmountable as I retired after my first full day of pre-flight training.

The next day, Sunday, Lieutenant Heath prohibited us from going to church for the first two weeks of training. He confined us to barracks to reduce the spread of any communicable diseases the new cadets might have been carrying. Instead, we spent a beautiful Sabbath morning giving our barracks a GI wash.

Lieutenant Heath called us together after lunch for a meeting with the base chaplains, each chaplain presenting a little speech and inviting us to come to church as soon as our leaders permitted.

Of course, it didn't matter which church we attended, they said, as they would attempt to please all denominations. The presiding chaplain gave the assembled soldiers permission to smoke and distributed copies of the New Testament to those who desired a copy. I felt a sincere respect for these dedicated men.

On Monday morning I still felt sleepy when the braggart Ute shouted out throaty commands and marched us to a post theatre to watch training films. Then it was back to the barracks where persnickety Lieutenant Heath inspected our beds and found them too loosely made, or not made at all in some cases, since we cadets were now separated from our wives and mothers. Not to worry, Lieutenant Heath was "kind" enough to show us how to make a bed hospital style, stretching the top blanket so tight that when you dropped a quarter on it the coin bounced like a Mexican jumping bean. Gratefully, we stood at attention as the considerate lieutenant departed.

We followed the Ute several blocks to a supply depot where a sergeant explained in detail the uncomplicated procedure we should follow to obtain our first uniforms. First, a bag flew out of nowhere as I entered the room. I caught the bag, removed my civilian clothes, and stuffed them into it, then stood completely nude with a battery of soldiers eyeing me and, without inquiring as to my customary clothing sizes, tossed me shorts, undershirt, and socks, which I was more than happy to put on. Next came shirts, a pair of suntan trousers, and a pair of olive drab trousers, followed by an overcoat, a raincoat, flight caps, belts, and finally, two pairs of heavy GI shoes. The person following me shoved me forward regardless of whether the clothes fit properly, the buttons were fastened, or shirttails tucked in, forcing me through the line with amazing rapidity. To give the clothing dispensers credit, they were skilled technicians or great guessers; only the trousers needed alteration—my legs were too short. I tied a knot in the bulging barracks bag, slung it over my shoulder, as I had done with a gunnysack of potatoes last harvest season, and trudged to my quarters, red tags stuck all over my outer garments.

Several devilishly grinning sergeants greeted us at Barrack C, ordered us to dump our bags on our beds, and report for instruction on footlocker organization as per Army regulation. To prepare for inspection the next morning, we rolled our socks, folded our towels, packed our shorts, arranged our shirts, etc., etc., as per instructions, and once the locker had met the sergeant's approval, I wasn't about to touch the contents.

CHAPTER 5

Aptitude Determinates

The first series of aptitude tests began the next morning to ascertain which branch of aviation best suited us—pilot, bombardier, navigator, or none of the above. Of course, I wanted to be a pilot—so did ninety-nine percent of the other inductees.

The first day of testing examined our ability to solve mathematical problems and read photographs. The tests were timed. As we struggled with an answer, lost in deep concentration, the gruff-voiced officer in charge would abruptly shout, "Stop! Lay your pencils on the desk." By day's end I felt jumpy as a hare in a rabbit drive.

The second day of classification took place in the hospital, where we underwent an extensive physical examination that eliminated a few of the men from consideration and left the rest of us fully prepared to "wash out," too. As I expected, the doctors examined the pneumonia scar on my back, and I rehearsed the particulars of my bout with pleurisy.

To test my reflexes, a large enlisted man whacked me on the knee with a mallet with sufficient force to guarantee a knee-jerk response. Frankly, I believe the Army doctors administered this test to verify we were still alive after the preceding tests. Even the eye tests would give anyone eyestrain. After hopping up and down several times, doctors measured our blood pressure, which everybody seemed to have.

At the conclusion of the day of testing, the doctors ascertained that I could see, hear, move, and react. My limbs, joints, and feet were normal. With little fanfare the brusque medics pronounced me physically fit to remain in the Army Air Corps as the lowest of the lowly — an aviation cadet.

Three days after my arrival, I had a long interview with a psychologist who assessed my mental state by prying into my past life. After answering a variety of questions that I considered very personal and none of his business, the doctor thanked me and directed me to a building for another series of aptitude tests. To my surprise, the first test was rather simple. Facing a board containing sets of lights organized in a diamond shape, I was directed to focus where one light came on and turn on the opposite light as quickly as I could. To my amazement, I did fairly well with the required hand-eye coordination.

My euphoria was short lived. The following test consisted of a flat board with square holes filled with pegs painted blue on one side and yellow on the other. All of the blues faced me at the start, and the doctors timed me as I removed the pegs and placed them back in the holes with the yellow sides facing me. In my haste I dropped a peg or two and turned one of them too far, but I felt I did pretty well, nonetheless. Considering my ambition to be a pilot, I might have muffed a few more pegs if I had understood that bombardiers, to be successful, needed great concentration and fine finger dexterity.

I couldn't do the next test to save me. The set up was simple: a record player with a disc on it. On the disc was a small copper-plated circular spot. I was given a stylus and instructed to hold the tip of it on the copper piece as the plate rotated. If the rotation of the disk had followed regular circles the test would have been easy, but it spun in an elliptical arc. A light went out whenever the stylus left the copper spot, and my grade depended on the percentage of time I could keep the circuit intact.

Piloting aptitude was clearly under evaluation when I sat in a chair with a rudder I controlled with my feet and a stick I controlled with my hands. I received points for lining up pairs of lights as they flashed on and off, using the rudder for the horizontal row and the stick for the vertical row. But just as soon as I aligned them, the lights went out and another set appeared and I had to start over. Certainly my eye, hand, and foot coordination would have improved with practice, but at the time of the test it was pitiful.

None of the tests, however, were as challenging as the final test. Five of us sat at a table facing a distinguished looking gentleman. We each held a pointed metal rod by the insulated handle, with our arms outstretched, keeping the point of the rod inside a tubular hole the circumference of a dime. We were not to allow the point of our rod to touch the side of the hole. If it did it completed an electrical circuit and elicited a loud nerve-wracking noise. The object was to remember sets of numbers or letters read to us by the examiner, and after a pause, repeat them back to him, while being heckled by the racket and by the difficulty of holding the rod steady. If we failed to repeat the letters or numbers correctly or if we failed to hold the rod steady, we lost points.

After that hectic day of testing, the guard at the gate of the psychopathic ward must have wondered if he should let us leave the place. We looked—and felt—awful. Moreover, I confess I was too psychologically uneducated to connect the results of the tests to our aptitude as pilots, navigators, or bombardiers. As a result, my fate hung in limbo for days until the test data were analyzed and my destiny announced.

Aptitude tests behind us, we marched to a base infirmary for inoculations early the following morning. Lining up in alphabetical order, we went in one door with trepidation and out the other with pale faces. Survivors related horrible tales to those of us unfortunate to have surnames in the latter end of the alphabet, and stories passed through the ranks about the square hypodermic needles and horrific side effects we could expect from immunizations

Queasiness increased as I watched a medical technician stab a needle about an inch deep into the biceps of the man in front of me. I shuddered, closed my eyes, and kept them shut through the remainder of the line. Medics immunized against small pox, tetanus, typhus, and typhoid fever. After the tetanus shot my throbbing arm felt like it had been kicked.

Nauseous and weak, I staggered out the immunization room door and headed for the barracks, but the torture wasn't over. A medic dragged me to another station where a doctor took blood samples for a venereal disease test and blood typing. I closed my eyes again as I squeezed my hand open and shut to pump blood into the vials. Suddenly I heard a thump. Behind me a cadet lay unconscious on the floor, the first of many I saw faint that day. I confess I became very light headed and swooned a bit, but luckily, I wasn't among those who mopped the floor with their faces.

Days passed and the Army assumed a dull routine. I didn't realize when I volunteered that training would include so much close order drill. "Right face. Left face. About face. To the rear. March," filled hours and days on end. To reduce the strain on them, our instructors alternated shifts marching us through our drills. Since we were to become officers before this segment of our training ended, we cadets also took turns running our squadrons through their paces.

On April Fool's Day the flight sergeant called me out of the ranks to demonstrate to the squadron how to execute, "To the rear. March." After sending men in the wrong direction several times and being laughed at each time, I succeeded in directing the squadron to the sergeant's satisfaction. Fifteen days later I had a chance to redeem myself—but it didn't turn out well, either. I marched the flight into a telephone pole, counted cadence out of step, and topped it off by giving them a "Right flank," and turning left myself. I barely caught up with the flight before they reached the barracks.

One afternoon Lieutenant Heath drilled us on "falling out," blowing his whistle and timing us as we scrambled out of the barracks and lined up in formation. We had barely returned to the barracks to relax when he blew the whistle again and we fell out. After several more calls to rush to formation, we caught on that Heath wouldn't be pleased until we could accomplish "falling out" in thirty seconds or less. We eventually succeeded, but Heath still kept us standing at attention while the surly lieutenant gave us a stern tongue-lashing. Suddenly, in the middle of Heath's lecture, a cadet nicknamed "Big Red" toppled over in a faint. Unfazed, Heath continued facing and marching the rest of us while a couple of the cadets assisted Big Red into the barracks. Big Red broke out with measles the next day, resulting in another quarantine period for our barracks, and exonerating Lieutenant Heath to a degree. But I resolved never to make men under my command stand at attention without first telling them to relax a little at the knees.

At last, classification into navigators, bombardiers, pilots, or wash-outs was posted, and to my astonishment, the Army classified me as a bombardier. Now, I was channeled into training I found much more interesting; we learned to identify aircraft, ships, and targets, and we studied mathematics, physics, signaling, and gunnery. This phase of our training was called "pre-flight."

Physical exercises became a big part of our routine over the next few weeks, including calisthenics (which is synonymous with "tiring quickly") and a variety of exercises in cadence. Occasionally, we played basketball, soccer, or softball, but mainly we ran the obstacle course, circling the perimeter of the base's large parade grounds. After running about a quarter of a mile we jumped ditches, scaled walls, climbed ropes, jumped obstacles, crossed a set of overhead pipes hand over hand, and jogged through an area of rough ground. For me, the only difficult part was the rope climb. Most often, Perkins, one of my Mormon friends, and I were among the first of the group to finish the obstacle course.

Physically, I felt I was in great shape, so one afternoon when our flight held a race around the parade grounds, I brashly vowed

I would win the competition. Perkins took the lead early in the race with me tagging his heels. We soon outdistanced the other runners and I felt confident of winning, until we reached a point about one hundred yards from the finish line. All of a sudden Perkins took off and left me far behind as I finished a distant second. Later, my friend told me he was a long-distance runner on the University of Utah track and field team.

While stationed at Santa Ana, I cut three wisdom teeth. When I asked the dentist to examine them, he decided he needed practice, and for a couple of days I lost a tooth per day in the hour just prior to my physical education period. I made each formation, even if I did spit a lot of blood on the parade grounds. Thank goodness, the fourth tooth came in later, because by that time, I had had about all of the torture I could take from that brutal dentist. Even the enemy couldn't have been more unsympathetic and cruel.

The most exasperating experience of pre-flight training was KP, or "kitchen police." On KP day we were awakened before dawn, marched to the mess hall, and assigned a part of the mess for the day. The bosses took pride in directing the only crew of running waiters in the Air Force, so by the end of each excruciatingly long day waiting tables, I was exhausted. All of the other bases where I trained had cafeterias, but Santa Ana insisted on doing everything the hard way, for the cadets at least.

Cleanliness was next to Godliness at Santa Ana, and every Saturday we washed the barracks, GI style, pouring hot soapy water on the floors, scrubbing, rinsing, sweeping, and drying them by hand. It seemed to me, Santa Ana's parade grounds were bare dirt just so cadets would track the dirt into the barracks and have more to clean. Early one morning the Colonel informed us that the Inspector-General of the Army was coming to inspect our camp. We never did see the general, just plenty of parade grounds as we picked up every scrap of paper on the base.

Ill fate plagued our squadron every time we were due for a weekend pass. Inevitably, one of the cadets caught a contagious disease, and we were again quarantined and restricted to base. Finally we were judged healthy, and on a weekend pass I attended church services at an LDS ward in Santa Ana. There I met Ellsworth Brown, who became one of my good friends.

Throughout pre-flight, Santa Ana's allure and Ellsworth's friendship continued to draw me into town on weekends. I made one trip to Los Angeles while stationed at Santa Ana, but it was disappointing. I became separated from my companions, and the night was so dark and the city so crowded that I couldn't even get a hotel room. I returned to the base in disgust.

With the war in full swing, the camp stayed on the alert. Late one evening after we had retired for the night, an air raid alarm bell rang. We all jumped out of bed, dressed hastily, and evacuated the base, our hearts pounding. We ran about five miles into the country and hid in some brush until the all clear sounded. As it turned out, a colonel who decided we were too comfortable, had ordered the air raid drill.

We regularly received guard duty assignments at the camp, keeping strangers from entering the base and protecting the Women's Air Corps (WACs) barracks from intruders. In the wee hours of the morning I could often be seen, walking my post, a lone sentry loaded down with a rifle, gas mask, steel helmet, a heavy overcoat, and a cartridge belt, everything a guard could possibly ask for—except shells for my gun. Generally, I was a happy boy when my relief arrived a few minutes after sunrise and I could drop off into sweet slumber in my comfortable bed.

The day I officially went on the United States account of war costs, my first payday, I received seventy-five dollars for my first month of army service. For some peculiar reason, my pay began on the day my orders were dated, rather than the day I reported for duty. I felt like a million dollars as I walked over to the post office and sent home money orders for fifty dollars and eight dollars. The fifty-dollar order went into my personal savings account, and the eight dollars, to the Church for tithing.

The camp throbbed with activity and optimism. On the fine spring evening we were issued cadet uniforms, we started to sing on the way back from the formation. Lieutenant Heath didn't allow such frivolity, but Captain Bell approved. Naturally, the Texans wanted to sing, "The Eyes of Texas," and "Dixie." The Californians insisted we sing, "California Here I Come". To prevent disharmony we sang both group's songs, but an argument evolved between the two factions and we neutrals were kept awake all night while they boasted about their states.

On Easter Sunday in the middle of the night, an alarm sounded, and in a few seconds our whole flight was awake, grabbing our clothes, gas masks, and overcoats. Our hearts again pounding hard in our chests, we fell out of our barracks and lined up, some of the men half dressed, one wearing only shower slippers and an overcoat. Flight Lieutenant Foster quickly organized us and ordered all of us except for the fire guards, who were to remain behind in the barracks, to march double-time to the dispersal area. Our favorite officer, Lieutenant Rice, ran up alongside our flight and shouted, "Nice going, boys."

Puffing hard, we ran headlong into the intensely dark countryside. Car lights and base lights were all extinguished. No one could even smoke. Searchlights shot long beams of light into the dark sky, circling and crossing each other in amazing brilliance. Behind us P-38 fighter plane engines roared, and we heard them take off into the darkness from a nearby airfield. After a minute or two, the searchlights stopped moving, focusing on a single airplane caught in the beams. In due time the plane was identified as friendly and we plodded wearily back to camp to try to snatch an hour or two of slumber before reveille.

As the days turned into weeks I gradually slipped into my new role as a bombardier in the Army Air Corps. Stories of the bombardier's role in combat circulated freely, one teacher telling us the bombardier's nose compartment is the most vulnerable spot in the plane. "Oft times the bombardier is washed from the airship with a hose at the end of the mission," he said. I didn't pay a lot of attention to the nonsense. Common sense told me that no one station in the plane was safer than another. Perhaps such tales served to scare the faint of heart to wash them out of the training and keep them out of air combat.

By the end of May, I received my last tetanus vaccination, and as usual, I was feeling fine until I reached for my shirt I had removed to expose my arm. A sharp pain hit me that felt as if someone had whacked me with a club about the size of a fence post. Nonetheless, I felt great relief at having the inoculations over once and for all. Needle-carrying medics still give me alternating chills and fever.

Meanwhile, news came from Los Angeles of fights between sailors and Marines stationed in the city and Mexican American, African American, and Filipino youth, who called themselves "Pachucos." They distinguished themselves by their flamboyant *zoot suits*: a long coat with baggy bell-bottomed pants, a pork pie hat, a long key chain, and shoes with thick soles.

Angry about the Pachucos' anti-war attitudes, the sailors accosted them on the streets of Los Angeles and forcibly removed their zoot suits. In the fighting, several men were stabbed, resulting in an order from the West Coast Training Command, making Los Angeles off-limits to all service personnel. From then on, men on weekend passes went to Pasadena, Santa Ana, Newport, or Balboa.

Slowly our training progressed, eventually introducing us to a pressure chamber to simulate flying at altitudes of up to 35,000 feet. We learned that gas expands to twice its original volume at 18,000 feet, making it imperative that we expelled gas freely from any part of our body where it may be trapped. Lectures covered the physiological aspects of the phenomenon, and films illustrated how even a cold or gas pains could knock a man out. Moreover, if a cadet couldn't pass the gas as he ascended, the pains increased exponentially. Similarly, with a head cold, pressure in the ears and sinuses from blocked air passages, such as the Eustachian tube, cause pain, and unless pressure is released, it could rupture the eardrum.

As the altitude increases, the percentage of oxygen remains constant, but the air itself becomes so thin that at about 15,000 feet, anoxia dulls bodily functions, resulting in unconsciousness or even death. To prevent anoxia we were fitted with oxygen masks before entering the chamber. At extreme altitudes, we also learned to watch for the bends, in which nitrogen bubbles that form in the bloodstream at low pressure collect around the skeletal joints and cause unbearable pain.

In the chamber our instructors simulated ascent by removing a specific amount of air to simulate different altitudes, then observed our reactions through windows. If a cadet showed signs of distress, he was removed through one of two side chambers and immediately treated without interfering with the other cadets.

Our first test simulated ascent to 5,000 feet, then dropped us to ground level conditions, and some of the men had to be removed because of earaches. On the second hop we were to don our oxygen masks at 15,000 feet as we ascended to 35,000 feet and leveled off. Cadet Salzburg contracted severe abdominal cramps, although he tried to belch and pass gas. But he couldn't and was quickly extricated. Bill Salisbury was attacked by the bends, and the pain was so severe in his knee joints that he, too, had to be carried from the chamber. As we descended, our wily instructor asked Jake Rives to remove his oxygen mask and write his name, but before Rives put pen to paper he passed out. The instructor gave him a few whiffs of oxygen and he swiftly recovered, smiling a sheepish grin. Thankfully, I got through the session without a problem.

Altitude training under our belts, we slid back into everyday army life, and soon after, I drew another KP stint, doing such a good job waiting tables at lunchtime that the men at one table gave me a seventy-five cent tip. Encouraged with my success, two of my envious friends, Adamcik and Bayer, decided they would impress their customers into giving them tips at the evening meal. To prime patrons into a generous mood, they placed two dimes in a saucer on the table. Clearing dishes after the meal they discovered a cadet had filched their dimes.

One night our flight was assigned guard duty at the PX. Around midnight I challenged a soldier who was so drunk that he had come to the wrong barracks area. Not knowing what I ought to do with him, I sent him to the parade grounds. For a lack of a better idea, the parade ground sentinel sent the sauced soldier back to me. Throughout the wee hours of morning we kept the poor guy walking between our respective stations until he sobered up enough to remember the location of his barracks. Lieutenant Gersting, officer of the guard that night (and our maps and charts teacher), was so impressed with our performance that we became his star students thereafter.

One summer day an order from headquarters arrived at the bombardier-navigator detachment, requiring us to sing as we marched on our way to and from classes. After a good laugh, we complied as ordered, but our flight could scarcely carry a tune and we sounded terrible. Since a "shavetail," a disparaging name for a newly commissioned officer, monitored every corner around which we marched to see that we sang, we picked our favorite jingle that went as follows:

The 2nd lieutenants will win the war, parlez vous,
The 2nd lieutenants will win the war, parlez vous.
The 2nd lieutenants will win the war, so
what the hell are we fighting for?
Hinky dinky parlez vous

After a while, someone got the bright idea to spice up the lyrics. As we passed the lieutenants, we sang heartily:

The WACS and WAVES will win the war, parlez vous,
The WACS and WAVES will win the war, parlez vous,
The WACS and WAVES will win the war,
so what the hell are we fighting for?
Hinky dinky parlez vous

The humorless lieutenants didn't like what they heard and gave our section march master a demerit. Some people are just hard to please.

Of all the officers, I most admired Lieutenant Rice, an oddity in the officer's corps. He believed men would do more if treated well, than they would if forced or treated badly. He avoided assigning us many of the distasteful details we saw neighboring barracks perform. They had lieutenants who did their best to be feared, even hated. As an example of his fairness, Lieutenant Rice inspected the attic of our barracks one morning and found it laden with empty liquor bottles. While some officers would have had a fit, Lieutenant Rice climbed out of the loft, lined up the bottles, and said, "I wouldn't have minded finding bottles in the attic if they were full."

On another occasion when Cadet Sam Snell cursed during a morning march through the compound after he remembered a dental appointment he had forgotten, we all laughed at the fuss he made. But it wasn't funny, because missing a dental appointment was a serious breach of conduct. Lieutenant Rice interceded and saved Sam from receiving several demerits and a batch of extra duties.

When gigs—demerits—given by other officers to cadets under his command reached Lieutenant Rice's desk, they disappeared. As far as I know none of the gigs were sent to headquarters for recording on a cadet's permanent record. One day I was assigned to be in charge of quarters—answering messages, reminding men of their formations, and generally assisting the clerk—when a gig slip came in on an infraction calling for five demerits on a specific cadet. When the clerk asked Lieutenant Rice what to do about it, he replied, "Give him two. No. Hell, just give him one."

Rice's colleagues criticized him for his humane attitude, but we would have done anything for the good lieutenant. Near the end of our stay at Santa Ana, the base held a comprehensive tournament between the flights featuring drill and athletic contests. Our flight was the overwhelming winner, much to the satisfaction of Lieutenant Rice. I resolved to be like him if I ever had command.

On Friday, June 25, 1943, pre-flight training ended and I was still in the program; I hadn't washed out. My grades were good, especially in Morse code and physics, in which I had a 98 percent and a 97 percent average, respectively.

Internally, we felt grateful that the ambiguity of what lay ahead had at least partially disappeared with our specific assignments in hand. Moreover, the understanding we gained on how our respective assignments fit into the overall scheme of the war augmented our confidence. Outwardly, in our relief we became brash and lighthearted. Pranks increased. One evening a mischievous soldier entered the barracks and threw Cadet Silva's coat hangers into the attic. Silva searched every corner of the barracks without success. Finally, a helpful cadet suggested he look in the attic. Silva had crawled through an opening and retrieved his property when we heard a cracking noise. In the darkness he stepped between the rafters and crashed through the plaster ceiling. He spent half the night patching up the hole and no one got any sleep.

CHAPTER 6

Bombing Basics

Speculation on where we would attend bombardier school caused a group of us to each place a dollar in a hat and hold a drawing, the winner to collect the cash when we received our orders. Several options existed, including Deming and Roswell, New Mexico; Big Springs, Texas; Chandler, Arizona; and Victorville, California. I drew Roswell, New Mexico, for my chance. I lost. By now it was July, and we were acclimated to the cool sea breezes of Santa Ana but ill prepared for our transfer to Victorville, California, an oasis in the desolate, scorched Mojave Desert. It was the last base any of us would have chosen given a choice.

Traveling the sixty-four miles northeast by army bus, we nearly had an accident when a tire blew out about a mile from San Bernardino city limits. While the driver fixed the flat in the hot sun, we filed out of the bus and, not finding a particle of shade in the barren desert, sat in the barrow pit breathing stifling air. We nearly passed out from heat exhaustion. The asphalt was so blisteringly hot we were lucky all of the tires on the bus didn't blow.

Victorville Army Air Base was a sharp contrast to Santa Ana; the barracks were clean; the food was exceptionally good; the schedule was well organized; and the base boasted one of the best safety records in the Air Corps. Major Charles Sampson was an officer in charge of training and, in my opinion, largely responsible for the excellent organization of the school.

The only major camp disadvantage, besides the intense heat, was the bad attitude of a few crazed taxi pilots who flew us on our bombing runs, flying small AT11 training planes. They would rather have been in combat overseas, flying large bombers or the coveted fighter planes. Frankly, I couldn't blame them for complaining about taxiing bombardiers around familiar flight patterns. It wasn't very exciting.

We didn't have time to waste at Victorville as we had often had at Santa Ana. Reveille started our day at 4:45 a.m. one morning and 5:30 a.m. the next, with lectures, films, hands-on training, KP, and guard duty until 9:00 p.m. Night after night we fell into bed worn out, sleeping soundly until morning.

> **ON SATURDAY, JULY 10, 1943**, four British divisions under the command of General Sir Bernard Montgomery and four American divisions of the United States 7th Army under Lieutenant-General George Patton — 478,000 troops — landed on the island of Sicily.

In Victorville, two inspections and a parade commanded our close attention. The first was a standby inspection of our quarters requiring us to stand at attention while inspectors scrutinized our living area with fine-toothed combs. Lieutenant Harbaugh ran white-gloved fingers over windowsills and behind footlockers in a fruitless search for elusive dust. Behind his back we dubbed him "Inspector Hawkshaw." With an audible collective sigh of relief, we passed the inspection with flying colors and headed out of doors to suffer through an open ranks field inspection, standing at attention on the searing parade grounds. Removing my shoes back in the barracks, I expected to find blisters covering my feet, but thankfully, my toes were a rosy pink with nary a sore.

Between the inspections we marched around the parade grounds, saluting officers as we passed an ostentatious reviewing stand. Then, puffing out our manly chests like cocks strutting before a clutch of hens, we marched boldly past the Women's Air

Corps barracks. When the attractive WACs cheered, more than a few cadets stepped out of sync, furtively observing to each other the women at Victorville were much prettier than their peers at Santa Ana.

Bomb dropping from an airplane was several weeks in coming, but in the meantime, we spent hour after hour manipulating bombsight controls on a mechanical training platform above a simulated bombing range, dropping imaginary bombs on miniature targets painted on the floor about ten feet below. Calculating various factors after we released the mock bomb, we determined whether we would have hit the target had our training platform been an airplane and the miniature target, a military objective.

What ought to have been an enjoyable experience became miserable as our instructor criticized us no matter how well, or poorly, we did, evoking within us a desire to throw him off the platform. His mood shifted 180 degrees when the day arrived for us to fly in real airplanes. After introducing us to our assigned aircraft, he magnanimously dismissed us to an hour of free time — a rarity indeed.

Bright sunshine, blue sky, and blooming cactus greeted me the summer morning of my very first flight in a real airplane. I dropped several practice bombs into the lonely Mojave Desert on nearby bombing ranges, each containing a shack surrounded by concentric rings. Hitting the shack dead center was the primary goal of each bombing run. Then using the concentric circles we could measure exactly how far from the shack each bomb hit.

When bombs hit the ground, a puff of smoke or at night a flash of light made by a small explosive charge told us the precise location of the strike. At that moment my good friend and bombing partner Cadet Jack Ryder snapped a photograph of my bomb strike and plotted the bomb hits on a chart. After I photographed and plotted his hits, we calculated the circle of error — the average distance of our hits from the center — and turned in the chart to our superiors following each mission. At the end of the training if the circle of error of all our bomb statistics averaged more than 230 feet, we were washed out as bombardiers.

Some bombardiers falsified the record of a bomb dropped far from the intended target by a dishonest practice called "raking bombs." The recording photographer would simply fail to take the picture, then covertly plot the strike location closer to the target. Pilots normally turned in dishonest cadets for the deception, washing them out of the program, but pilots weren't all that observant and many bombardiers got away with the sham. Cadet Ryder and I decided from the start we would be honest and photograph all our bombs wherever they hit. Ultimately, the resolution proved advantageous to me at graduation time.

As we progressed, the height of our bomb runs increased from 500 feet to 10,000 feet. At high altitudes the temperatures in the desert cooled, and the scenery was beautiful around Arrowhead and Big Bear Lakes. When we flew at night, the flights were peaceful and quiet. Generally, we disliked having our annoying instructor along on our missions because he was such a nuisance, and he practically sat on us as he evaluated our efforts.

Early one morning after dropping my first bomb, the instructor shoved me aside, glared at the bomb-sight synchronization and, even before the bomb hit the ground, began cursing me for dropping it so poorly. As luck would have it, the bomb struck twenty feet from the target, the best I had ever dropped. On the next run, I released the second bomb and again the irascible instructor shoved me to the side, cursing my ineptitude. But this time the bomb fell even closer to the shack. Embarrassed and red faced, the little gnat shut up for ten wonderfully peaceful minutes.

Obnoxious officers seemed to be the rule rather than the exception. When a chain broke on the bombing simulator, the instructor detailed me to run to the office and ask a maintenance man to fix the machine. Instead of knocking before entering an open office door, I barged through and began to ask for help. Lieutenant

Jascyk interrupted and asked if I knew how to report to an officer.

"Yes," I told him.

"Then go back outside and do it properly," he replied.

I did as he asked. Standing before him at attention he and another lieutenant cursed me. Several minutes later Lieutenant Jascyk asked,

"Are you sick?"

"No, sir," I replied.

"Then get out of this office and run fifteen laps around the hanger."

Fifteen minutes later I completed the laps, running about a mile and a half. When I returned to the office the lieutenant assigned me calisthenics on top of the laps. I almost passed out from exhaustion. I felt chagrined and angry about the whole affair. Adding insult to injury, during calisthenics meticulous Lieutenant Harbaugh gave me two gigs for failing to have my shoes tied. It was a grim war and I hadn't met the enemy yet.

Our short-tempered instructor habitually arrived late for our practice bombing runs. One morning Lieutenant Field, Ryder, and I sat in the unbearably hot plane for about half an hour, waiting for him to accompany us. Suddenly, Lieutenant Field cursed loudly and said, "That guy went through pre-flight with me and was late for every formation. We're taking off without him." Ryder and I buckled up as Field started the engines and we took off.

At one thousand feet, Lieutenant Field ordered me to enter the nose compartment to begin the drop. As I stumbled along the catwalk, past the copilot's seat and into the bombardier's chair, Ryder pulled the arming pins from the bombs. I quickly donned my headset and throat microphone, uncovered the bombsight and began my computations. Taking the air temperature at intervals of one thousand feet, I determined an average outside temperature. At twelve thousand feet, I donned my oxygen mask and adjusted it for the bombing runs. A minute later I had the trail and disc speed set into the intricate Norden bombsight, a top-secret analog computer developed to ensure accurate bomb drops. By now I could see the target in the distance, so I leveled the stabilizer and opened the bomb bay doors, as directed by Lieutenant Field, while Ryder prepared the camera to take pictures of the bomb impacts.

When the bomb run started Lieutenant Field transferred control to me and I flew the plane using the Norden bombsight through the Automatic Flight Control Equipment (AFCE). Stabilized by directional and vertical gyroscopes, the bombsight computed ground speed and crosswind drift, air density, wind force and direction, bomb configuration, plus a variety of other factors to gradually focus two cross hair sights on the target, indicating the exact position to drop the bombs.

Developed by the U.S. Navy in the 1930s, the bombsight was a marvelous instrument but it had two basic problems. First, the bombardier had to see the target before he could hit it. This wasn't a problem in clear weather or when the enemy wasn't firing on you, but add in a cloudy sky, battering by prop wash from neighboring B-17s in tight formation, bursting flak, and adrenaline flowing through the bombardier's veins during a fighter plane attack, and conditions change measurably. Second, the bombsight was complex, temperamental, and didn't always work. Since it was top-secret, from the beginning of our training we pledged to destroy it if we were shot down.

Picking up the dim blur of the target rapidly approaching, I engaged the directional and disengaged the secondary switches. My hands automatically engaged the gyro, turned on the instructor switch, raised the trigger, and switched on the telescope motor, killing my course so I could get a level bubble reading by turning the leveling knobs until the bubbles—similar to those found on a carpenter's level—were even.

Once the bubbles were level, my eyes went back into the sight and I finished killing the rate and course. The cross hair indices passed, the release rattled, and I broke out into a sweat as I yelled, "Bombs away, sir." (The "sir" was a very important part of the procedure.) Hastily I turned off the switches, caged the gyro, re-engaged the secondary and disengaged the directional, and gave the plane back to Lieutenant Field.

The descending bomb was a beauty. At one hundred feet and three o'clock, I said to Lieutenant Field, "Okay to turn, sir." My voice was much calmer than it had been earlier and I began to prepare for my next bombing run. Soon all five of my bombs were away and Ryder and I exchanged positions. On the way back to base he and I calculated our statistics and discovered my circle of error was one hundred and forty-seven feet, which was good. Perhaps I can be a bombardier after all, I thought.

With the stress of the run over, Ryder and I began to worry about how angry our instructor would be about us leaving without him. True to form, he was furious, but Lieutenant Field defended us and accepted all of the blame. A few weeks later Field submitted his report of the mission to our superiors and word leaked out that our instructor hadn't been on board. The colonel was furious and reprimanded our instructor, confining him to base for several weekends. After that our obnoxious instructor was a little bit easier to live with.

Had all of our officers been as fair and decent as Lieutenant Field we would never have had anything to complain about. On a flight with Lieutenant Field, I realized after I dropped my bombs and retired to my seat in the rear of the plane that I had left my pencil in the bombardier's compartment. I ran through the plane to retrieve it, picked it up, and briskly returned to my seat. Moments later Lieutenant Field called me on the interphone to come to the cockpit and fly the ship. As soon as I took over the controls, Field climbed out of his seat, went to the back of the plane and stomped around. To my amazement, the airplane became unstable in my hands. This was Field's way of impressing me with the importance of staying stationary while on the bombing run.

Field was suitably cast as a pilot—solid, knowledgeable, with a practiced understanding of aircraft machinery, and fun to be around. But he was a dyed in the wool practical joker. Late one afternoon as we returned to the base after a flight, Field, without warning, decided to practice maneuvers, throwing the plane into a dive just as I reached to close the cover over the camera hatch. The force of the descent slammed the cover hard into my face, then sent it rolling out of reach in the back of the ship. Rubbing my head with one hand, I hastily chased after the cover that was taking headers in every direction. Field eventually leveled the plane and I returned to the hatch and was securing the cover when Lieutenant Field yanked back on the throttle, lifting the plane upward and throwing me against the floor. I found myself peering through the open hatch at the ground, the earth below moving rapidly in a dizzying pattern.

Violently ill, my stomach churning, I felt the contents slide up my throat, ready to leap out of my mouth—along with my tonsils. Finally, Field again leveled the plane and I, swallowing hard to force the acidic lump back down my gullet, closed the cover and sat limply on the floor, praying for the dizziness and nausea to subside. Then Field landed the plane with a jerk, and the jar was the final straw. Holding my hat below my mouth, I pitched my cookies. Unruffled at my distress, Lieutenant Field simply laughed heartily and thanked me for not messing up the airplane. I silently hoped I would never ever be that sick on a flight again.

The summer heat of Victorville held, and back on the ground we continued our daily classes. Behind Lieutenant Griego's back, a Hispanic who was one of our flight's bombardier trainers, we began to call him "El Toro." Cadet Harold Reeves, thinking that was his real name, referred to Griego as El Toro while speaking with another instructor. Later the instructor told Griego what Reeves had called him. Griego sought out Reeves, informed him El Toro means "bull" in Spanish, kidded him about his mistake, and asked Reeves to call him by his appropriate name. Griego endeared himself to us, because he was such a good sport. Unlike some shavetails, Griego didn't let a little authority destroy his sense of humor.

Meanwhile, I suffered my own name troubles. During roll call I regularly caused a titter among the troops when I interrupted a new instructor to say, "The name is Ririe, sir," pronouncing the first syllable with a long "i" and the second with a long "e." But no matter what I did, the army spelled and pronounced Ririe every way, but seldom the right way. Then when I revealed my hometown was also named Ririe, it confused clerks completely. One frustrating day I reported as ordered to the personnel office at the far end of the base, where the clerk accused me of entering my last name in the "city" space on a form I had submitted.

I laughed about it after the war with my younger brother Clive, who experienced a similar mix-up when he boarded his first Navy submarine. The boat's yeoman met sailors at the gangplank, collecting their names, addresses, and next of kin for the Navy to notify in case of a calamity. Clive was last on the list and the ship was behind schedule when the petty officer asked Clive his name. "Ririe, Clive Perry," he replied. The officer wrote down "Riley," and Clive corrected him. The yeoman erased the name and wrote "Ryre." Clive corrected him again. The officer berated Clive for holding up the departure and wrote "Clyde." Clive protested. The officer changed the name to, "Glide." Again Clive protested. "V as in victory," Clive told him. The officer swore but corrected the name to "Clive." In the space for Clive's middle name, he wrote, 'Terry." Trying to be calm, Clive said, "No, my middle name is Perry." This time the officer got it right. He repeated, Ririe, Clive Perry. Clive agreed, thanked him, and went on, naming our father as the relative to be notified. Then the officer asked, "And your father's address?" Clive began to say, "Ririe, Idaho," but the officer sternly interrupted him. "No, not your name again. Your father's home address!"

Later, I attempted to convince the army of my birth date error, March 20, not March 19, 1922, as it appeared on the birth certificate from the state of Idaho. Confidentially, I'm sure that it would have been impossible. In the end, I gave up trying, and March 19 became my birthday during my army days.

In spite of the buzzing that went on at Victorville, the morale and safety record remained high. Unless cadets caused problems, instructors allowed us some privileges, such as drinking Cokes in the simulator. Unfortunately, when an empty Coke bottle tossed from the simulator cracked Cadet Sal Schenk on the head he made such a fuss that the instructors forbade us from drinking Cokes on the simulators for the duration of our class. The cadets bemoaned the loss of cold soft drinks to counteract the intolerable heat, often reaching 115 degrees Fahrenheit. As it happens, during a physical about a month before we graduated, too many airmen were over weight. Doctors blamed Cokes for the weight gain, and the base commander banned the soft drink from the premises. I lucked out. I didn't care for Cokes anyway.

CHAPTER 7

Wings and a Commission

On July 22nd, the U.S. 7th Army captured Palermo, Sicily, forcing Italy's Grand Council of Fascism to depose, arrest, and incarcerate its dictator, Benito Mussolini. Three days later, July 25, the British Bomber Command began Operation Gomorrah, sending 791 aircraft with 1,000 to 8,000 pound bombs containing 1,346 tons of high explosives and 931 tons of incendiaries in a massive air strike on Hamburg, Germany. An estimated 1,500 Germans were killed, 20,000 made homeless, and 12 Luftwaffe bombers shot down. We read about Mussolini in the newspapers but didn't hear much about the air strike until after the war. Due to government policies most battles, won or lost, were seldom reported to the general public during the war as a measure of national security.

At noon, on Saturday, July 24, our instructors set us free for the weekend. With little else to do, I went into Victorville, where the only thing happening was a Roy Rogers film at the local movie theater. I thought the deportment in our little movie house in Ririe was rowdy, but Victorville moviegoers were downright disorderly, shouting loudly when the hero yanked the black hat villain off his horse, rolled down a hillside with him, and punched him to a pulp.

Melvin J. Rich, Ellsworth Brown, and I hitchhiked to San Bernardino, an hour away, on our first Sunday morning off, to attend church. Standing on the side of the highway just outside the base, a California highway patrolman offered us a ride. We accepted the offer and on the drive I looked up the address in the little Church directory Dad had given me before I left home. The patrolman dropped us on the edge of town and a hotel clerk directed us to a beautiful Spanish-styled meetinghouse.

"We're at the right place," Rich said. "Look at all the kids."

The church was swarming with children chasing each other around the building.

Sunday School began shortly. After we introduced ourselves, Jack Parry, a soldier from nearby Camp Hahn, introduced himself as my cousin. He explained he had married my father's cousin Lois Lovell after I reported to Santa Ana. The class members laughed at our coincidental meeting. Jack was very glad to see us because he was homesick for his bride.

To our surprise, the commander of our bombardier school, Major Sampson, led the congregation as bishop, and the base supply officer Lieutenant Hollingshead was the bishop's counselor.

After Sunday School, the ward clerk, Brother Koldewyn, and his wife invited us to their home for dinner. In the evening we returned with them to the San Bernardino chapel to attend Sacrament Meeting. Unexpectedly, Bishop Sampson asked me to open the meeting with prayer and Brown and Rich to give impromptu sermons. Major Sampson publicly congratulated us for attending church on our first military pass. After Sacrament Meeting a member family by the name of Skousen invited us to their home for ice cream. We stayed with them until we caught a bus back to camp, ending our pleasant day in the appreciative warmth of the church.

Since attending church in San Bernardino required a cumbersome journey, I attended church at the Victorville Branch for several Sundays. The tiny congregation worshipped in a small house, but I enjoyed the services and the members' hospitality. It affirmed for me the truism that when a few are gathered in Christ's name, there the Holy Spirit will be.

Sunday, August 1, on an ill-fated air raid on Ploesti, Romania, 164 American bombers took a wrong turn and alert German defenses shot down 41 planes and killed 300 airmen. Again we never heard anything about the incident until after the war. The same morning, a Fast Sunday in Victorville (a monthly meeting during which members fast and donate the money they would have spent on food to the Church for the needy), Brown and I hitchhiked to San Bernardino and attended church services. We shared our testimonies in Fast and Testimony Meeting. Being in church made me think of my family and during my testimony I became so homesick that I choked up with emotion and could scarcely speak. In the afternoon after evening services, a young man in the ward loaned us his car and we went for a drive with the young man's sister, Gwen Wahlen, and two other cute girls, Dayle Davis and Jody Irwin, whom we had just met at church. As we drove into the mountains to visit scenic Arrowhead Springs Hotel, Dayle obviously liked Ellsworth. Jody, who disapproved of her flirtations, said little during the drive and didn't impress me very much. Little did I realize how much that pretty blond girl would one day mean to me.

Lazily, we wandered around the hotel and admired the striking panoramic view of the San Bernardino Valley until one of the girls looked at her watch. We had barely enough time to get to the station and catch the last bus back to the base. Rushing to the car, we jumped in and Ellsworth stomped the accelerator to the floorboards, speeding down the mountainside so recklessly that I feared for our lives. Even so, we barely arrived at the station in time.

Victorville residents must have hated us constantly buzzing their homes. Fortunately, there were very few houses in the area of our bombing ranges, but even wild animals couldn't have slept well as planes roared over them night and day. One morning Jake Rives and I had a mission to each drop three bombs from an altitude of one thousand feet. Our run took us directly over a house on top of a small hill. After dropping the bomb the pilot buzzed about thirty feet above the house just as a woman walked toward it. Frightened, she high tailed it into a shed. When we circled and came off the second bombing run, the pilot again buzzed the house.

The frightened woman again ran into the shed. Frankly, I think pilots were bored and did ridiculous pranks such as buzzing houses in the hopes that someone would complain, forcing the military to send the pilot into combat.

A few days later, Lieutenant Makarov flew over the river seeking migrating ducks resting on the sloughs on their way to Canada as he returned to base. When the two cadets who were on the flight with him remarked they couldn't see any ducks, Makarov dived the ship toward the water. Frightened birds flew in all directions as Makarov pulled the plane out of the dive a few feet above the river. Inside, the cadets pitched their cookies, figuring their duck, I mean, goose, was cooked.

Near one of our ranges, the Bicycle, a group of antiaircraft soldiers used one of our runs for training. Cadet Harold Scherer was bombardier on a mission over the range when his pilot had trouble finding the target. Seeing an oval-shaped ring in his sight, Scherer assumed the ring was the target, calculated its position and released the bomb. Minutes later the pilot realized the assumed target was actually a well-camouflaged antiaircraft battery. Luckily, Scherer missed the emplacement by seventy-five feet, but the angry GIs manning the battery immediately aimed a canon at the plane. Before they could fire, the pilot gunned the engines and cleared the area. Apparently the battery either didn't have rounds for their gun or the positioning crew was too slow getting a bead on the plane.

To increase my flying time, which counted toward my qualification, I flew copilot on a bombing run with a bombardier who was a lieutenant, one of several officers in my class who elected to train as bombardiers. Despite his rank, the lieutenant proved to me that I was certainly not the poorest bombardier in the class. The lieutenant's bombs fell all over the Mojave Desert and afterwards he used a rake to cover up the bad impacts. At graduation, if given my way, he would have received a pearl handled miniature rake in the center of his wings instead of the customary bomb insignia.

On my first night bombing run, I dropped two water bombs. Our irritating instructor accompanied me, and when I dropped the first bomb at eighty feet from the target, he beamed. When the second bomb hit twenty feet from the target, he crawled all over me, slapped me on the back, and complimented me for the first time in six weeks. At that point, I decided I might survive and receive my wings.

It took luck as well as skill to operate the temperamental Norden bombsight. Actually, night targets were well lighted and easier to see than day targets. And it was simple to distinguish them from the bright streetlights of Victorville, San Bernardino, and Barstow. Additionally, the night air on my first flight was smooth as glass, which favored accurate bombing. Unfortunately, on night runs we had to contend with gyroscope toppling resulting from the gauge lights sucking up the electrical power like a sponge.

On my second night run I had a weak gyro and dropped my bombs helter skelter. The gyro was so far off after my last bomb dropped that the rate wasn't killed as it normally is when the bombsight works properly. The instructor shoved me away from the sight, looked in, frowned, and exclaimed, "It will hit three hundred feet over." We were both amazed when the flash lit up about fifty feet to the right of the shack. That's what you call compensating errors.

As our training progressed, men began leaving the ranks one by one. Melvin C. Rich washed out and received orders to attend radio school in Sioux City, Iowa. Jim Snyder also washed out, but he transferred to pilot school and wasn't disappointed about abandoning bombardier training. To bolster flagging morale, a hundred beautiful chorus girls arrived at the base and put on a show for the troops. I didn't attend and later heard the show was corny. No one cared, however, because the girls' beauty lived up to their billing. That night the girls stayed in the WAC quarters and swam in the pool before leaving. Men lucky enough to ogle them went gaga.

On September 2, the day before General Guiseppe Castellano secretly signed the armistice between Italy and the Allied Armed

Forces in the village of Cassibile, near Syracuse, Sicily, I flew my final record mission. Even though I had a hectic time, my conversion of circle of error calculated at 231, one foot over the 230 required. Jack Ryder's circle of error hit 232 feet. Although neither of us believed we would wash out for bombing only one or two feet over the mark, especially since our grades were quite good, we still faced desert training, a couple more classes, and a final interview. Clearly, we weren't out of the woods yet.

> **ON SEPTEMBER 12, 1943**, seventy German Waffen-SS commandos, flying nine DFS 230 gliders and wearing parachutes, assaulted the Campo Imperatore Hotel in Northern Italy and liberated Benito Mussolini from his prison in a daring raid ordered by Adolf Hitler. Not a shot was fired. Once the dictator was free, Hitler set him up as leader of the Sato Republic, a fascist regime in Northern Italy.

In late September one of the Victorville pilots hit two ducks, and the birds became so entangled in the propeller that it stalled out the motor. Thankfully, the pilot landed the ship safely and after examining the damage, wrote on the report, "Two ducks in the left motor." When the crew chief removed the ducks from the engine the next day, he wrote, "Left engine all right. Removed two ducks." I silently prayed that if we ran into any birds while I was upstairs, they would be either hummingbirds or sparrows.

The closer we came to graduation the greater the pressure on the troops. To relieve the tension we fell into the habit of hitting each other over the head with our rolled up Mercator charts as we marched to our navigation class. All was fun until Silva and Sherman, the main perpetrators, whacked cadets too often. Disgusted with their performance, our flight leader decided to teach them a lesson. He called the formation to attention, put all of us in a brace, and then cracked Silva over the head with a blow so hard it almost knocked him out. All of us laughed at Silva—which probably hurt him more than the blow to the head.

Days later my name appeared on the list of graduates as either a second lieutenant or a flight warrant officer, and I received an allowance to buy new uniforms. To my delight, the blouses, trousers, etc., were stylish. When I dressed in the officer's uniform I thought, "I am wearing the best clothes I have ever worn."

The Indian summer weather held for a training bivouac in the desert near Helendale, California, with Lieutenants Walker, Menzies, and Harbaugh in charge of the exercise. Designed to prepare us for field operations in the desert, the training area contained two small buildings, dust one-foot deep, two runways, an outhouse for the officers—and the probability that a snake or scorpion lay under every rock or clump of brush.

Dumped off the truck with our gear, we pitched tents the moment we arrived, including a mess tent, a large tent for the guard, and latrines near the runways, and by evening a bedroll lay stretched out on every army cot. We raised the folding cots about a foot off the wooden floor because a cadet in an earlier bivouac had the misfortune of having a snake slide into bed with him. Cut brush topped with dirt camouflaged the top and sides of the tents. I thought, now every time we walk in or out of the tent a pound or two of dirt will fall off the roof and slide down our necks.

The lieutenants informed us reveille would sound at 5:00 a.m., and the day concluded with a meeting every evening at 8:00 p.m. We didn't have to shave; any uniform was permissible. In our shorts and sun helmets, with mess kits and canteens, we looked like the wild animal hunter Frank Buck. And never fear, there would be plenty of work to keep us busy since we were to fuse and load our own bombs. Water was so scarce the lieutenants told beer drinkers they could buy beer after 5:00 p.m. Those of us who didn't drink beer had to manage on highly chlorinated water.

Ryder and I, on guard duty the first night, were awakened at four o'clock in the morning, having slept at the guardhouse. Assigned to guard the gate for a boring four-hour shift, we only saw one car, Lieutenant Brooks' on his way to the gunnery range. At

7:30 a.m. we took turns going to the mess hall for a breakfast of stew, hard biscuits, candy, and cocoa extract. To wash our mess kits after eating, we formed a line and dunked them in several large water basins. If you were first in the line you could do a good job of washing. If you were at the end of the line, the water was so greasy that you could do a better cleansing job scraping the kit with a branch of sagebrush.

The following night I slept in the mess tent so I could be more conveniently awakened for breakfast duty in the kitchen the next morning. I wondered if I would ever sleep on the cot in my own tent. Compared to the miserable KP duty I worked at Santa Ana, in the desert it was a pleasure, since much of the food was prepared at the main base and trucked to us. All we did was serve food, pump fuel into the gas stove with a tire pump, and wash pots and pans. Best of all, the detail only lasted half of the day.

Lieutenant Simmons drank a beer as he taxied Ryder and me to the range for our first mission to drop bombs from one thousand feet above the desert. Right after dropping the first bomb, Simmons dove the plane to a few feet above the sand, buzzed everything in sight, then climbed back to bombing altitude, giving us barely enough time to synchronize the bombsight and drop the next bomb on the target. Despite being terrified, I managed to score two very good hits. I had to release one of Jack's bombs with a screwdriver because the release failed to work. Ironically, the bomb fell for a direct hit. Regardless of our success on the range, we didn't want to fly with Simmons again. He was a menace to safety.

With limited water and no baths, we were all dirty. One afternoon after we had installed fuses and loaded our bombs, the lieutenants packed us into a truck and transported us to a mossy farm reservoir. Not much bodily cleansing resulted, but we enjoyed cooling off.

A couple of days later, a posting appeared on the bulletin board announcing the bombardiers selected to represent our class in a regional bombing contest at Carlsbad, New Mexico. With my squeakby circle of error in mind, I didn't even bother to look at the posting, until a cadet called out in passing,

"Hey, Ririe, you're going to the contest."

"You must be mistaken," I answered.

I rushed to the board and saw that I had been chosen to be the team's photographer. My picture taking of bomb impacts was the best on the base. If Ryder and I hadn't decided at the beginning to be honest and photograph all our bombs, I might have been tempted to miss photographing the impact of a bad bomb. To me this was a lesson in honesty. Unfortunately, our participation in the contest didn't materialize, because on our way to Carlsbad, a storm forced our plane to land at Luke Field in Phoenix, Arizona, where we spent the night. Lieutenant Field made sure we had a good time anyway.

Meanwhile, other cadets received their commissions, but I was still waiting. Apparently, the colonel couldn't decide whether to make me a second lieutenant or a flight officer, because personnel called me in for a second interview. As the questions began, I felt nervous and apprehensive until the officer startled me by asking a question I hadn't anticipated.

"What is your religion?" he asked.

"I am a Mormon," I answered. I hope he isn't bigoted, I thought.

"What do you believe in?" he asked.

I was on the hot seat until the Church's thirteen Articles of Faith I memorized in Primary came to mind. "We believe in God the Eternal Father, and in His Son Jesus Christ, and in the Holy Ghost," I began.

A lively discussion followed. The interviewer must have been impressed because we didn't get to the second Article of Faith before he ended the interview.

After anxiously waiting a few days, I received orders awarding me a commission in the army as a second lieutenant and the coveted bombardier's wings. After long hours of study, considerable bombing practice, incredible tension, and the desert heat sapping my strength, I achieved my goal. Better still, I earned a furlough.

CHAPTER 8

Days of Tedium

Newly commissioned Second Lieutenant Ellsworth Brown and I met the train at the station in Victorville with our furlough papers happily in hand, but the train from Los Angeles was jam-packed with passengers and we were unable to buy tickets to Salt Lake City. After pondering our situation we took a chance and boarded the train without tickets. When the conductor discovered us we humbly explained we only had a short furlough, our last leave before going into combat. The good man accepted our money, sold us tickets to our destination, and somehow found two seats in a passenger car for us. Despite our luck I was so keyed up about the prospect of being at home again I couldn't sleep. I doubt that if I had been in a Pullman berth it would have made any difference.

Brown and I parted company at Salt Lake City. I had an hour layover before my train departed for Idaho Falls, so I went to a nearby restaurant for breakfast. Enlisted men swarmed the café, and I found myself taking salutes and being addressed as "sir" for the first time in my life. I admit the attention felt good.

Back on the train the journey to Idaho Falls was slow and boring. As soon as I arrived at the station, I ran to a phone booth and called home. Mother and Dad drove quickly from Ririe, and we were soon hugging each other. My family wanted to hear a firsthand account of my experiences, and we talked into the wee hours of the morning. For the second night in a row, I didn't sleep much.

After breakfast, I accompanied Dad to the Kraft cheese factory to deliver milk and eat handfuls of curds while the cheese maker turned a blind eye. When we returned home I borrowed the family car and drove into town to purchase a haircut from Red Larson, the local barber. Elated that I had recommended him for a reference when the army investigated my background, Red talked so much that I had difficulty getting away from him.

Stepping out of the barbershop, I ran into my parents' neighbor Etta Tirrell, who insisted on taking my picture in my uniform. The following day I attended a funeral service with my parents and came across Ruth Bright, my third grade teacher, who made a big fuss over my uniform. Clearly, I was a celebrity in my small country town.

Friday afternoon Dad, Max, Clive, Wayne, and I drove to a reservoir on the North Fork of the Snake River. We made our beds by the shadowy pines along the shore, built a roaring fire, and shot the bull until we dropped off to sleep beneath the stars. Arising early the next morning, we fished all day without catching a single trout, but I didn't care because I was with the most important people in my life.

Late Monday afternoon, my furlough over and bags packed with my Mother's sweet delicacies, I boarded a slow moving train headed south to Salt Lake City for my next posting at the Utah State Fair Grounds. Even though my orders required I report for duty on Tuesday I traveled the night before to arrive relaxed and in control when the army posted bomber crew assignments, due the same day. A fussy baby on the train cried every time I dozed, and I arrived in Salt Lake City exhausted and in a dither. In any case I shouldn't have worried. In typical army fashion weeks passed before crew assignments came through.

To spruce up after my restless night I visited a barbershop and received my first shave from a professional barber before reporting to the commanding officer to answer questions, present orders, and fill out a questionnaire. A group of buddies from Victorville showed me our quarters in a slightly remodeled Utah State Fair Grounds cowshed, one of several buildings where in pre-war days 4-H youth groups groomed, fed, and stabled their prize animals on clean wheat straw. Some of the men complained of the lingering odor in the barns, but I assured them that after fifteen minutes in a barn you can't smell anything anyway. My own chagrin at having to bivouac in a renovated cowshed evaporated when I discovered my assigned space lay adjacent to my Victorville friend Ellsworth Brown.

> **IN ENGLAND ON OCTOBER 9**, the U.S. 8th Air Force created diversions in Woensdrecht and Leeuwarden in the Netherlands, plus sent 100 bombers to Anklam, Germany, and lost 18 planes. Meanwhile, the main force of 246 B-17 and B-24 bombers attacked Gdynia and Danzig in Poland. The airmen also destroyed the Focke-Wulf aircraft plant at Marienburg in East Prussia, but Germans damaged 51 planes and wounded 25 men before they got away.

With very little to do in Salt Lake City, I obtained permission to leave the fair grounds to visit my mother's sister Melba Barnes, from whom I learned that my Barnes cousins were all active in the war effort, either as members of the armed services or as defense workers. Florence was in Santa Ana, California, with her Army Air Corps husband; Jeanne worked in a hospital in New York City; and Fred, a U.S. Navy Lieutenant Junior Grade, served in parts unknown. For the life of me I couldn't figure out why so many of my relatives opted for the Navy, because few of us had even seen an ocean before the war.

A few days after taking up residence at the fairgrounds, my father's cousin, Ray Lovell, married a beautiful girl named Florence Lindsay in the Salt Lake LDS Temple. Being Ray's only male relative in the area at the time, I agreed to serve as his best man at the reception. Mercifully, he promised I wouldn't be required to wear a tuxedo, because in my new army uniform I looked sufficiently fashionable for the occasion.

I soon found myself in an uncomfortable formal reception line, between Aunt Harriet Lovell and Ray, introducing guests to the groom, most of whom I did not know. The vast majority belonged to the bride's family. Bashful Ray received a kiss from nearly every woman I introduced to him, each kiss causing him to blush a brilliant red. Luckily, I survived the evening without a kiss.

After the line disbanded for the evening, the bride and groom danced. Left to my own devices, I danced with a beautiful bridesmaid, who was gracious but also married. She tolerated my sweaty hands and didn't complain too loudly when I clumsily stepped on her feet.

Notwithstanding the delicious food, the loving atmosphere, and the melodious dance music, the evening was long for me, a bashful farm boy. Late in the evening the pace picked up when a gang of pranksters stole Ray's bride, stuffed her in an idling car and drove off as she screamed, "Ray, save me!"

Ray and I jumped into his car and chased after the kidnappers in an attempt to rescue Florence, but we couldn't find them. After burning up a lot of gas in pursuit, Ray dropped me off at the army base, thanked me, and resumed the search by himself. At three o'clock the next morning the scoundrels delivered a tear-stained bride to her anxious groom.

Living on the fairgrounds I could have appropriately quoted from Charles Dickens' *A Tale of Two Cities* that opens with the phrase, "It was the best of times, it was the worst of times." The Salt Lake base kept us on ice while we waited for our next assignment. More and more, I disliked living there. Morale among the troops, who had nothing meaningful to do, sank to record low levels. To occupy our minds and tone our bodies, the commander in charge prescribed several long, boring hikes in the desert between the airport and the brackish Great Salt Lake, as well as hour upon hour of close order drill, both of which we heartily despised. Day after day the only task we accomplished was compacting the sandy soil with our army boots. In close order drill, in which we took turns as drill leader, we marched each other back and forth, up and down, to the right flank, to the left flank, to the rear, and forward until "troops dismissed" returned us to our canvas cots in the smelly barns.

> **ON THURSDAY, OCTOBER 14**, the US 8th Air Force in England sent 60 B-24 Liberator bombers and 291 B-17 Flying Fortress bombers to attack ball-bearing plants in Schweinfurt, Germany. But due to inclement weather, the Liberators turned back and 26 B-17s aborted with mechanical difficulties. American P-47 Thunderbolt fighter planes escorted the remaining bombers to Aachen, Germany, before returning to base. German fighter planes shot down 37 bombers before they reached Aachen, but the rest of the B-17s hit the factories hard, causing ball bearing production to drop 60%. The 8th lost another 23 bombers on the way home and 200 bombers returned with heavy damage. Losses were so high, the 8th labeled the day Black Thursday. If we had known about the air strikes and heavy losses we might have been a little less anxious to receive our assignments.

Fortunately, we obtained passes fairly easily, and Brown had many contacts in the area. Once off the base, we discovered a variety of ways to entertain ourselves. Even though we received enough wages to afford movies, to date girls, and to frequent restaurants, we often visited the hospitable serviceman's center sponsored by the LDS Church in the converted Missionary Training Center. Brown also introduced me to his two congenial girl cousins Beth and Barbara Hamblin, who lived nearby, and to his aunt, the wife of Hugh B. Brown, whom the Church designated as servicemen coordinator during the war. Furthermore, the homes of the Browns, the Hamblins, and my Aunt Melba became open houses for us on weekends.

The fall weather was beautiful, and one Saturday afternoon the University of Utah hosted the University of Nevada in a collegiate football game. With so many college age men in the service, I wondered how the two universities found sufficient players to field teams. In my postulations I determined the players were either classified 4F by the Selective Service or were elitist draft dodgers. From the way the Ute's leaky defense allowed an elusive runner from Nevada to return two punts for touchdowns, I concluded the Utah players were the 4Fers. The Wolf Pack from the Silver State beat the Utes by a score of 33 to 12.

> **DURING A STAFF MEETING** on November 3, British Air Chief Marshal Arthur Harris insisted sustained aerial bombing would cost Germany the war and asked Churchill to authorize the Battle of Berlin. The Prime Minister agreed. On the evening of November 18, 1943, 395 British bombers attacked Mannheim and Ludwigshafen, Germany, in a diversionary assault while 444 British heavy bombers attacked Berlin. But due to heavy cloud cover, the raid did little damage and lost nine planes.

Perhaps the uniform, the wings on my chest, the sense of achievement in becoming an officer in the army, the money in my pocket, the excitement of becoming involved in a world conflict in which I would prove my inner qualities, or a combination of all of the above enabled me to overcome my natural born shyness. With newfound confidence I dated several girls, especially Beth Hamblin, who was pretty, pleasant, and easy to be around. In no time at all I had a crush on her.

One quiet weekend, Mother and Dad drove down from Idaho to visit me in Salt Lake City. As I gave them a tour of the base and introduced them to the troops, Mother became agitated. Our living conditions in the overcrowded cowshed, devoid of privacy, appalled her. But mainly, she worried about me and earnestly prayed that my new crew would contain safe pilots, accurate gunners, a talented navigator, and that all would be morally clean. A few days after my parents' visit the army posted my crew, and over the next few months it became clear my mother's prayers were answered.

My flight crew consisted of the pilot, 2nd Lieutenant Edmund J. Ely; copilot, 2nd Lieutenant Frederick H. Pratt; bombardier, 2nd Lieutenant David Ririe; navigator, 2nd Lieutenant William L. Ellis; engineer gunner, Staff Sergeant Leo K. Kornoely; radio operator, Staff Sergeant John M. Russell; ball turret gunner, Sergeant Vincent J. Muffoletto; right waist gunner, Sergeant Harvey L. Ringer; left waist gunner, Sergeant Constantine G. Scourbys; and tail gunner, Sergeant Thomas Neill.

Now that I was part of an official flight crew, no airman in the Army Air Corps was more eager to get on with the war than I. I impatiently made preparations to leave the base. Sorrowfully, I said goodbye to my newfound friends, wished Ellsworth Brown safe flying, and got up enough nerve to kiss Beth Hamblin a fond farewell.

> **ON MONDAY, NOVEMBER 22, 1943**, Churchill and Roosevelt met with Chinese President Chiang Kai-shek in Cairo, Egypt in a highly reported summit. What wasn't reported was the same evening 764 British bombers attacked Berlin inflicting heavy damage. They returned the following night and destroyed 30 major industrial complexes, killing 9,000 Germans and making 200,000 homeless.

At 4:30, the afternoon of Wednesday, November 24, in company with a Lieutenant Stevens, I boarded another slow, overcrowded train in the Salt Lake City terminal and headed for Ardmore, Oklahoma, for the next phase of my training as a bombardier. As the miles clicked away, I remembered a prediction made by Aunt Melba's husband Joe Barnes, a railroad engineer. After the war, he said, air corps pilots who survive combat would be hired to fly commercial airplanes. Passengers would fly and trains would carry only freight. Twisting and turning in my uncomfortable seat on that puffing conveyance, I wished his prophecy had already come true. The trip was miserable.

CHAPTER 9

Flying High

On Thanksgiving Day, November 25, 1943, Lieutenant Stevens and I sat on a cold train chugging through the Royal Gorge in Colorado, as colored porters served us a superb turkey dinner, liberally seasoned with dysentery bacteria. Consequently, the meal was not exactly one we were thankful to receive. Deathly ill, we reported for duty on Friday, November 26, at Ardmore Air Force Base, Ardmore, Oklahoma, to receive Phase Training, and that evening I met all the crew except Ely, the pilot, and Ellis, the navigator. Ely arrived on Saturday in his own car, a large Packard. Originally from Pennsylvania, Ely was married, good looking, tall, jovial, and spoke authoritatively with an Eastern accent. Ellis showed up a few days later.

Unbeknownst to us, on Monday, November 28, Churchill, Roosevelt, and Soviet Premier Josef Stalin met in Teheran, Iran, to discuss war strategy. The same day our instructors introduced us to B-17 Flying Fortress combat warplanes, and we began flying long missions in the winter weather, acclimatizing us to cold conditions at high altitudes. These heavy-duty fighting machines were specifically designed for high-altitude combat, built at a cost of $204,370 each. The four engined B-17 had a good reputation as an airplane, having progressed through several evolutions in its development. During the war the U.S. sent 12,677 B-17s to Europe. More impressive is that between December 1942 and August 1945 the U.S. organized 29,370 bombardment crews, like mine, Number 858, to fly them.

Each individual B-17 required ten men to operate. The interior was generally stark. An exterior aluminum skin, so thin you could easily punch a hole in it with a penknife, held in place by thousands of rivets, covered a framework of aluminum ribs. Monstrous wings extended 100 feet from tip to tip, hiding internal wing gas tanks. Ironically, the space inside the fuselage was miserly. The pilot and copilot sat side-by-side in a five-foot-square cockpit with a view of the sky and the curve of the horizon, but they were unable to see the earth or sea or whatever lay below. Surrounded by 150 gauges, switches, cranks, and dials, pilots monitored air speed, manifold and fuel pressures, ground speed, position and direction, barometric pressure, altitude, and wind drift—any one of which if misread might jeopardize the integrity of these 60,000 pound behemoths.

Below the cockpit and further forward in the nose sat the navigator and bombardier. On the port (left) side the navigator sat behind a small desk, containing instruments and maps to chart the plane's course. With a pair of windows on each side of the fuselage, a large Plexiglas astrodome above, and the large Plexiglas nose cone in front, the navigator had the brightest position in the plane. The navigator's gun stuck out a large window on the right side.

The bombardier sat in the most exposed spot in the plane, directly behind the Plexiglas nose cone. Bent over the bombsight, he aimed and released the payload, ranging between 2,600 to 8,000 pounds of explosives. He also protected the plane from frontal attacks, manning two guns. One gun protruded through the right side of the nose section. The second was a revolving chin turret under the nose armed with two forward-firing .50 caliber machine-guns.

Directly behind the pilot sat the flight engineer, the chief mechanic who kept the engines running and doubled as the top turret gunner. He manned two .50 caliber guns strategically placed in a hydraulically-controlled revolving turret covered with a bulletproof Plexiglas bubble protruding through the roof of the fuselage.

Behind the flight engineer, through the bulkhead, the yawning bomb bay held the payload, packed floor-to-ceiling with racks of bombs on both sides of the plane. Great gaping bomb bay doors opened in the floor. Only by traversing the narrow 18-inch wide catwalk between the doors could men access the other part of the plane. Once airborne, the bombardier used the catwalk to reach individual bombs to remove the firing pin before dropping them. If a bomb became stuck during a run, the engineer manually dropped it, usually with a good swift kick. If for some reason the bay doors failed to close after the run, a fail safe hand crank lifted them into landing position.

In a separate semi-quiet compartment behind the bomb bay, the radio operator sat alone. He manned a hand-held .50 caliber machine gun, its barrel pointing out an open slot toward the tail. Behind the radio operator stood two waist gunners, positioned so close together, in combat their backs touched. They defended the middle of the plane. Below them, in a thirty-inch diameter revolving Plexiglas bubble, hung precariously beneath the plane, sat the ball turret gunner. In his tight quarters, he could only shoot at whatever appeared between his knees. The space was so compact, he entered the bubble only after the plane took off, and he hung his parachute on a hook by the access door at the rear of the plane, because there wasn't room to wear it in the turret.

At the far end of the plane, alone and isolated from the rest of the crew, the tail gunner sat in a Plexiglas bubble under the tail, on a padded bicycle seat. Looking behind and below the plane, hunched over a .50 caliber machine gun, he protected the plane from rear attacks.

The plane was functional, though not designed with our comfort in mind. It usually reeked of grease and sweat, with the smell of cordite filling the air after every shot. Before takeoff, men smoked in the plane, filling the interior with tobacco smoke. Only the front section of the plane was heated: the cockpit, the nose, and the radio room. Initially crews flew a single 25 mission tour of duty before rotating back to the U.S.A., but as more planes were shot down and manpower waned, tours extended to 35 missions, and later to 50 missions.

We often made our flights at 25,000 feet, where the air was not only cold but also very thin. To protect us from the cold, thin air, the army issued us flight clothes—coveralls, fur-lined trousers, jackets, boots and mittens, all made of very good materials, and oxygen masks. By the time we had all of this paraphernalia on, plus a parachute, we were weighted down.

The training was hard work, but our crew quickly evolved into an efficient team, appreciating and respecting each other. Even though I was an officer, I tried to be friendly with all of the men and not act arrogantly, as did some of my fellow officers. Personally, I found it difficult to maintain the aloofness expected of officers, and Ely occasionally chastised the enlisted men for not addressing me as Lieutenant Ririe.

From our base at Ardmore we ranged over Kansas, Nebraska, Arkansas, Louisiana, Oklahoma, and Texas in flights simulating combat bombing missions, giving us long hours of instrument and formation flying. The mock bombing missions intrigued me, but the instrument and formation flying were tedious and difficult. A miscalculation meant unimaginable catastrophe. Two airplanes breaking formation on one of these practice flights ran into each other, killing my good friend and bombardier school partner Jack Ryder. Prior to the accident, Ryder's crew made one of the best records in the entire training group.

The problem was the battle-weary planes received inadequate maintenance, and failures of the bombsights, instruments, equipment, and even the airplanes themselves were common. What so exasperated us was that many of the planes had survived tours of duty overseas and had logged many hours of operation. One morning after checking out an assigned B-17 with the engineer, Ely announced he wouldn't fly the plane because it wasn't air-worthy, and we returned to the ready room. An obnoxious superior officer entered the room, demanding our pilot explain why we weren't in the air. Ely informed him that the plane wasn't in condition to fly. The disgusted officer turned and asked another crew to fly the plane. The second pilot wisely said, "If Lieutenant Ely says the plane is unfit to fly, I won't fly it either."

That afternoon Ely turned in his report stating why he had refused to fly the plane, but our superior officers regarded his opinion lightly. The very next morning another crew took the plane up. As the crew circled the field to obtain altitude, the airplane fell apart and dropped to the earth, killing all of the men aboard. After that we had an even greater respect for our pilot's good judgment.

Nonetheless, we experienced some equipment failures of our own. On a high altitude bombing practice mission, we donned our masks and turned on the oxygen. On the first run my bomb hit very close to the target, but on the second run I didn't do as well. By the third run I couldn't synchronize the bombsight controls and called the pilot to request he circle around to make another approach and I would try again. In spite of my failures I felt extremely self-assured, but on the third run I was even less able to cope with the manipulations necessary to drop the bomb. Finally, the navigator glanced at me and frantically yelled to the pilot to drop the plane to a lower altitude. Upon reaching a breathable atmosphere I removed the mask and discovered two little holes near the nose had lost their plugs, allowing the oxygen to escape and nearly causing me to lose consciousness. Not having enough oxygen proved to be a peculiar feeling, because in all my life I had never felt more confident.

The hazardous Oklahoma winter weather often made flying and navigation dangerous. While returning from one night mission, thick fog forced us to make an emergency landing at Shepherd Field, in Wichita Falls, Texas. It was one of the coldest nights I had ever endured. On another flight we joined a formation to bomb imaginary targets in the Texas panhandle. Ellis neglected to wear his flying boots, and the cold temperature froze his feet. Several days passed before he recovered.

Bad luck rode with one of our companion crews. First, a gun turret mechanism malfunctioned, painfully injuring one of the gunners. Then the landing gear of the plane wouldn't lower, forcing them to make a belly landing. A week or so later as they made an emergency landing on the newly-constructed Ada, Oklahoma, airfield, they buzzed the town, and were reportedly met by a highway patrolman, the mayor, and a delegation of prominent citizens. I never found out if the report was true.

Ardmore administrators had a ridiculous rule requiring that we drop all our practice bombs before returning to base, no matter the weather or even if the bombsight, the automatic pilot, or other crucial equipment malfunctioned. Failure to do so brought a serious reprimand. Consequently, we salvoed many practice bombs into a nearby lake and reported otherwise rather than carry out the bombing run in unsafe conditions. Not all pilots were as wise.

One blustery night our superior officers sent us and several other crews out in an extraordinarily strong wind on an abnormally confusing exercise to drop bombs on a practice target located near the small town of Phillips, Oklahoma. As I flew the plane during one of the runs, concentrating on dropping the bomb, Ely suddenly took control from me and dived the plane. The bombardier in another plane directed his crew to the target on a collision course with our plane. The quick action by our alert pilot pulled us out of the way.

A couple of days later in the ready room a photograph was posted of Phillips as it appeared the morning following that hectic bombing run. Some errant bombs dropped on the town miraculously missed the houses but destroyed several front yards. Fortunately, no one was hurt, but a military court reprimanded the bombardier and removed him from the crew. On another confusing mission a bombardier yelled, "Bombs away," and inadvertently dropped a tank of gasoline. Normally, we loaded a gasoline tank into one of the bomb bays for long missions and the bombardier pushed the wrong control button by mistake.

ONE-MISSION MAN

> **HEAVY BOMBING WAS ESCALATING** dramatically in Germany. On the evening of January 30, 1944, five hundred ninety-nine Eighth Air Force B-17 and one hundred four B-24 bombers attacked industrial sites around Brunswick, Germany, dropping 1,747 tons of bombs, losing 18 B-17s in the process. On February 4, four hundred ninety-three First and Third Division B-17s and ninety B-24s attacked Frankfurt am Main. Two B-24s and 18 B-17s were lost. On February 10, one hundred forty-one B-17s attacked Brunswick. Twenty percent of the planes and two hundred ninety-five crewmen were lost. On February 24, one thousand two hundred fifty-one American heavy bombers struck Gotha, Kreising, Posen, Rostock, and Schweinfurt, losing 16 B-17s and 33 B-24s, with 484 missing crewmen. On February 25, nine hundred sixty-four heavy bombers attacked Augsburg, Stuttgart, Furtand, Regensburg, and Prüfening. Due to the inadequate number of long-range fighter escorts, the bombers suffered a twenty-four percent loss.

With the numbers of lost planes and missing crewmen increasing at an alarming rate, the army was anxious to give us practical experience in long-range high altitude strategic bombing missions and required each crew to lead one long mission during our training period. When our turn arrived, we led a 740-mile round-trip flight to Houston, Texas, and pretended to bomb a couple of ships in the harbor, plus the stadium of the University of Texas in Austin. All went well on our mission until I pre-checked the bombsight and discovered the temperamental machine didn't work. In a hasty conversation with Ely, I advised him to allow the second plane to take our place as lead. "Nothing doing," Ely replied, not about to relinquish his place. "Just aim over your toe," he advised.

As we approached the harbor I zeroed in on the target ship, and as Ely suggested, I sighted over my toe as we started the run. Taking a calculated guess, I started the timer for the camera, pressed the switch to release an imaginary load of bombs, and yelled, "Bombs away." The camera clicked and took a photograph of what we would have hit had we dropped a real bomb. A few seconds later Ellis charted a new course and we headed for Austin, Texas. As we passed over the stadium I again sighted over my toe and snapped a picture of our target. Ironically, if either location had been a real target we would have scored direct hits.

The next day, to my chagrin, the commanding officers hung my photographs of the targets with accompanying legends reporting our air speed, altitude, location, and other pertinent information in the briefing room as a perfect example of good bombing technique. To my mortification, the photographs remained in the briefing room for several weeks, embarrassing me every time I saw them. Thankfully, no one let our secret out.

The strain of long flights and intensive training took a toll on men as well as on equipment. One afternoon after we landed the plane and taxied into a line with several other bombers, I thought the pilot had shut off the engines. I slipped out of the hatch and started to walk away when suddenly Sergeant Kornoely grabbed me by the shoulders and yanked me backward, stopping me from walking into a nearly invisible spinning propeller. He saved my life or at least rescued me from serious injury as a result of my momentary lapse of attention.

On weekend passes, we often went into dull little Ardmore to relax and attend the movies. But if we desired excitement, fun, or even if I just wanted to go to church, we sought larger towns. I visited Fort Worth, Texas, where I attended Sunday School in a small branch of the Church. One evening Ellis and I attended a dance in Paul's Valley, Oklahoma, that turned out to be a Wild West affair. During the dance I expected to see a Jesse James or a Billy the Kid start a gunfight at any moment. Frankly, some of the girls at the dance were hunting mates—as if flying with inexperienced crews in poorly maintained aircraft in bad weather weren't hazards enough for flight crews. Needless to say, Ellis and I never returned to Paul's Valley again.

We attended dances at Texas State College for Women, in Denison, Texas, when we sought female companionship, because Ellis had at cousin there. In sharp contrast to the girls that we met at Paul's Valley, TSCW girls were very poised, modest, and pleasant.

As a crew we had fun together in Oklahoma. Ely liked to fly the plane low and we often chased a herd of beef cattle to the other end of a pasture. Once we buzzed a lake, causing a couple of fishermen to jump out of their boat. We were typical aviators in the Army Air Corps: cocky and conceited. Everything in our demeanor exuded confidence and daring. Our hats were jaunty, our salutes undignified. Men of the other services must have found us extremely annoying.

Ardmore introduced me to Southern charm and ugly racism. In my small Idaho hometown there were no colored people, except for an old hermit who lived near Willow Creek. Segregated drinking fountains, theatres, buses, and toilets shocked me. Naïvely, I didn't know such racism existed in the United States. As a white male in uniform wandering Ardmore I received royal treatment. In fact, in no other location where I served in the military was I invited into homes or offered rides as frequently, or treated as cordially as I had been in Ardmore. So it baffled me to see such gracious people treat fellow human beings so badly. I felt sorry for the colored people, forced to sit in rear seats on a hot, stuffy bus, or sit in the stifling balcony of the movie theater. It just didn't seem fair. No wonder tension between the races came to a head after World War II.

Back at home, my brother Max joined the army, and a few days before reporting for duty, he married MarDean Dalley on January 28, in the Logan LDS temple. He passed through Oklahoma while I was stationed at Ardmore, but we couldn't coordinate a reunion.

CHAPTER 10

Numbered Days

Phase Training ended at Ardmore as abruptly as it began. Following the final lecture, within hours our crew flew to Grand Island, Nebraska, for final staging prior to a combat assignment in Europe. Cold, blustery March weather met us with vengeance. A fierce blizzard swept down from Canada and lowered the freezing temperatures several degrees. Wind blew the deep snow into drifts taller than I had ever seen. Yet, no matter how cold it was in Nebraska, our instructors insisted it couldn't compare to the cold we would endure over the Arctic's polar regions on our flight to Great Britain.

To warm us up on the long flight to England, the army issued us woolen underwear, fur-lined jackets, and fleece-lined over boots. After I dressed in the woolen underwear, I developed a terrible skin rash, an allergic reaction to the wool. Discarding the underwear, I bought cotton gym clothes to wear under my flight gear. Having grown up in Idaho, acclimated to freezing temperatures, I didn't much mind the cold.

At Grand Island we met the plane we would fly to England: a sleek, shiny, brand-spanking new B-17G Flying Fortress. The plane wasn't the familiar olive drab camouflage color we had been flying in Oklahoma. In early 1944 the army stopped painting B-17s, primarily because paint increased the plane's weight and drag, which decreased gas mileage. Besides, not painting meant lowered costs and shortened production time. The decision made perfect sense economically but proved disastrous when flown with painted planes, because the shiny aluminum made them easy targets for enemy guns. To compensate, many bomber groups didn't send silver planes out on missions until they had a group of them on the tarmac.

The grim weather continued and as the time for our departure from Grand Island came nearer, I telephoned home, over a miserable connection, to say good-bye to my family. Although I enjoyed visiting, I felt dissatisfied that the static on the line prevented me from expressing myself clearly in my final farewell. I gathered my gear and boarded the plane. Just as we took off a gust of wind blew us off the runway and delayed departure as mechanics inspected and repaired the plane. Playfully, we accused Ely of purposely running off the concrete and into the mud and snow so he could spend more time with his wife, who had come from New Mexico to bid him farewell.

Once we took off, we had little time for brooding. On March 12, 1944, we flew the first leg of our flight over beautiful snow covered country with lakes, farms, and millions of trees, landing at Presque Isle, Maine, our last stop in the scenic United States. Snow and cold blanketed northern Maine, and with three days in Presque Isle and little to do, we rented skis from the Officer's Club and headed for the slopes. The very first hill spoiled our fun when Ellis, a Southerner who had never been on a pair of skis in his life, fell and sprained his ankle so badly we had to help him stumble back to the barracks.

At Presque Isle we attended a dance, and like the dance in Paul's Valley, it was a wild affair. We sat at a table where everyone drank alcoholic beverages except me. A crew member asked the waiter to bring me a glass of milk and everyone enjoyed a good laugh. I calmly drank the milk without saying a word, and such ridicule never occurred again.

On March 15, 1944, we continued our flight to England, flying over eastern Canada, with its spectacular waterways and evergreen forests, to Goose Bay, Labrador, the staging area for the European theater of operations. As we crossed the border into Canada, Ellis remarked, "Now I'm considered overseas and need not file my income tax until I return. I just barely made it."

Huge snowplows had piled the snow on both sides of the very quiet, very white, and very isolated Goose Bay runways, and as we landed it felt like we had descended into a deep canyon. On the ground, the hard, frozen snow crackled under our feet. Fortunately, the barracks were warm and cozy, and we slept well before taking off early the following morning. I felt a little disappointed, because I had wanted to fish through the ice as some crews had done.

Darkness enveloped us as we flew over Greenland, the land emerging from the blackness as a frozen, snowy mass. The moon rose in the dark blue sky like a ball of fiery red neon lights and cast a rosy glow on the plane's wings, revealing a thin layer of ice. For a while we worried the ice would sink us into the sea. Luckily, the layer never thickened more than a few centimeters, and we reached Iceland without incident. The Icelandic landscape reminded me of the snow on jagged lava rock out-crops in Idaho's volcanic areas.

We spent the night in a relatively comfortable Nissen hut. We found the weather much less wintry than in Labrador but very changeable; snow and rain fell, followed by bright sunshine. The natives teased us that the weather might be sunny when you entered the hut, but stormy before you could walk to the other end of the building.

Early the next morning we continued our journey. Clouds surrounded us as soon as we lifted off Iceland and enveloped us throughout all of the final leg, our longest yet. At length Ely lifted the plane above the clouds and Ellis attempted to get a sextant shot of the sun through the astrodome above his station. His instruments nearly froze in his hands in the cold, thin air, and he began to worry about the accuracy of his readings. After seeing the immensity of the ocean below in the broad daylight, I also worried.

When we reached our estimated time of arrival we couldn't see land in any direction, due to the thick cloud cover beneath us, but

Ellis insisted we were over Prestwick, Scotland. He breathed a sigh of relief when Sergeant Russell called ground control over the radio and learned we were precisely on course and right on time.

Meanwhile, I finished reading a book, the copilot woke up from a restful nap, and all of us rejoiced to have successfully navigated the North Atlantic, when Russell received a radio communication directing us to alter our course and land at Nutts Corner, North Ireland.

Accommodating the air armada of the United States and Great Britain, composed of hundreds of aircraft during the war, required scores of airfields. As we approached Nutts Corner, we saw three airfields in the distance. We established radio contact with ground control, and Ely aimed for the nearest field, when the control tower told us we were heading for the wrong field. After a good laugh, Ely changed course and entered the traffic pattern of the correct airfield. We soon touched down on Irish soil. We made it.

Lieutenant Murphy, one of the pilots of our formation group from Grand Island, missed Nutts Corner altogether and attempted to land at neutral Dublin. On his way in, the Irish objected, but Murphy radioed back, "Clear the runway, you Irishmen. I am out of gas, and I am landing this airplane."

Immediately after landing and being assigned barracks, we desperately needed to shower and clean up. We asked an Irish soldier to direct us to the lavatories, but we couldn't understand his thick accent. We asked him several times, and finally he led us there. When he instructed us how to flush the toilets, he said, "You pull the chine, you know." We eventually figured out what "chine" meant.

After bathing we wandered through camp looking for a place to shave and encountered a damp, smelly room with several little tubs on a bench or shelf around the edge of the room, but there were no mirrors. We ran hot water into the basins and helped one another shave, all the while joking about the deplorable Irish plumbing. Returning to our barracks we saw men shaving in a very modern washroom with nice sinks, mirrors and bright lighting. We had shaved in the laundry room. At least we learned they didn't have washing machines.

True to Irish tradition, weather alternated between brief showers and bright sunshine. In the mess, cooks served meals in several courses and with so many pieces of silverware I pitied KP detail. We enjoyed fish, meat, vegetables, soup, potatoes, and a choice of desserts at every meal. Following the meal, diners retired to a separate room for coffee or tea and alcoholic drinks. Excited to try a local soft drink, I ordered a ginger ale but found it too strong for a Mormon boy to imbibe. Ironically, in Ireland, as in other places in England and Europe, I discovered asking for a glass of cold water was unheard of, especially if you requested ice.

On March 20, 1944, I celebrated my twenty-second birthday by visiting Belfast. The bus ride through the green countryside into town was pleasant, but when we entered the city we saw block after block of nothing but bombed houses and buildings, a very sobering sight.

After a couple of days at Nutts Corner, command transferred us to a seaport town near Belfast and ordered us to remain on the base, but we slipped into town to the movies as soon as possible, since there wasn't any fence around the camp. When the shavetail lieutenant in charge discovered our absence he sent a contingent after us. Halfway through the movie the reels stopped, the lights came on, and a soldier announced all airmen were urgently needed at the base. Naively, we returned to base where the lieutenant bawled us out and confined us to our quarters.

The following day, still grumbling about being hoodwinked, we received orders to move again. We boarded a ferry and sailed across the Irish Sea to the Firth of Forth and enjoyed a train ride to Stoke-on-Trent, our new residence while we waited to become a replacement crew.

Stoke-on-Trent is an attractive town, but thanks to the testy lieutenant, we were still confined to base. Occasionally, however, we walked off the post or rode bikes to town. On the way back to base on one of these ventures, we saw a pretty English girl on a bicycle. Thinking we would ride along with her for a pleasant conversation, we sped up, but when she saw us she smiled, kicked her bike into high gear, and raced off. Try as we might, we couldn't catch the saucy lass. I suspect she had outrun American soldiers before.

After a few days at Stoke-on-Trent, command sent us to Knettishall, the location of the 388th Bomb Group. As the train rushed along some of the men amused themselves by shooting sheep grazing in the pastures. American Air Force boys not only disgraced their country with their obnoxious behavior, they revealed why we lost so many planes. These boys were very poor shots.

Airmen called Knettishall the Country Club of the European Theatre of Operations, but we didn't stay long enough to know if the name was accurate. We reported to headquarters and were assigned to the 563rd squadron with a Colonel William B. David as our group commander.

The Eighth Air Force was in England at a crucial time for the Allies. Hitler was dominating Western Europe and the war in Japan was going badly. Great Britain's resources of men and machines were eroding. Due to the lack of support from its already-captured neighbors across the channel, the Brits attempted high-altitude strategic bombing, the only tactic available to strike back at Nazi encroachment. Yet, daylight bombing of industrial targets had been so disastrous the Royal Air Force (RAF) resorted to night raids exclusively, flying bombers in, one at a time, over a target to reduce the risk.

The United States Army Air Corps held to a different strategy, bombing only military and industrial installations during daylight hours with hundreds of bombers, each bristling with deadly machine guns. We flew in tight formations with minimal fighter plane support, four miles above the earth's surface. The purpose of the bombing was simple: to end the war quickly and resolutely, without town-to-town, door-to-door, face-to-face combat.

Now, in the spring of 1944, the Allies were doubling their sorties, and the Eighth Air Force was fully engaged in bearing down on Germany with a constant daily barrage of long-range, high-altitude strikes. Furthermore, the Eighth was an elite outfit, composed almost wholly of volunteers who had enlisted before Roosevelt's 1943 order that ended voluntary enlistments. The bomber crews contained men from every occupation, location, religion, creed, and ethnic group, bonded together to defeat a common enemy. Since most of the men, including me, had never been on a plane before the war, the ability to stay alive relied more on the men supporting each other than it did on an individual's ability to do the job.

Walking around the base it surprised me that civilians accessed the airfield with such ease. Grain grew adjacent to the runways, and one afternoon a funeral procession crossed the air base, the mourners walking solemnly in their black attire. The grey sky overhead and the dirty snow they trudged through completed the somber scene. How did the Allies keep spies from learning all of our secrets, I wondered.

> **DURING THE NIGHT** of Friday, March 24, 1944, Britain again attacked Berlin with 811 bombers. In the battle the Germans shot 72 planes down, killing 392 crew members and taking 131 as prisoners. The attack marked the 10,000th sortie the Brits made against the German capital city since August of 1943, making the bombing campaign the longest and most constant offensive against a single target in the war. Now, after nine months and 30,000 tons of bombs, Britain declared the Berlin strategy an operational defeat and called it quits.

At Knettishall we quickly learned the life of bomber crews consisted of days of boredom interspersed by short bursts of frenetic activity. While we waited for our turn in the fight, we had little to occupy our minds. One morning we flew to a field near London, but without even leaving the field we turned around and came straight back to Knettishall. A practice flight on a mock bombing range followed a day later, then nothing. A group of airmen held a party on the base, but thankfully I didn't attend, because it ended in a drunken brawl. Afterwards, Pratt came home fighting mad because someone at the party stole his overcoat.

Some airmen saw an opportunity in the misfortune of others. They began collecting bikes belonging to fellows who didn't return after their bombing missions. They would sell the collected bikes to newcomers, earning a tidy profit. Bikes changed owners frequently as more and more planes failed to return.

One afternoon Pratt flew a combat mission as a substitute co-pilot for another crew. He returned depressed by the bad weather and confusing orders. It proved to be a foretaste of things to come, as the colonel summoned us to appear in the briefing room the next morning. All night our hearts were in our throats. Our preparation soon would be put to the test in our first—and final—mission.

CHAPTER 11

Dulag Luft

My mother later told me she was at home when the telegram arrived from the War Department informing her I was missing in action. She said she climbed into the car with her sister-in-law Edna Ririe, Jimmy and Carma, picked up ten-year-old Wayne from school and drove toward the dryfarm where Dad was working. They met Dad on the highway about three miles from the house walking toward town with a piece of damaged equipment in his grease-soiled hands. The farm implement he was using had broken down and the old truck he drove that morning refused to start. Dad read the telegram, embraced Mother and they cried in each other's arms. Wayne burst into a flood of tears. "My whole world collapsed," he wrote years later. "I thought 'missing in action,' meant David was dead."

The next day my photograph appeared in the local newspaper with a short announcement of my disappearance. Mother said that night she and Carma each had a lucid dream. Mother dreamed she saw me limping as I walked along a road. Carma dreamed she saw me thin and haggard in a building hobbling from room to room. From these dreams they concluded I was alive. After breakfast, Clive retrieved my Patriarchal Blessing that I had received as a boy from Mother's dresser drawer. He read to the family the same phrase that had given me peace on the first night of my incarceration, "You shall return home rejoicing."

Mother later told me those simple words sustained her during the long anxious weeks when my fate was unknown and my family's fervent and oft-repeated prayers focused on my return. Six weeks passed before a telegram arrived with the news I was a prisoner of war.

"Our faith was tested and family ties welded together more tightly during the days we waited further word about David," Carma wrote years later. "I had no doubt as to his safety."

Lying terrified on my wooden plank bed that first lonely night, locked up in the damp, cold cell in Rostock, Germany, I thought morning would never break. I had sprained both my ankles in the crash and they throbbed with pain. When a few rays of light finally broke through a chink in the window shutters, I saw marks running across the cell wall, left by a previous inmate, ticking off the days of his internment. I visualized myself going crazy if that many days of solitary confinement were my lot.

From the next cell I heard scuffling, but I couldn't tell who was making the noise. Then came the most dreadful suspense of my life. Heavy footsteps resonated down a very long corridor, beginning far away, but drawing ever nearer. Keys clanked, doors banged open and closed, and deep muffled voices spoke words I could not understand. What was happening? Were prisoners being removed and killed? Or were they just being fed? After what seemed hours, the footsteps stopped outside my door. A moment of silence. Keys clanged in the lock. The heavy steel door shrieked open and two soldiers barged into the cell.

The soldiers could have stepped out of a Hollywood movie or been typecast for starring roles in a propaganda film. Their uniforms were impeccable, right down to their gleaming knee-high leather boots. They glared at me in menacing silence through cruel eyes. They spoke to each other as if discussing a loathsome creature, and then, to my relief, they departed without making any effort to communicate with me. Apparently, their visit was only a routine check.

A while later the shutters outside my window folded back and bright, warm light flooded the cell. Through the barred window I could see nothing but sky, but my mood rose from hopeless to hopeful.

Later in the morning, a third man, dressed in a soldier's uniform but without much military bearing, opened the door. His face was kind and gentle. He carried a slab of coarse dark brown bread, a jug of water, and a small dish containing a milky-white, sweet syrup, which I later learned is called *ersatz* (artificial) honey. He placed the food on the table and left without a word. After the anguish of the last 24 hours, I didn't have much of an appetite but wanting to keep up my strength I choked down what I could of the rough bread.

By the time the guard reappeared to remove the dishes, I mustered courage to ask him out of desperation where to find the restroom. Not knowing any German vocabulary, I used every word I could think of to describe the latrine. When I finally said "toilet," the man brightened and ushered me to the restroom located midway down the long echoing corridor. In my short excursion I saw another man in an air corps uniform but had no opportunity to talk to him. After I relieved myself, the guard returned me to my cell.

Late in the afternoon, the guard entered my cell with a large pot of steaming potatoes, handed me a dish, and poured out a few of the potatoes. I smiled, remembering how we fed animals on the farm in a similar manner. Seeing my smile the kindly guard gave me more potatoes. Compassion existed even in the enemy camp. Still, I didn't have much of an appetite, and after the guard left I wrapped a couple of hot potatoes in my clothing and pressed them against my swollen ankles, easing the pain and giving me something useful to do.

Sometime during the next day I discovered Pratt occupied the cell next to mine. We talked by shouting close to the wall. Frustrated at not being able to communicate more than a few simple thoughts, we decided to call the guard at the same time and were rewarded with a simultaneous trip to the restroom. Pratt appeared calm, as usual, and while standing at the urinal we quietly spoke a few words to each other. Another American prisoner, who happened to be in the latrine with us, told us an errant B-17 accidentally dropped its bombs on his plane and forced it out of the air.

On April 13, 1944, two days after we crashed, the guards removed us from our cells and loaded us onto a clean, modern passenger train. Guards watched us constantly but allowed us to converse among ourselves. One of the prisoners, dying for a cigarette, scavenged butts out of the ashtrays on the coach. I pitied his desperation and realized one form of imprisonment comes from our own addictions. At least, that prison didn't hold me.

At Leipzig we transferred to a second train. Hobbling painfully the several hundred yards through a recently bombed rail station, I saw blue sky through countless broken windows in its ceiling. I also saw hatred in the eyes of passengers who glowered at us as we hustled through the station on the guards' heels. Clearly, these Germans would kill us, given the opportunity. Someone called us "Chicago gangsters" and other disparaging names. It dawned on me that our own literature and movies supported the Nazi propaganda and contributed to the poor image of our country in the minds of foreign peoples.

I struggled to keep up with the other prisoners but fell hopelessly behind. Alone, injured, and unguarded, I felt all eyes turn upon me in vicious disgust. My heart raced and I expected to perish by the hands of the angry crowd at any moment. To my relief, one of the guards noticed me and fell back, glaring at the mob. He patiently escorted me to the train. Never in my life had I been happier to be so closely guarded. I believe the brave guard preserved me from serious injury, or worse.

As we rode through the German countryside both guards left our compartment and the train almost stopped. Briefly I contemplated escaping, but my screaming ankles convinced me against the scheme. Why the men with me did not take action I do not know. Later I realized opportunities to escape come very, very seldom.

ONE-MISSION MAN

Late at night we arrived at Oberursel, a beautiful city nestled in a mountainous section of the country, near Frankfurt am Main in southwestern Germany. Guards hustled us off the train and up several flights of stairs to a room in the station where they watched over us until a bus arrived to haul us to Dulag Luft, a collection center for captured Allied airmen.

> **DURCHGANGSLAGER DE LUFTWAFFE** (Transit Camp Air Force), abbreviated as Dulag Luft, existed to extract as much information as possible from captive fliers before shipping them off to permanent prison camps scattered around Germany. Detaining each prisoner in solitary confinement upon arrival, psychologists quickly analyzed each individual's weaknesses before determining the most efficient way to break his resistance.
>
> If the prisoner became nervous or afraid, the Germans tortured, threatened, and otherwise mistreated him. If these tactics still didn't work, they bribed him with cigarettes, a comfortable living area, food, or other amenities until he broke. The Germans treated prisoners they couldn't break well but retained them in solitary confinement longer than their broken buddies.
>
> Eight thousand prisoners passed through Dulag Luft in 1943, but as the Allies increased their high-altitude bombing campaigns, the number of captured airmen escalated to 29,000 by the end of 1944.
>
> Due to the high probability that airmen would eventually become POWs, the air corps taught them how to react to interrogation tactics and illustrated with graphic case histories what had happened when information did slip out. Instructors drilled into airmen the only information the Germans had a right to know was their name, rank, and serial number, as agreed to in the Geneva Convention's rules of warfare. Nothing more.
>
> Nonetheless, the Germans were so adept at extracting useful information from airmen that Dulag Luft became an important information-mining operation. Built on 500 acres of flat ground, Dulag Luft had

> twin twelve-foot high fences, spaced ten feet apart, surrounding it. Between the fences ran a deep channel filled with razor-sharp barbed wire. Deadly watchtowers rose every hundred yards on the outside perimeter fence, manned by vigilant guards who patrolled the boundaries with vicious dogs to prevent escape from the compound. Heavily armed pillboxes guarded the area beyond.
>
> To prevent the Allies from accidentally bombing the compound, the Germans wrote "Prisoner of War Camp" with white rocks on the large grassy lawn in front of the main building. They painted the same words, in large white letters, on the roof of the buildings.

It felt like the middle of the night when the guards ushered us into private cells at Dulag Luft. After the long tense day, I climbed into a comfortable bed, and dropped into a restful sleep. No one disturbed me, though apparently, I was an isolated case. Some of the men found an extra airman in their bed the next morning. After breakfast a German officer barged into my cell and demanded I fill out a form with information he purportedly needed to notify my folks of my whereabouts. Wary of his motives, I wrote down my name, rank, and serial number as sloppily as I could manage. Frankly, I trembled so violently in fear of the man, it wasn't hard to write illegibly. When I finished, he snatched the form, cursed at me, and said, "A child could have written more legibly." To my relief, he then stomped out of the room.

Apparently, the Germans soon realized I had little information to divulge. They interrogated Ely, our pilot, several times, using various approaches, but after my sole interview the guards moved me to a compound for airmen awaiting assignments to prison camps. When I arrived at the compound, the scene was both humorous and pathetic. Many of the U.S. Air Force fliers had been shot down in baby blue flight suits, looking like they fled a burning building in the middle of the night wearing their flannel underwear.

The men, I noticed, were scratching; the camp — and prisoners — were lousy. Men had large blotchy sores on their skin, brought on by allergies to the vermin bites, scratching, and filth. Moreover, nearly all of us wore beards, having gone varying lengths of time without shaving. Before long, a razor and a couple of blades appeared out of nowhere, and we drew lots to see who would shave first. By the time my turn came, the blades were so dull I couldn't even scrape dirt off my face.

Worse yet, the camp received little medical attention. My ankles still pained me, but as I evaluated the men in the compound, some suffered far worse injuries than I. Bandages covered the heads of a couple of flash burn victims; only their eyes peering out. Another man had lost his lower leg.

As I assessed the camp, one of my old instructors from Ardmore leaned out of a window and spoke to me. He had joined a flight crew and been shot down on their second mission. The irony was humorous. Only a few months before he trained us to avoid the situation in which we now found ourselves. We laughed despite our dire circumstances.

When the guards lined us up to be counted, I stood next to Ellis who had run into a man from his class in navigation school. When the guards finished speaking, Ellis's classmate asked me,

"Where are you from?"

"Idaho," I replied.

"Do you belong to the Church?" he asked.

"Yes," was my happy reply.

From that point on, I couldn't have had a finer buddy. Robert Dean Matheson, *Rocky* to his friends, was a returned LDS missionary, who hailed from McGill, Nevada. He and I decided to get church services going when we arrived in our permanent camp.

Several intolerable days later, our guards herded us together with news they were transferring us to a permanent prison camp. We had a long walk to the train station, they said. They gave us a choice: we must either surrender our shoes or pledge not to attempt an escape along the way. We looked at the rocky road winding into town and all, except one man who surrendered his shoes, took the pledge. I admired that man.

On the long, miserable walk, Rocky and Ellis stuck with their hobbling companion (me), bringing up the rear of the disorderly column. After what seemed like sixty miles (probably four or five), we reached the train station where guards herded us like sheep into boxcars.

About thirty men and seven guards boarded each rail car. In German style, the guards took the center half of the car for themselves, roping or wiring the section off with a demarcation line. At night the prisoners on each end of the car huddled together and attempted to sleep. The close proximity to our companions helped us to keep warm, but that was the only advantage of our crowded conditions. Having been denied baths for several days, we stunk, and we had barely enough room to lie down.

As the train rumbled slowly through the country, we received no food or water to drink for a whole day. Nearly choked from thirst, we set up a wail, yelling, "wasser, wasser, wasser," until the guards tired of our chanting and placed a full milk can of water at each end of the car. Our thirst quenched, we needed to answer nature's call but the insolent guards refused to allow us off the train in the stations. Whenever the train stopped, no matter where we were or who watched, we furtively got behind as much cover as we could find and relieved ourselves. Europeans, I soon discovered, were not as self-conscious about toilet privacy as Americans. At any rate, the guards didn't care if we were embarrassed or uncomfortable.

In truth, our guards weren't the brightest bunch. Privately, we referred to them as the Seven Dwarfs, naming them individually Doc, Sleepy, Dopey, etc. Early one morning as the train slowly bumped along, Ellis and I awoke and found them all asleep, with two of their rifles within easy reach. As a joke, Ellis stuffed their gun barrels with bread crumbs.

On the outskirts of Kassel the train parked on a siding, and through cracks in the walls of the car we watched searchlights and antiaircraft fire as British planes bombed the city. The raid took a long time, because the British dispatched their planes to the target area one at a time. We watched enthralled as each new plane brought new action, searchlights, and bomb bursts. Admittedly, this method seemed safer than our massive daylight raids, but the Royal Air Force bomber command also lost scores of planes and by the end of the war registered a twenty percent casualty rate. In any case, sequestered in our frigid, reeking rail car we enjoyed the spectacle, which by contrast, petrified the guards.

CHAPTER 12

Stalag Luft 1

On April 20, 1944, the third and final day of our boxcar ordeal, swastikas and photographs of the Fuehrer commemorating Hitler's birthday hung in the windows in every town we passed. Upon arriving at Barth, a small town on the Baltic Sea about 100 miles northwest of Berlin, the guards unloaded us and marched us through town amid quips and jeers from the local residents. We passed under Dammtor Gate, a 14th century tower on the main street, and through Barth. The guards led us two abreast for two miles, passing beautiful farmland before stopping us at a gate leading into Stalag Luft 1. Officially named Kriegefanglager der Luftwaffe (Prisoner of War Camp of the Air Force), it was the German POW camp for captured U.S. Army Air Force and British Royal Air Force officers.

Built in a backward "L" configuration on a desolate sliver of land protruding into the Baltic Sea to the north, the compound followed the natural curve of the bay estuary to the west. Thick pine forests hemmed us in to the southwest and scrubby bushes covered the peninsula to the east. Besides the prison, the Luftwaffe maintained an antiaircraft artillery school near the west side of the compound. We didn't know it until later but on the far side of the bay the Nazis also operated a chemical warfare experimental station and carried out deadly experiments, and Polish slave laborers assembled aircraft an airfield two miles to the south.

The camp contained multiple individual "lagers," or compounds, to house prisoners: North 1, North 2, North 3, South, and West. Communication of prisoners between compounds was strictly forbidden. The guards' compound, the "Volager," located in the heel of the L, contained an administration building, hospital, workshops, and stores, all surrounded by lush green grass and shrubbery.

Double ten-foot-high barbed wire fences enclosed each compound. Two twelve-foot-high barbed wire fences surrounded the entire camp. Guard towers strategically positioned along the fences bristled with trigger-happy guards, constantly aiming deadly .50 caliber machine guns and, during the night, blinding searchlights along fence lines. Guards prowled the compound at night with Schmeisser machine pistols and growling dogs.

As we entered the compound, it appeared most of the Army Air Corps had been shot down already and were there to welcome us. Corpsmen lined up along the fence and greeted the men they recognized, asking questions and making wise cracks, such as, "Did you bring your golf clubs?" "Is Hoover still President?" "Welcome to the Balkan Rest Camp." Thankfully, I recognized no one in the lineup, but I appreciated the warm welcome by friendly faces after the Nazi scowls, slurs, and spitting. Inside the camp we became "kriegies," an abbreviated form of the word "kriegesgefangenen," the German word for "prisoner of war."

Upon entering the camp, guards photographed, fingerprinted, and assigned us a number. Then a guard escorted us to a washroom where we showered and were deloused by guards, who threw an insecticide powder over our naked bodies. The guards spoke roughly and treated us like we were the vermin, but we appreciated the opportunity to clean up. Smelling sweeter than we had for some time, we each received a bed sheet, two thin army blankets, a burlap mattress cover filled with wood shavings, a small linen towel, a small bowl, a cup, and a knife, fork and spoon.

Built for Hitler Youth activities, North 1 became a part of the prison after the numbers of captured airmen dramatically increased in early 1944. North 1 contained a large communal building housing a kitchen and mess hall that we also used for a theater and recreational area. North 2 and North 3, hastily built after I arrived, were not as developed as North 1. Originally, the South compound was the prison; it was where the British POWs resided.

Frame buildings built of rough-hewn lumber served as our barracks. Each contained numerous small dormitory rooms of various sizes, branching off both sides of a central corridor. At the end of each barracks was a smaller room, designed for a leader and his aide (revealing typical German regard for rank), a latrine, and—almost as welcome—a sink and faucet, supplying us with fresh water suitable for drinking. Wooden posts elevated the barracks floor eighteen inches above ground level.

Each dormitory room originally held twelve to fourteen men in double-decker bunks. By war's end some rooms contained triple-decker beds and eighteen to twenty or more men. In the beginning, Rocky and I were assigned to Room 5 of Barrack 11 in the North 1 Compound, with 12 other men. Each room also contained a small wooden table, two or three wooden chairs, a bare light bulb dangling from the ceiling, and a small cast-iron wood-burning stove, sufficient for cooking but not sufficient for heating the room. Large double hung glass windows brought in natural light during the day but the Germans shuttered and locked them every night at 10:00 p.m. At the end of the barracks was a latrine for use at night. During the day we used a central toilet/laundry, housed in a separate building several yards away.

The barracks in North 1 surrounded a central parade ground where, whether the weather were fair or foul, we lined up twice daily, at 6:45 a.m. and at 4:30 p.m., for "appell," the German word for roll call. The Germans were very regimented in their procedures. For twelve months roll call did not vary in any detail or in the officious manner it was conducted, regardless of weather or circumstances.

The counting squad marched in, split us into smaller ranks five men deep by barrack blocks, and we stood at attention with two guards facing our ranks and two behind. The number of men varied from barrack to barrack. Once the barrack commander had his men in ranks he reported to the compound commander that his men were ready for the count. The count was oral and guttural—eins, zwei, drei . . . up to acht and achtzig for our group. At the conclusion of the counting, the soldier at the back reported to Herr Hauptman, one of the officers facing our single files. The salute was the same each time as the soldier at the back said, "Acht and achtzig, Herr Hauptman." The captain marched to the center of the parade ground with military drill and precision and the guards added up the numbers.

We often teased the guards and on warm days made counting difficult. On cold or rainy days we could depend on the count being incorrect and the procedure repeated, sometimes as many as ten times. We stood, wet to the skin from the rain or snow, since we wore no protective clothing. In winter we nearly froze and from the exposure to the elements our feet developed chilblains, painful acral ulcers that damage capillary beds in the skin, triggering blisters and inflammation, and causing skin to slough off. Worse yet, whenever we warmed up, the chilblains made our feet itch and smart until it was almost unbearable. Luckily, my feet never became infected, as did those of some of my friends.

After the counting the Germans saluted our officers who dismissed us. The rest of the day we did what we pleased under the direction of our camp officers until 10:00 p.m. when our captors barricaded the barrack doors with heavy wooden poles and shuttered the windows, locking us in until morning. They shut off power for electric lights at 6:00 p.m. and didn't turn it back on again until morning, making our rooms dark in the evenings, especially on long, melancholy winter nights. To counteract our lack of light, an enterprising kriegie devised an innovative process of dipping the heavy waxed paper wrapping from Red Cross parcels into hot water, then skimming off the wax with rags. He rolled the rags, saturated with wax, into candles, which we lit with a match provided by the Germans. The flame gave us light, inadequate but preferable to darkness.

American prisoners were managed separately from the British but with very close liaison. Colonel Jean R. Byerly, as Senior American Officer (SAO), and a small staff, oversaw the activities of the four American groups through an organization entitled Provisional Wing, headquartered in North 1. Provisional Wing directed internal affairs, disciplined disobedient kriegies, kept records, and communicated with the Red Cross, the Young Men's Christian Association (YMCA), and otherwise maintained order in the camp.

Provisional Wing officers also acted as intermediaries between the Germans and the Swiss government, the camp's "Protecting Power." The Geneva Conventions in 1929 compelled countries at war to accept the assistance of a neutral third party in settling POW disagreements. As Protecting Power for Stalag Luft 1, the Swiss government inspected the camp every four months to confirm living conditions were as outlined in the Geneva codes of conduct. The International Red Cross, and the YMCA, as independent humanitarian organizations, also inspected Stalag Luft 1 every four months. The Red Cross generally supplied food, uniforms and blankets while the YMCA supplied sports equipment and requested supplies. Red Cross food parcels were handled through a central warehouse and issued at the rate of one per person per week.

Provisional Wing administration contained four divisions: A1, personnel records; A2, intelligence; A3, education and athletics; and A4, supply. In addition, every compound organized internally, with each barrack forming a squadron led by officers within their ranks. In North 1, our barrack commander, Captain John Paul Carson answered to compound commander, Colonel Ross Greening. Greening answered to Colonel Byerly.

ONE-MISSION MAN

On our first Sunday in Stalag Luft 1, Rocky, Al Strom, and I went to a church service conducted by a Protestant chaplain, who had been captured in North Africa. The service was well attended, but Rocky was unimpressed. The next day we visited every room in the compound and located six LDS men: Robert McGregor, Salt Lake City, Utah; Blaine Harris, Soda Springs, Idaho; F. H. Betenson, Cedar City, Utah; W. N. Rasmussen, Mt. Pleasant, Utah; Rocky and me.

Harris and his roommate graciously agreed to offer their double room every Sunday for an hour allowing us to hold Sunday School undisturbed. The first Sunday we met, after an opening prayer, blessing and passing of the sacrament, and a scripture reading from a library copy of the New Testament, we held a testimony meeting. Each man stood individually, and to a man, we each expressed thanks to God for his deliverance from death.

In his testimony Rocky said that after his plane crashed he hid from the Germans for several days. A local man became suspicious when Rocky was unable to answer the man in German when he spoke to him; the man turned him in to the authorities. Rocky said he appreciated being captured. He had nearly frozen to death during his days of freedom. Due to his miserable experience, Rocky seldom participated in our escape attempts.

Harris told us, as the pilot of a B-24, a Liberator Bomber, he commanded a crew of nine men. Feeling keenly the responsibility as their leader, he had prayed that in the event of serious emergency, he would have the ability to save the lives of his crew. During combat, a shell hit his plane, igniting an uncontrollable fire. Harris commanded the crew to parachute to safety, but when the ball turret gunner reached for his parachute pack he discovered the fire had destroyed it. Without a moment's hesitation, Harris felt inspired to instruct a man with a good parachute pack to attach one hook to his harness and the other to the gunner's harness, and the two men jumped out together. When all the crewmembers were out of the plane, Harris bailed out. The jump injured a couple of the crewmen but everyone lived. Harris thanked God for his kindness in answering his prayers.

After sharing testimonies we closed the meeting. We didn't sing, hoping to avoid the ridicule of others who may have listened in, and also because none of us were good singers. Encouraged by our successful start we met regularly, alternating responsibilities to take charge, pray, speak, administer the sacrament, and keep the minutes.

The minutes of our Sunday School on December 24, 1944, illustrate how we conducted our regular meetings:

In Charge:	Matheson
Invocation:	Matheson
Sacrament:	Ririe and Harris
Scripture Reading:	Harris read Romans 1, 2, and 3
Attended:	Ririe, Harris, Matheson, Rasmussen excused
Lesson:	Chapter 8 in 2 Nephi by Matheson
Talk:	Ririe—The Story of the First Christmas and Childhood of Jesus
Closing Prayer:	Harris

During our first meeting Rocky and I prepared the sacrament but struggled to recall the sacrament prayers. Rocky approached the chaplain and asked him to obtain a Book of Mormon for our little congregation. When the book arrived from Switzerland, it was a French translation. Ironically, Rocky had served a mission in French-speaking Canada before the war and read French fluently. Each Sunday thereafter he translated part of the Book of Mormon and shared it with us in our group. We were greatly relieved when he translated the sacrament prayers from the Book of Mormon, verifying we had remembered them correctly.

Rocky, Harris, and I had been active members of the Church before the war; the other members, for one reason or another, proved less regular in their attendance at our services. After the war Rocky turned in the minutes of our meetings to the Church authorities.

Our ritual attendance at church each Sunday aroused the curiosity of our companions and stimulated interesting conversations. Our ability to hold church meetings on our own, without the benefit of a clergyman, awed one of the men. When we explained our lay clergy organization it duly impressed him. One of our roommates wanted to know about temple marriage and expressed admiration for our doctrines. Yet, as missionaries, Rocky and I failed to convert anyone to the Church while in captivity. In fact, we were unable to discuss our religion much at all, because religious and political discussions inevitably led to arguments among the kriegies. And all of us had seen enough fighting to last us a lifetime.

Even though our Sunday School meetings were simple, I felt the Spirit of Christ as we worshipped together. His gospel meant a great deal to me. More than at any other time in my life, I appreciated the scripture which I had first noted in the little Victorville Branch, "For where two or three are gathered together in my name, there I am in the midst of them." My appreciation of the Book of Mormon also increased while I was imprisoned. And to have Rocky with us to read and translate this wonderful book from French was a godsend.

CHAPTER 13

Unrelenting Boredom

The realization that we were prisoners of the Third Reich and out of the war became more obvious by the day. We had little to do. Killing enemy combatants was replaced by killing endless hours of monotony. It challenged us from the moment we opened our eyes until we closed them again at night.

After morning roll call we dedicated our day to reading, talking, cooking meals, playing cards, tossing footballs, and sleeping. Some days I studied Spanish or agriculture in structured classes; other days I participated in athletic competitions organized by A3. In the evenings we walked around and around the perimeter of the compound, just inside the fence. Walking gave us exercise and was a change from "sitting around." One walker calculated that if his steps could have been oriented in a straight line he could have walked home.

For endless hours Ellis and I played chess to pass the time away, but even then the minutes crawled by. Fortunately, the YMCA sent books we could check out of the camp library. I read many volumes to preserve my sanity, including, *The Hunchback of Notre Dame, The Mill on the Floss, Botany Bay, Gone With the Wind,* and *Dombey and Son*. Often in the evening, especially in the wintertime, small groups of men gathered in one of the rooms and sang. One current popular American hit had new meaning for us: *Don't Fence Me In*.

Colonel Byerly insisted we have calisthenics after roll call each day. Normally, these sessions weren't long or strenuous and were cancelled during inclement weather. The captain assigned to our barracks obeyed the order as commanded but not wholeheartedly, generally leaving us in good spirits by adding his own original exercises. His calisthenic orders went like this: "Extend index finger. Bend index finger. Extend index finger. Bend index finger." As we bent our fingers he counted, one, two, several times. Then came the order, "Dismissed."

Despite our dire circumstances we generally found things to laugh and joke about. The Germans never figured out our game of Flinch. It was too simple, I suppose. If a man walked by, motioned as if to strike you and you flinched, he could have an uncontested punch to your body, usually applied to the upper arm. Flinch must have looked silly to the Germans, for a smile never creased their serious faces.

A pair of comics named Herbert Bunde and Fernando Tellez shared our room and provided us with entertainment on a regular basis. We had a good laugh when they constructed a ladder to climb up to their top bunk. We didn't exactly need labor saving devices. One day during a rainstorm a leak developed in the roof above Bunde's bed. The enterprising airmen entertained us by building an elaborate drainage apparatus to carry the water from the ceiling to the window. The structure would have made an engineer jealous.

The center of North 1 Compound contained a sports area, and thanks to the generosity of the YMCA, who supplied us with balls and bats, A3 organized softball leagues and scheduled games between the barracks. Occasionally, the Germans allowed inter-compound games on the playing field west of West Compound, watching them with interest, especially since our umpires and players had seen enough major league games to stage very authentic *rhubarbs*. North 1 also had a basketball court, but the game wasn't as popular—quite likely because basketball required too much energy from us on our guaranteed-weight-loss diet.

When the POWs selected members for inter-compound softball teams, my ankles still hurt too much to play. Later in the summer I joined one of the teams, the *Elegantes*, and played in a few games. *Elegantes* was the brand name of a cheap cigarette available in the camp that smokers said tasted awful. Our team slogan was, "If you think *Elegantes* are bad, you should see us." Despite the negative connotation of our slogan, we won several of our games.

Football became popular in the fall. Each barracks organized a team with unusual names, such as *Barley Bashers, Kriegies, House of Adolph, Big Timers,* and *Has Beens,* and played against each other in the cool autumn weather. Our barracks forged a good team and we won most of our games. In one of the games, I ran headlong into an opposing player, nicknamed *The Body,* due to his great physique, and he knocked me down hard, giving me one of the worst blows I ever received as a football player. My chest ached for days. Not surprisingly, Colonel Byerly cancelled competitive football halfway through the season. Too many casualties.

For a while we played competitive volleyball. On my team I played setter for a tall athlete named Anderson, from Los Angeles, who could spike the ball better than anyone I ever played with back home. Unfortunately, Anderson's superiority far outdistanced the competition and league volleyball didn't survive. Moreover, as our food supply dwindled, our energy level dropped. We just didn't have the strength for volleyball.

Individual airmen's talents surfaced in a variety of activities. The camp band entertained us during our meals and on special occasions, playing musical instruments donated by the YMCA. A group of thespians wrote plays and presented dramas, wearing homemade costumes, with airmen playing roles of both sexes. One fellow made a nice looking girl, and some of the plays were quite risqué.

A skinny man named Johnson and his buddy, a real collection of muscles, often presented the camp's favorite act. The big man, after much groaning, straining, and sweating, lifted a large set of weights over his head. Then Johnson entered the stage and carried the weight off with one hand. Another act featured Johnson's buddies tossing him high in the air and catching him with a blanket held taut between them.

One of the rooms put on a special act for new arrivals as they entered the camp. Walking with the new men into camp, a large prisoner feigned an epileptic fit. As he frothed and shook, his eyes darting wildly about, three or four of his companions struggled to subdue him. When he invariably passed out, they announced, "Don't be too alarmed. After two or three months here, all of us have seizures." Then they carried the seemingly unconscious man into the barracks and disappeared. A few hours later they revealed the truth and everybody had a good laugh.

Men in an adjoining barracks developed a show for their own amusement they called "The Séance" and invited us for an evening performance. Since the guards locked us in our barracks at night, we brought our blankets and slept on the floor after the show. The program consisted of card tricks, skits, and ended with a séance, introduced by several half-naked men dressed up as Eastern magicians. In the shadowy candlelight, we asked questions, and their table mysteriously tapped once for no, twice for yes, or an appropriate number of taps for numeric answers. Common questions were: "When will the next air raid occur?" "When will the war end?" "When will mail arrive?" The evening was memorable, but the table's answers were seldom correct.

Bridge and poker were the most popular card games and many of the men were excellent players. Poker games usually involved gambling with cigarettes used as money. Normally, stakes consisted of matches or something even less valuable, like *I owe yous*. Players won everything from bank accounts to the Brooklyn Bridge, but I doubt that anyone collected their winnings. I played an occasional game or two but always lost, my obvious lack of experience proving my downfall.

> **IN THE EARLY SUMMER** of 1944 the war got serious in a big way. On Monday, June 5, a contingent of 1,047 British bombers dropped 5,000 tons of bombs on French batteries along a 50 mile strip of beach on Normandy's coastline. American and British navies then pounded coastal cities with heavy bombardments. Shortly after midnight on June 6, a black, overcast night, 5,000 ships and 13,000 aircraft ferried 155,000 Allied troops to the beaches and were met with heavy German fire. The Allies incurred 11,000 casualties, including 2,500 dead, but pushed the Germans inland far enough to secure a foothold in France. The invasion became known as D-Day.
>
> A week later, on Wednesday, June 14, two hundred and twenty-one British Lancaster bombers hit Le Havre, France, in a daring daylight air raid, killing 1,000 German sailors and securing a major deep water shipping port for the Allies. Both attacks took the Germans by surprise.

As the war progressed, we plotted the battles on a large map in the mess hall, relying on the news we received from the Germans. The guards normally notified us of bad news immediately, but if they said nothing, it meant the Allies were winning. Moreover, bad news wasn't always bad; from the last known area of reverse, we often realized the Allies were making great gains.

Of course, we received first-hand news about V bombs, jet planes, sports, and the latest songs from new prisoners, but the most reliable news about world events we read in the camp's unauthorized secret newssheet, the *Pow-Wow (Prisoners of War Waiting on Winning)*, a two-sided, two-column per page underground newspaper, founded and edited by fellow prisoner Lowell Bennett, an International News Service correspondent. The newssheet was printed on legal-sized tissue paper, no doubt obtained from a nicotine-addicted guard, and circulated each evening. The camp had its own *authorized* daily newspaper containing news harvested from newspapers, radio broadcasts, and interviews with new arrivals, as well as other soft news supplied by the Germans. But it was only a ploy to help distribute the *real* news.

The Germans discovered the *Pow-Wow* when they found a copy in Bennett's room during a search, but they believed Bennett obtained the information he published by listening to a radio hidden in North 1, where he was imprisoned. Despite extensive efforts to find the radio and destroy the newssheet, the Germans never discovered the source of intelligence: two secret radios and a Morse code keyer, secreted in West Compound.

The *Pow-Wow* newssheet was the product of a team of exceptionally brave men. Two RAF radiomen built the radio in 1943 from smuggled parts. They concealed the receiver between wall panels behind a bed in a dormitory room, a map covering the position. Two barely discernible holes indicated points where listeners attached an antenna and an earphone cable to hear BBC broadcasts.

British kriegie D.J. Kilgallen listened to the broadcasts, transcribed the news in longhand on small sheets of toilet paper and delivered it to Warrant Officer R. R. Drummond, liaison between the senior American officer (SAO) and the senior British officer (SBO) headquarters, via the false bottom of a powdered milk can. Drummond folded the transcribed sheets and hid them in a hollow wristwatch before returning to North 1 on his daily rounds.

In Barracks 9 of North 1 Compound, Drummond read the news to First Lieutenant D. McDonald, who typed it up on a legal sized sheet of tissue paper and duplicated copies using homemade carbon paper, attached a copy to the authorized newspaper and delivered it to all fifty-some barracks each evening. The POWs read the news silently in groups of three, burning the sheet after everyone had seen it. I looked forward with keen anticipation to reading the newssheet each day.

Observing the sky also gave us bits of information on what was happening on the front lines. American and British planes often turned south over Stalag Luft 1 on air raids to Berlin. Many nights we lay awake and listened to British planes flying overhead one after another all night long. Fighter planes often sparred in dogfights near the camp, occasionally plunging in fiery balls to the earth. One afternoon an Allied fighter pilot bailed out of his burning plane a few miles from Stalag Luft 1, and the wiry airman joined us in the barracks a couple of days later.

We cheered loudly when American and British planes appeared overhead until an order arrived forbidding us to leave our quarters when the air raid alarm signal sounded. One Sunday morning while we were preparing for church, the air raid alarm signals rang and one of our men didn't hear the warning. As was often our custom, after he finished dressing he stepped nimbly through an open window in the barracks. Without warning rifle shots rang out, killing the airman instantly.

We kriegies were furious. There was no excuse for this act of cold-blooded murder. A simple warning from the guard would have reminded the man, and with a gun pointing at him, he would have complied. The colonel complained to the commandant about the incident and it was investigated, but none of the guards were charged.

On another occasion just as a German plane was taking off from the Barth airbase, an RAF mosquito bomber made a pass. We heard gunshots and explosions as the plane flew over the airfield, and we cheered when it came up behind its hapless victim. In a matter of seconds the German plane went down in flames and the mosquito bomber headed out to sea, presumably on its way home. Suddenly, the air raid alarm sounded and guards ushered us inside the barracks, even though it was after the excitement was over.

Prisoners never tired of telling their *true* stories whenever they could find a listening ear. Every airman had his own "jump story," and it was interesting to hear about the fateful *last trip*. Fighter pilots seldom confessed to being shot down by an enemy fighter pilot. Usually, they were downed by a lucky ack-ack shot, by engine malfunction, or they ran out of fuel or had some stupendous accident, such as losing a wing in a thundercloud or striking the earth with the propeller while strafing.

One of the most popular fighter pilots in camp was Colonel Henry Russell Spicer, compound commander of North 2. Spicer floated in the English Channel for two days in a small lifeboat after he was shot down May 3, 1944. On the Fourth of July, 1944, we held a celebration in the camp and the German commanders attending requested permission to speak. Every time one of them spoke or looked at the audience, a group of us made Churchill's famous *V for Victory* sign with our fingers. The Germans ordered us to stop. Colonel Spicer, sitting behind the speaker, refused to comply. Whenever he made the sign, we responded with laughter. When the Germans eventually caught on, they promptly ushered Spicer out of the compound and into solitary confinement, or the *cooler* as we called it.

After his release, early on an exceptionally cold October morning, Spicer gathered his men for roll call and stood a miserable two hours in the bitter cold while the Germans counted and recounted. Fed up, Spicer dismissed his men before the guards finished their count. As the men walked back to their barracks the Germans issued violent threats, but they allowed the kriegies to leave the parade ground.

Later in the day Spicer recalled the men to his barracks and addressed them. Earlier in the week the Germans sent an American officer to the *cooler* for not saluting a lower ranking German officer. This violated the Geneva Convention rules that stated we were only required to salute officers of higher rank. At Stalag Luft 1 the German administrators demanded POWs salute all officers, including lower ranking officers. Speaking in a loud voice so the Germans could overhear, Spicer reminded the men of the Geneva code and told them they were only to salute officers of higher rank.

Spicer then chastised the men for becoming too friendly with their captors, reminding them of German atrocities. "Don't let them fool you," he said. "They are dirty sneaks that can't be trusted."

The men cheered and applauded. An hour later Spicer stood before Commandant Oberst Scherer, who charged him with defaming the German character and inciting prisoners to riot. Scherer held Spicer in custody until a military court sentenced him to six months solitary confinement followed by execution by a firing squad. Thanks to fate, Victory in Europe Day arrived before the execution date.

Due to its proximity to the Baltic Sea, Stalag Luft 1 was damp in winter, with a penetrating, chill wind entering the un-insulated wooden barracks. Each week the Germans issued one small box containing a coke-like material and briquettes of compressed processed peat to heat our quarters. Since the entire week's supply of fuel wouldn't have heated our room for one day, we rationed it, burning a small fire for a short time each morning to take the chill out of the air. After the fire burned out the room became very cold in just a few minutes.

The Germans didn't issue clothing to prisoners and they confiscated anything we received from home that remotely resembled civilian attire. The Red Cross supplied uniforms and blankets to the camp on a regular basis. A large shipment in the summer of 1944 provided each man two complete uniforms and two blankets, but as the numbers of prisoners arriving at the camp increased, supplies dwindled rapidly. In February 1945, the SAO ordered a redistribution of uniforms because so much of the clothing the men wore was threadbare and patched.

In the bone-chilling cold of winter nights, instead of undressing for bed, we donned socks, underwear, shirts, sweaters, trousers, and even our overcoat before crawling under our lone, thin blanket. If we warmed up, the chilblains began to itch and ache. More often, we shivered all night, a result of having so few calories in our diet that our bodies couldn't generate sufficient heat. The next morning, come rain or shine, sleet or snow, the Germans forced us to stand outside while they counted us.

Occasionally, the SAO called for a barracks inspection. Generally, we growled about inspections, but on these occasions we washed our clothes, shined what little equipment we had, and scrubbed our living quarters with a good GI cleansing to remove potentially dangerous germs. While our health mattered little to the Germans, it did concern our Allied medical personnel, who attended to us when anyone fell ill. We prayed hard that nothing contagious would afflict the camp, and we were blessed. In all cases, the injections we received in the training and staging camps proved to be good preventative medicine. The rugged physical conditioning to which we had been subjected served us well, also. In an emergency we could visit the dentist, who admittedly had a larger practice than he could handle. Fortunately, I was never one of his victims.

After I developed a number of canker sores in my mouth I did visit the camp medical doctor. He looked in my mouth, swabbed an astringent on the sores, and said, "The pain is exquisite, isn't it?" *Exquisite* wasn't exactly the word I would have used. Since I also complained of a stomach ache he gave me a liberal dose of physic. The laxative induced vomiting and diarrhea at the same time and nearly killed me. In a few days I did feel better, however.

CHAPTER 14

Tunneling Out

"Freedom lies in being bold," wrote the poet Robert Frost. If there is poetry in confinement, it is the poetry of boldness. I not only yearned to be a free man while imprisoned at Stalag Luft 1 but felt it my patriotic duty to reenter the war at the earliest possible moment. Escape never left my mind. Day after day with little to do but think, my roommates and I devised several plans to break out of the camp but never came up with one that was practical.

A POW could escape on his own volition, but if he first ran his plans past the camp's underground Central Security Committee, and if the plan appeared to be sound and didn't conflict with other plans underway, the committee helped potential escapees. The committee supplied expertly forged, custom made identification papers, travel permits, camp passes, ration cards, plus civilian clothing, wire cutters, food, and other necessities.

Part of the reason POWs could work clandestinely without the Germans becoming aware of our activities was the imbalance of the guard-to-prisoner ratio. Only a small number of the 500 guards assigned to the camp were on duty at any given time, while the POWs, who numbered in the thousands, were in constant motion all over the compound.

After reviewing a variety of options, tunneling out became the only logical way of escaping we could devise. Since our room was on a corner of the barracks, we decided to dig a tunnel in a diagonal line toward the guard tower and exit directly underneath the tower on the far side of the fence. We submitted our plans to the Escape Committee, who approved them with little alteration, and we went to work sawing a hole in the floor, large enough for a man to slide through, under a bed in our room. Since the barracks were built with the floor about eighteen inches above the ground, they provided just enough room for a man to crawl around on hands and knees under the building.

Whenever the camp began a clandestine activity, such as our tunnel, the Escape Committee assigned men, called stooges, to guard the tunnel entrance. If a German drew near, the stooge would shout, "Goon's up," and work stopped until given the all clear. The term *goon* came from a 1920s comic strip character in the Popeye cartoon, drawn by Elzie Segar. Alice the Goon was a good hearted but simple-minded creature. Her body was shaped like a pear; she had a baldhead, a big nose, and hairy arms and legs. But when the Germans asked what the term goon meant, we kriegies informed them it was an anagram for "German Officer or Noncom."

Tunneling was tough, demanding work. We quickly discovered the soil beneath the barracks was mostly sand and easy to dig, but highly prone to cave-ins. Furthermore, due to the high water table on the peninsula, water often flooded the tunnel, adding to our discomfort when digging. We referred to our tunnel diggers as "moles," a very accurate description of us dressed in our grimy underwear, or sweat suits, worn out from crawling and digging, giving us a grey and grisly appearance. We dared not dig in our regular clothing, because fresh soil has an easily recognizable smell. The odor also made it extremely difficult for us to get rid of cubic yards of dirt.

We worked in two-man teams, crawling on our stomachs, using our elbows to propel us along the tunnel floor, slowly scraping the dirt away by hand with shovels made from flattened tin milk cans. We carried the dirt away from the shaft on pieces of cardboard. To provide air in the confined space, we pumped in fresh air with handmade bellows created from empty milk cans and operated by hand. We learned that if we cut the tunnel in elliptical cross sections, we lowered the risk of cave-ins and avoided the need for shoring.

To divest ourselves of the dirt as we dug, we disposed of as much of it as we dared in the attic of our barracks and in the fire prevention water barrels that stood at each end of the hallway. The hall was so poorly illuminated that we were able to fill the barrels with soil to within one or two inches of the water surface.

The more we dug the more our disposal problem intensified. No matter what disposal solution we concocted, the soil kept coming. When the attic and water barrels were full, we filled the stove chimney pipe up to the point where the pipe went through the wall into the main chimney, which provided us several inches of empty space. When the stovepipe was full we placed cardboard over the wooden slats on our beds and poured several inches of soil under the straw ticks. The extra soil didn't affect our sleeping comfort because the beds weren't exactly inner spring Beauty Rests.

Finally, our tunnel cleared the fence, but our progress toward the tower suddenly slowed when we ran into a gravel formation. Digging through it was arduous. Just as we were overcoming the gravel strata, our beds filled to overflowing with soil, we decided to chance spreading the dirt from the final few feet of our tunnel under the barracks.

Tunneling activities came to an abrupt halt one morning when a stooge nervously yelled down the hole, "Goon's up!" as a German search party marched stiffly and sternly through the gate. We quickly climbed out of the hole, hid our digging clothes and tin cans, closed up the opening under the bed, and appeared as innocent as possible while the Germans searched the camp. Despite our protective measures, the Germans discovered our tunnel and abruptly collapsed the project. Colonel Byerly followed the Germans around on their search and after inspecting our tunnel, jotted down our names and said, "Good show, men."

ONE-MISSION MAN

Later, Colonel Byerly himself participated in a tunneling project and was caught trying to escape. As a punishment the Germans put him and his accomplices in the cooler. He had probably pulled his rank to be the first one out and it backfired. Solitary confinement for periods measured in the weeks was standard punishment in Stalag Luft 1.

After the discovery of our tunnel, we learned the reason for the sudden search by the Germans. In another barracks a group of men were digging a tunnel simultaneously with ours. To hide the excavated dirt, the POWs placed it in their attic like we had done but incorrectly estimated its weight. The load soon exceeded the carrying capacity of the trusses and the roof caved in, alerting the Germans to the men's tunneling activities.

Nonetheless, after our botched attempt, we immediately started another tunnel but had to abandon it when the chosen route encountered a hard, rocky strata our miserable tin cans couldn't dent. Our third and fourth tunnels were also abject failures. On one of them we were caught almost before we had cleared the edge of our barracks.

ON DECEMBER 13, 1944, the U.S. 3rd Army captured Metz, France. On the following day, Colonel Hubert "Hub" Zemke arrived at secluded Stalag Luft 1 and relieved Colonel Byerly as SAO. Son of German immigrants, thirty-one-year-old ace fighter pilot Zemke spoke fluent German and Russian. A slender man of average height—5 foot 9 inches—with an open face, he was a natural leader, inclined to speak his mind. This former commander of the celebrated U.S. 8th Air Force fighter group Zemke's Wolfpack had 19 victorious strikes under his belt when his P-51 Mustang lost a wing in a thunderstorm high above Hanover, Germany, and he parachuted into enemy hands.

Long sought by Hitler, the American ace joined a distinguished list of captured warriors at Stalag Luft 1 permanently tucked away in the backwater camp to prevent them from creating further havoc against the Reich. Among them were Lieutenant Colonel Francis (Gabby) Gabreski, an air ace, who shot down 28 enemy fighters; Major Gerald Johnson, an ace with 18 kills; fighter pilot Lieutenant Colonel Charles

> "Ross" Greening; and Medal of Honor recipient John "Red" Morgan. Gabreski and Johnson had served with Zemke in the 56th Fighter Group's Thunderbolt outfit.
>
> On December 16, along a densely forested 60-mile front from Monschau, Germany, to Ecternach, Luxemburg, 200,000 German tank and infantry troops surprised 83,000 American troops in an attempt to split the British and American lines, encircle and destroy the Allied armies. Named the Ardennes-Alsace campaign by the U.S. Army, the month-long battle became known as the Battle of the Bulge, due to the "bulge" the Germans created in the front line.
>
> Surprise not withstanding, General George Patton's Third Army with 500,000 to 840,000 troops pushed the Germans back to the Siegfried line on January 25. The U.S. suffered 70,000 to 84,000 casualties, including 19,000 deaths, making the Battle of the Bulge the bloodiest and costliest battle in the war.

Even before Zemke arrived at Stalag Luft 1, unceasing, gnawing hunger was the most constant of our discomforts because the Germans intentionally kept us hungry to subdue us. Cooks prepared meals in a central kitchen and POW volunteers distributed it to the compounds. Meals usually consisted of boiled culls (potatoes we Idahoans leave in the field because they're too small to peel) and sauerkraut so foul that we flushed much of it down the toilets. We couldn't let the Krauts know we hadn't consumed it, since they would cut our rations further if they knew. We also received sugar beet jam that was inedible, a little sugar, dried turnips, black bread, and a thin barley soup. Several times we received tasteless Italian cheese packaged in tubes like toothpaste that was fairly palatable toasted. Generally, we couldn't save our food supplies for a leaner day because the Germans confiscated hoarded food. Consequently, we never had any reserves.

The Germans seldom gave us meat. One rare exception was after an Allied pilot shot a couple of horses near the camp. When the two cats that hung around North 1 for a while disappeared, a rumor arose suggesting kriegies ate them. We accidentally discovered an additional source of nutrition when a large prisoner who often beat us to the mess hall to wolf down more than his share of the barley soup suddenly turned ghostly pale and left the table. We realized he had noticed weevils in the soup, but the rest of us figured that since the worms were well cooked, we might as well eat them. In fact, we elevated the status of barley to the best protein source available in our provisions.

Frankly, if not for the food parcels sent to us by the Red Cross we would not have survived. A single parcel, designed to keep a man going for one week, contained one pound of Spam, one pound of corned beef, one pound of powdered milk, one pound of margarine, one-half pound of cheese, twelve biscuits, one-half pound of salmon, six ounces of liver pate, a one pound bar of chocolate, one-half pound of jam, one ounce of salt and pepper, twelve vitamin tablets, one pound of raisins, one-half pound of sugar, and one hundred cigarettes.

If the Red Cross and the German food issues had been regular we would have eaten quite well, but sometimes weeks went by without a shipment, and if a consignment did arrive, most often there weren't enough parcels for each man to have a box of his own. Just before Christmas 1944 we suffered a hungry period. Red Cross parcels arrived and our hopes soared, but there weren't enough parcels to go around. Just as we were dividing our Christmas food at the rate of two men per parcel, a new contingent of prisoners arrived and we had to divvy up the contents at three men per parcel.

We prized all of the items in the Red Cross parcels and traded the items we didn't consume. Cigarettes especially became valuable units of exchange for those of us who didn't smoke. Even under conditions of semi-starvation, many smokers traded us food for cigarettes. The POWs' coffee addiction was almost as severe. As soon as camp cooks announced hot water was available, men ran to the kitchen with coffee cups in hand like a herd of thirsty cattle stampeding to a water hole. Generally, there were no serious casualties, but occasionally a man fell down and the other men unavoidably trampled him.

In the early days of my confinement at Stalag Luft 1, the camp band played in the mess hall as we ate. The music was enjoyable — we had so little of it. Fine china and fresh linens were not a part of our meals, but a gifted artist painted several lovely girls smiling upon us on the mess hall walls. Occasionally, I took a turn on KP, but it wasn't much of an assignment with so many men in camp, so much time on our hands, and so little food to prepare.

One morning the sirens sounded, but instead of an air raid, we saw flames rising from the cookhouse. The Germans rushed to the burning building carrying a fire hose while the POWs cheered and called out their wish that the fire would burn down the whole camp. In a very dignified manner the Germans fastened the hose to a hydrant, pointed the nozzle toward the ferocious fire, and opened the valve. Everyone expected a great gush of water, but to the Germans' chagrin, and our delight, only a stream about the size of a pencil trickled out the end of the fire hose.

The Germans dropped the hose to investigate. Suddenly water spewed out of the hose with great force, tossing the nozzle in frantic convulsions on the ground, watering kriegies, jerries, and everything within range — except the burning mess hall. We lost no time in voicing smart remarks as the Germans tried in vain to regain their dignity. When, at last, they brought the gyrating hose under control, the cookhouse was too far destroyed to save. It wasn't much of a loss because by that time the only food leaving the kitchen was a bowl of unsalted dried turnip soup per man per day, After the fire, we improvised cooking utensils out of powdered milk cans and prepared all of our meals ourselves in our dormitory rooms.

Just before New Year's Day 1945, Oberst von Warnstedt replaced the commandant Oberst Sherer and conditions at the camp deteriorated considerably, at times becoming grim. In early January von Warnstedt installed a knee high, single wire fence around all compounds just inside the double barbed wire fence. Soon after he issued an edict stating prisoners who touched the wire, accidentally or otherwise, would be shot without challenge.

Foodstuffs from German sources, notably potatoes, began to arrive late. In addition, the Germans put a limit on the amount of food that an individual could save from his Red Cross parcels. When the Red Cross parcels were down to a two-week supply, the Germans confiscated reserves of canned jam and other foods stored in the central compound stores.

I later learned back home in Ririe by all outward signs nothing had changed in our small community yet the war was all around. Sunday evenings Franklin Roosevelt spoke to my family over the radio, asking them to work harder to produce food for the "boys overseas." This was disconcerting because several Ririe residents had abandoned their farms and moved to California to work in munitions and aircraft factories. The shelves of the local grocery store were nearly bare, since most items required a special "ration" ticket to purchase them. "Everything was scarce," remembered Wayne. "Never did a candy bar taste so good as the rare times when our grocer received his allotment." Even six-year-old Jimmy felt deprived. "Mother would give me one little cube of chocolate and the remainder [of the bar] would be mailed to David," recalled Jim in a letter years later. "It seemed everything I liked was rationed."

Early one morning, Uncle Hy and his son Perry saw a large bomb dangling from a balloon descending from the sky. The 33-foot diameter balloon was one of 9,000 "Fugo" balloons launched by the Japanese who wanted them to set the forests of North America ablaze and cause widespread panic. Armed with four bombs weighing about ten pounds each, plus a 30 pound incendiary bomb, the balloons did little damage. Most were intercepted by high-altitude fighter planes before they reached the states. Calibrated to explode at a low elevation, Uncle Hy's bomb was prevented from detonating by Ririe's mile-high altitude. A naive deputy sheriff hauled the bomb away in the back of his truck without diffusing it. The government adopted a policy of silence on the balloon bombs to quell panic and the news media never reported on the attacks. When the Japanese didn't read news items about the bombs in the newspapers they surmised the campaign was a failure and brought it to an abrupt halt.

Far from his bride, Max celebrated Christmas in Hawaii, preparing for the invasion of the Japanese mainland. Clive, 17, was eagerly anticipating his April birthday when a third star would be added to the small flag hanging in our living room window, representing three family members serving in the armed forces. Wayne said the mere mention of my name at church or school brought a chorus of concern for my wellbeing.

Dad continued farming, serving in state politics and church work, and keeping up with the progress of the war, all without allowing world events to distract him from his immediate responsibilities. His formula for beating hard times was to be up with the sun and in the fields every day.

With Max and me away, Mother helped Dad bring in the harvest in the fall, even though she was six months pregnant with Elaine, who would be born four days after Christmas, two days after Mother turned 45. In a stake conference, she played the piano to accompany visiting church leader Spencer W. Kimball as he sang *Where Is My Wandering Boy Tonight?* Aunt Velda sat in the congregation sobbing uncontrollably.

"Mother never complained, never acted sorry for herself, or blamed others but was cheerful and optimistic, as interested in others, as pleased to see them and to be with them, as ever," recalled Wayne. Clive, who saw Mother daily, as close-up as only a son could, wrote, "I seriously doubt that much time passed when she wasn't thinking and praying for her prisoner son."

ONE-MISSION MAN

The Ririe/Lovell Family in 1898 in the settlement which became Ririe. Leah Ann and David Ririe, standing in front of the wagon to the far right, had eight children.

David Ririe, my grandfather for whom I am named, was a prominent farmer in Southeastern Idaho. In 1914 he petitioned the Oregon Short Line Railroad Company to build a spur to serve communities north of Idaho Falls and helped the company obtain right-of-ways. Railroad executives were so grateful for his help they dubbed the new station "Ririe."

As I boarded the train my grandmother, Leah Ann Lovell Ririe, took a five dollar bill from her purse, pressed it into my hand, and with a tear in her eye, gave me a kiss on the cheek.

The Ririe Depot served the community until it was phased out by the railroad in the early 1970s. Unable to sell it the company tore the building down in 1985.

The James E. Ririe family in 1927. (Sitting) James E., Clive Perry (baby). (Standing, top to bottom) Verna Fanny Perry, David and Max Henry.

Me, Clive and Max about the time Max and I herded 124 ewes on my family's dry farm at Granite. At the end of the summer we each received the first money we earned from our own labor.

Even though we were ten years apart, my brother Wayne and I were best buddies. I taught him how to whistle and wherever I went around the farm he followed me like a puppy. When I left for the war the separation was hard on both of us.

The James E. Ririe Family in 1943: (back row, left to right) David, Clive Perry, Max Henry. (Front row, left to right) Wayne, Verna, James A, James E., Carma. During the 13 months I was a POW, my family continued farming, serving in state politics and doing church work. With Max, Clive and me away, Mother helped Dad and my brothers who were too young to join the fighting bring in the harvest even though she was six months pregnant with Elaine, who was born four days after Christmas, 1945.

I was born in this two-story, 14 room stone house that my grandfather David Ririe had built for my grandmother, Leah Ann Lovell Ririe, in 1906. The home still stands today.

Second Lieutenant David Ririe soon after I received a commission as a bombardier in the U.S. Army Air Corps. I was assigned to Flight Crew 858 in the 388th Bomb Group of the 563rd Squadron before being shot down over Rostock, Germany on April 11, 1944.

The Expectant Father crew posed for a photograph in March 1943 in Grand Island, Nebraska, shortly before flying to England. Kneeling, left to right: Edmund J. Ely, pilot; Frederick H. Pratt, copilot; William L. Ellis, navigator; David Ririe, bombardier. Standing, left to right: Leo K. Kornoely, engineer; Constantine G. Scourbys, right waist gunner; John M. Russel, radio operator; Vincent J. Muffoletto, ball turret gunner; Harvey L. Ringer, left waist gunner; Thomas Neill, tail gunner. The crew's first mission was also its last. After the plane was attacked over Germany all of the enlisted men bailed out over the Baltic Sea. Kornoely, Scourbys, Ringer and Neill did not survive.

ONE-MISSION MAN

One of the most well-known aircraft of all time, the B-17 bomber, with up to thirteen machine guns, became known as the Flying Fortress. A normal B-17 bomb load averaged around 6,000 pounds and boasted a ceiling of 35,000 feet, a range of 4,400 miles and a top speed of 300 mph, although it flew at about 160 mph on most raids.

Our plane, *The Expectant Father,* was a new "silver bomber," an aircraft with a bare metal finish. The Army discarded the familiar olive drab and neutral grey camouflage finish in February 1944 because its weight and drag took several miles per gallon from performance. Not painting the aircraft also lowered costs and decreased production time. Our crew felt the naked bomber attracted enemy fighter planes by singling us out as an inexperienced crew and was partly responsible for the plane being shot down on its second mission and our first mission as a crew.

The B-17 bombardier sat in the nose, directly behind the Plexiglas cone, the most exposed place in the plane. Besides flying the plane during the bomb run, the bombardier also controlled the bomb bay doors, the bomb release, and protected the plane from frontal attacks, manning two .50 caliber machine guns.

The Norden bombsight (above, bottom right corner) was a top-secret analog computer developed by the U.S. Navy to ensure accurate bomb hits. Although this wonderful instrument gave us a strong advantage over the enemy, it was very temperamental and didn't always work.

ONE-MISSION MAN

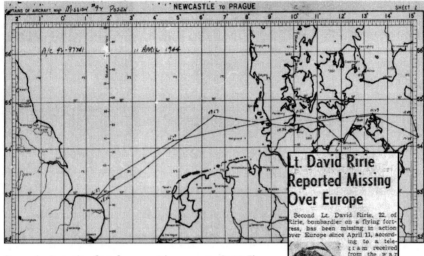

Our mission, the first for us with our new B-17 Flying Fortress bomber, was to bomb an aircraft plant in Posen, Poland. The flight was lengthy, 675 miles (1,086.5 kilometers) one way. The map on the wall of the briefing room didn't display the entire route. The above map is part of the official Missing Air Crew Report the U.S. Army Air Forces' prepared after the disappearance of T*he Expectant Father.*

Lt. David Ririe Reported Missing Over Europe

Second Lt. David Ririe, 22, of Ririe, bombardier on a flying fortress, has been missing in action over Europe since April 11, according to a telegram received from the war department, his parents, Mr. and Mrs. James E. Ririe of Ririe, disclosed Saturday.

Lieutenant Ririe was graduated from Ririe high school, attended Ricks college and entered the air force in March of 1943.

He received his basic training at Santa Ana, Calif., and his wings from the bombardier school at Victorville, Calif. He received operations training at Ardmore, Okla.

I had a card containing the theme of the LDS Church's youth group, the Mutual Improvement Association (MIA), in my pocket when I was captured.

The news that I was missing in action in Europe appeared in the Idaho Falls *Post Register* the day after my parents received a telegram from the war department.

This is the receipt the Germans gave to me after they stole my watch.

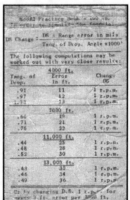

A card containing formulas for calculating bomb drops was among the personal effects which I surrendered to the Germans.

131

ONE-MISSION MAN

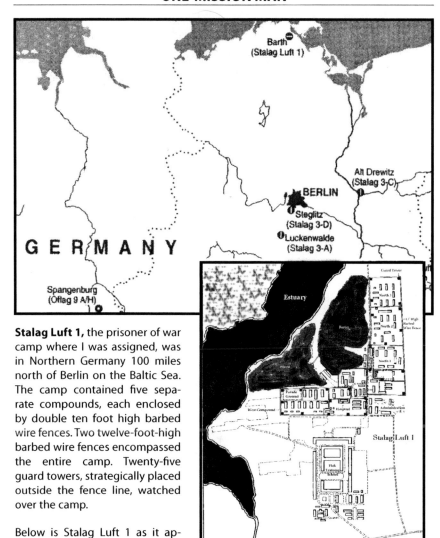

Stalag Luft 1, the prisoner of war camp where I was assigned, was in Northern Germany 100 miles north of Berlin on the Baltic Sea. The camp contained five separate compounds, each enclosed by double ten foot high barbed wire fences. Two twelve-foot-high barbed wire fences encompassed the entire camp. Twenty-five guard towers, strategically placed outside the fence line, watched over the camp.

Below is Stalag Luft 1 as it appeared in 1945.

I became POW 4454 and was assigned to Room 5, Block 11, of North 1 Compound, a small dormitory room in an un-insulated wooden barracks. I'm in the window on the left hand side.

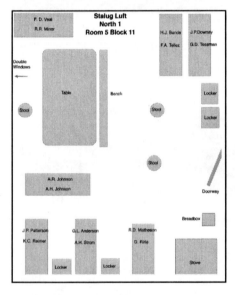

The layout of Room 5, Block 11, at Stalag Luft 1. Towards the end of the war when bombing increased and more men were captured as planes were shot down, living conditions at the camp became increasingly cramped with as many as 18 to 20 men sharing the same small room.

Robert Dean "Rocky" Matheson was my best friend during my captivity. Rocky, a returned LDS missionary from McGill, Nevada, and I were both ordained elders in the church. Soon after our arrival at Stalag Luft 1 we organized a Sunday School to partake of the sacrament and study the scriptures with other LDS prisoners on a weekly basis.

These are my dog tags from Stalag Luft 1 and the U. S. Army Air Corps.

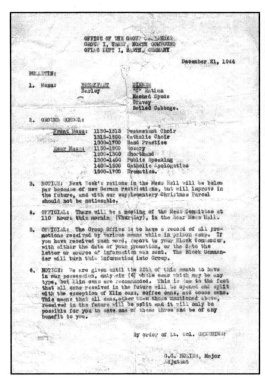

Max Henry Ririe, my brother, was stationed in Hawaii at the headquarters of the U.S. Army Forces in the Middle Pacific (MidPac) where he prepared top-secret communiqués for the high command staff, including one regarding the atomic bomb dropped on Japan.

In an effort to relieve the unrelenting monotony that challenged us POWs from morning to night, our leaders organized daily activities. Besides the usual camp and KP duties, we attended structured classes in a variety of subjects and participated in inter-compound sporting events.

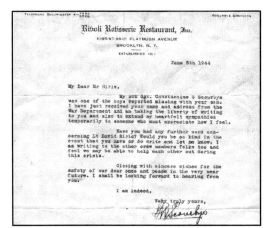

My father received this heartfelt letter from Scourbys' grieving father as he searched in vain for his son who was lost in the Baltic Sea.

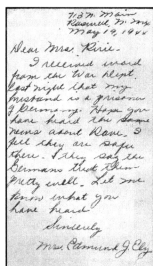

Ely's wife sent my mother this grateful note soon after she received news from the War Department that we were captured, expressing relief that her husband was alive.

ONE-MISSION MAN

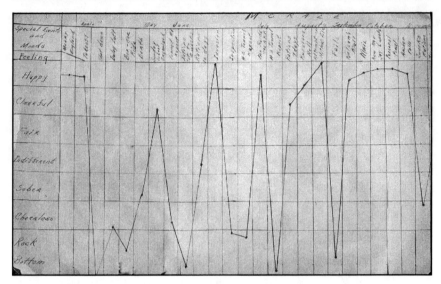

To help retain my sanity, I kept track of my emotions weekly on a morale chart, plotting war and personal events and activities on one axis and how I felt at the time on the other axis. Besides indicating that my lowest emotional points coincided with tunnel failures and periods when food was scarce while my high points matched successful air raids and Red Cross parcel arrivals, the chart also provided me with an accurate chronological record of my captivity.

I went to Paris on this 24 hour pass but the trip actually took 48 hours.

A telegram from my mother, answering one I had sent on July 14, 1944, arrived at Stalag Luft 1 on February 14, 1945, six months later.

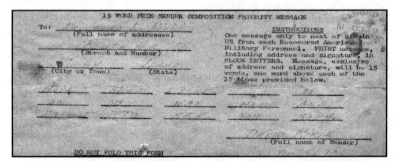

This is the content of the telegram I sent home to my family informing them of my liberation by the Russians from Stalag Luft 1 in May 1945.

135

An article in *Stars and Stripes* announcing our release from Stalag Luft 1 upset the bomber crews by glorifying the fighter pilots, who were in the minority at the camp, and ignoring the rest of us. Ace fighter pilot Lt. Col. Francis S. Gabreski's statement that all POWs were anxious to get into the Pacific war after gaining their freedom was particularly galling to us kriegies.

Jody, James and I pose for a family portrait in 1949. Ruth Joanne Irwin and I met in Sunday School in San Bernardino, California, while I was stationed at Victorville Army Air Base. She later was a major reason I selected Brigham Young University for my undergraduate degree. I had found my Ruth.

The surviving members of the crew of *The Expectant Father* reunited in 1999: (left to right), Vincent Muffaletto, William Ellis, Edmund Ely, John Russell, and me, David Ririe.

CHAPTER 15

Fighting Chance

Our fifth tunnel — our finest effort — came about in early January of 1945. The Germans segregated the Jewish prisoners, British and American, from non-Jews and sequestered them in a barracks in North 1. Though the German rationale never became clear, the relocation seemed a kiss of death for the prisoners and everybody knew it.

Few Jews practiced their faith openly in the camp but in South Compound Father Michael Charlson, a Roman Catholic priest and a British captain, allowed about 100 Jewish men to attend High Holy Days, Yom Kippur and Rosh Hashanah in a tent provided for Christian services without the Nazis' knowledge. In any case, gathering the Jews into one location appeared to be a precursor of an evil intention.

In the repositioning the Germans transferred my roommates and me to a fresh barracks where our predecessors had done very little tunneling. Under this barracks the soil was less dense and easier to move with our milk can scrapers. In addition, someone in our group stole a shovel and we were, as a result, much better equipped for a new tunneling adventure.

In preparation we discretely observed the Germans for several weeks and discovered that every fourth night our captors sent a crew of men, whom we called *ferrets*, and dogs to search under the barracks and check for seditious activity. With a window of four days before us, we determined we could dig a tunnel in a marathon tag-team effort between ferret crew visits by selecting a group of thirteen experienced moles for the tunneling job. A marathon dig meant we would have a minimal soil disposal problem, since we planned to be gone before our work came to light, therefore we could place the loose dirt in the crawl space under the barracks. We submitted our plans to the Escape Committee and were immediately given the go-ahead.

When the designated evening arrived we frantically started digging after the ferrets completed their inspection. We dug rapidly in shifts, stopping only when roll calls demanded, and kept a constant lookout. To remove dirt from the tunnel, we loaded cardboard slips with soil, jerked on an improvised rope and the dumpers quickly pulled out the slips and unloaded loose soil on the ground. The slip was then pulled back into the tunnel with another rope and reloaded. As we had done earlier, we dug in a straight diagonal line until we cleared the barracks, then turned the tunnel slightly, and headed straight under the yard, the fence, the road, and into the adjacent field where two large electrical wire spools lay unattended. The goal was to come up between the spools.

The job went well, but when we started digging under the road my digging partner and I became a little skittish. Vehicles driving directly over us along the roadway created a terrifying noise. We were already jumpy when someone came crawling down the tunnel toward us, and we heard a guttural, "Was ist dieses?" I froze, and my partner and I nearly collapsed from fright, only to realize we were staring into the dimly lit faces of two laughing Americans—our replacement crew.

By the third night we had completed the escape tunnel. We had saved food from our meager rations and obtained maps and gear from the camp Escape Committee. To further improve our chances of escape, we paired off into small teams and drew lots to determine the order of departure. K. C. Reimer, Al Strom, and I decided to escape as a trio. Strom seemed a good companion because he spoke Swedish, and Sweden was the closest neutral country to the camp. In the luck of the draw, our team was scheduled last to leave.

After lock-down two of our men entered the tunnel, two waited under the barracks, and two more stood ready to leave the staging room when the Germans burst in and caught us in the act. They had double-crossed us, bringing the ferrets around an evening earlier than usual. In panic the men struggled to get out of the tunnel. One of the guards fired a rifle shot down the entrance hole but he missed hitting the two men in the tunnel who, fortunately, were behind the protective bend. Guards quickly rounded up the escapees and tossed them in the cooler where they received a month's worth of solitary confinement.

Meanwhile, my two companions and I jumped into bed with our clothes on and yanked them off under the blankets. Our roommates, who were not part of the escape team, draped our clothes over the edge of the bed where we normally kept them at night before climbing into bed themselves. When the Germans burst through the door we sat up in our beds and rubbed our eyes as if just awakened. The guards never discovered Reimer, Strom and I were part of the plot, but they did confiscate our filthy mole suits.

The day after our failed escape attempt several German guards visited our barracks wearing broad smiles—which was unusual for them—and placed a sign next to our tunnel exit hole, which read: "Many Happy Returns of the Day. You Have Been Caught Digging Tunnel Number 100 From This Camp." They then filled up the tunnel with barbed wire entanglements, shoveled in the ends, and left chuckling.

The sign was a lot less than we had hoped for, but we also laughed at their little joke. It was a switch. In the past we had never known the Germans to consider anything humorous. That may have been an error. Inflicting torture and misery appealed to their more sadistic and sinister side.

Tunnel Five was my last attempt to tunnel out. We were disheartened, our digging clothes were gone, and the news from our sources suggested the Allies were gaining on all major fronts. Moreover, after every single tunnel in the camp failed, it became evident to our leaders that the Germans were using seismographic equipment to monitor below ground tunneling noises.

No matter who, where, or when we were digging, it seemed the Germans knew about it. They would patiently wait until the tunnel neared the outer fence, then rush in and destroy it with as much fanfare as they could muster. Apparently, allowing us to finish the tunnel before caving it in was a ploy to heighten our disappointment. As for my motley group of moles, we decided to stop digging and wait it out until the end — unless, of course, a good idea came along.

Escape attempts didn't stop. One airman rode out of camp submerged in the garbage cart but was recaptured when the garbage men dumped the cart. Another airman affixed boards to his back and, while his accomplices created a diversionary disturbance, crawled under the fence in broad daylight. Despite his bravado, he was quickly recaptured.

In fact, none of the 90 attempts to escape from Stalag Luft 1 ever got very far before the escapees were recaptured. Part of the reason for the quick captures was that after early escape attempts the Germans legalized the shooting of escaped POWs without warning if they were within specified forbidden areas. Both of the camp's commandants, Oberst von Warnstadt and Oberst Scherer, often imposed mass reprimands, punishing an entire barracks for one person's violation of a regulation. Von Warnstadt was particularly liberal in his "shoot to kill" regulations authorizing guards to use firearms and confining POWs to the cooler for minor disciplinary infractions. Conditions outside the camp became so dangerous that the SBO, Colonel Ginger Weir, forbade the British men who had attempted the majority of the failed escapes from further attempts.

In late February the Germans stopped delivery of Red Cross parcels, claiming the constant strafing by Allied fighters of rail lines and roads had made transporting the parcels too dangerous. Even though there were more than a million parcels stocked in warehouses in Lubeck, seventy-five miles away, we had no way to reach them. The U.S. government offered to provide trucks and gas to pick up and deliver the food supplies, but the Germans refused. The German objective seemed to be to starve us.

Rocky, several others, and I joined in a pact that if the war didn't end by the first of March, we would shave our heads. No sooner had we shaved them than the allies began to move offensively but not before the weather changed and we would have liked to have our hair back. Some of us looked pretty silly with our bumpy heads.

IN EARLY 1945 the Russian Army made a strong drive into German-held territory. On January 12, one hundred twenty miles south of Warsaw, Poland, and only three hundred miles from Berlin, seventy divisions of the 1st Ukrainian Front crossed the Vistula River. Two days later bombers destroyed rail targets and oil plants at Saarbrucken and Leuna, Germany. On January 16, bombers attacked Leipzig and Bruz. By the evening of January 17, the Soviets had liberated Warsaw.

Once the Red Army reached the Oder River in late January, Hitler turned his attention to defending Berlin, where about a million German soldiers manned the lines. Even so, Russians had the advantage, with General Georgy Konstantinovich Zhukov and General Ivan Stepanovich Konev commanding 2.5 million men.

The Russian Advance created chaos for Stalag Luft 1. Power lines were down in many locations in Germany, causing sporadic electrical shutdowns. Water often ceased to flow in the pipes. POWs continued to arrive daily from camps closing down in Poland and East Prussia, mainly enlisted men imprisoned at the Battle of the Bulge.

On February 14 and 15, Dresden was hit by two massive air blows of fire bombs by Allied bombers, causing the largest destruction of a big urban area in the war and killing 400,000 people. The fire burned for weeks afterward.

ONE-MISSION MAN

Around the middle of March we began to suspect that the German turnip crop had failed. Our one bowl of food per day became smaller and more watery. There was very little to eat. In our weakened state we lost our ambition and tended to sleep more and care less. We became irritable and stopped talking about food since even thinking about food made us hungrier. Although desperate for something to eat, an ironic sense of humor prevailed in the camp. One morning we received a tongue-in-cheek announcement that each man would receive a package from the Chinese Red Cross containing one pound of brown rice, eight pounds of opium, one pipe (extra long stem), and three pounds of soluble Saki.

Cutting the daily loaf of bread became a revered ceremony. We first admired the loaf and studied it as thoughtfully as a diamond cutter might examine a rough gem. Each loaf appeared delectable in spite of its black color and sawdust covering. After examining it from every angle, the slicer of the day cut the loaf slowly into seven portions, each as equal-sized as he could manage.

After slicing the loaf, we cut a deck of cards to select first rights to consume it. The man with the highest card chose his portion first. The bearer of the lowest card received the last piece. After the first man sighted, surveyed, and hefted the portions, he selected his choice. The next man repeated the process and all made their selections. The time required for this ritual became progressively longer in inverse proportion to the number of days since the most recent Red Cross parcels had arrived.

Normally, in card cutting, I usually drew the two of clubs. However, one day a fellow prisoner in the compound obtained a whole loaf of bread and held a lottery to sell it, each chance selling for a pack of cigarettes. I wasn't in my quarters when the POW offered chances, but Rocky bought one for me and I won the bread. In our time of greatest hunger we felt rich as we shared a simple loaf of bread. It was a happy day.

A week after my 22nd birthday our prayers for food were answered when a truckload of Red Cross parcels arrived. Colonel

Zemke had negotiated with the Germans to provide POW drivers to make collection runs to Lubeck using Swedish Red Cross trucks and gas. Two armed guards rode along with each truck. The POWs continued shuttling supplies until we had nearly 90,000 parcels tucked in storage. Once again we received one parcel per week apiece.

Early in our incarceration, to retain our sanity a few of us amused ourselves by recording our feelings on morale charts, plotting events and activities at the camp on one axis and our emotions on the other. For example, our charts indicated a sharp rise in morale on Easter Sunday when the shipment of food parcels arrived. After going home and showing these charts to Mother I discovered she knew through her great faith when I reached all of the high points on my chart. She told me the morning I won the loaf of bread she awoke with a happy feeling. "Something good happened to David today," she said she told Dad.

Later, in her personal history she wrote, "While David was a prisoner, it was made known to me each time he was in any great danger. I prayed earnestly for his safety." Once she saw me starving and it grieved her so much that when she took bread from the oven she remembered a story about a loaf disappearing from a mother's table and being given to her hungry missionary son in a distant land. She thought how nice it would be if something like that would happen to me. When I came home we compared my morale charts with her journal and discovered I won the bread on that day. We both decided I had received a direct answer to her prayers.

CHAPTER 16

Turning Point

Chaos, terrifying uncertainty, anarchy, death, and destruction enveloped Stalag Luft 1 as the final days of its existence came to a close. In April of 1945, history swirled in a vortex of tension in the world beyond the camp. We knew only a particle of what transpired on the wider stage, but many events had altered or would soon alter our existence.

A week after we received the long overdue Red Cross rations, U.S. President Franklin D. Roosevelt died of a cerebral hemorrhage at the *Little White House* on April 12. The International News Service broke the story to the world at 5:47 p.m. Eastern War Time (EWT). An hour later Chief Justice Harlan F. Stone administered the presidential oath of office to Vice President Harry S. Truman. We heard about both events via the BBC on the camp's secret radios and shared the news with our captors by wearing black armbands as a sign of mourning. The guards knew nothing about either event until we told them.

> **ON MONDAY MORNING,** April 16, 1945, as President Truman was giving his first address to Congress, Russian Marshall George Zugkov was concentrating 20,000 Red Army guns on Berlin from a bridgehead west of Kuestrin, Germany. Escaping German forces attempting to flee into western Netherlands attacked Canadian forces at Otterlo, as American bombers attacked Dresden.

From this news and other signs we knew the German defeat wouldn't be long in coming. Day after day younger guards disappeared from the camp and older men replaced them. Newly captured airmen and POWs transferred from camps too close to the front arrived at the gate at an accelerated pace, increasing our numbers to nearly 9,000 men. The number of airplanes stationed at the Barth air base diminished and no replacements appeared. American and British bombers flew overhead day and night, heading south to Berlin unchallenged. To the east we heard a constant roar of Russian cannons blasting away.

Fearing we might be caught in the crossfire should fighting reach the camp, Colonel Zemke appealed to Von Warnstedt for permission to dig slit trenches and foxholes near the barracks. The commandant relented and we halfheartedly dug trenches to hide in if we were bombed.

With full stomachs the stupor of mind and body caused by hunger rapidly waned and boredom intensified our restlessness. A3 organized new educational classes and athletic events to keep us busy and provide a cover for men training for the camp's commando unit. On a whim to encourage the men to stay active physically, Zemke, a model of vigor and vitality and an experienced boxer challenged the camp to a boxing match. The idea of fighting a colonel appealed to the men and several challengers stepped forward.

On April 18 the SAO's staff prepared a boxing card of ten matches and men fought each other for the privilege of boxing Zemke as the prize. Major Cyrus E. Manierre, an Office of Strategic Services (OSS) agent five years the colonel's junior but four inches taller and ten pounds heavier, won the privilege. In the end the Colonel won the fight by a decision, even though some of the curtain raisers looked better than he did, in my opinion.

Soon afterward Von Warnstedt summoned Colonel Zemke into his office and told him he had just received orders from *Oberkommando der Wehrmacht* (Armed Forces High Command) to move the POWs to an undisclosed location near Hamburg, 150 miles to the west. He ordered Zemke to prepare the men to move out in 24 hours. Zemke was dismayed. Heavy fighting had disrupted the rail system and roads, and since obtaining a fleet of trucks to transport POWs overland was out of the question, both men clearly understood the exodus doomed the POWs to a forced march.

> **ON APRIL 25, 1945,** British and American troops met Soviet forces at Torgau, Germany, on the Elbe River, 195 miles south of Barth. General Eisenhower ordered the U.S. 9th Army to suspend its march to allow the Red Army to capture Berlin. At 5:00 p.m., while the first United Nations Conference was opening in San Francisco, Truman received a phone call from Heinrich Himmler—General Plenipotentiary for the Reich's administration (Generalbevollmächtigter für die Verwaltung). He expressed a desire to surrender—but only to the western Allies, not to the Russians. Truman cabled Stalin immediately. That night 375 British bombers and one hundred U.S. Mustang fighter planes destroyed Hitler's residence at Berchtesgaden while fifty more aircraft bombed his villa, all to no avail. Hitler was not in either place. He was hiding like a scared rat in a bunker deep below Berlin.
>
> A BBC broadcast contained still more astonishing news. The Allies had captured Milan, Italy, and the Italian dictator Benito Mussolini had been killed by Italian partisans near Lake Como. In angry retribution, the partisans hung Mussolini's body upside down in a gas station for public viewing, like a slaughtered pig at market.

Zemke flatly refused to cooperate. After consulting with his staff that evening, Zemke called on Von Warnstedt the next day and informed him Provisional Wing X would not participate in a forced evacuation. If he tried to force them, Zemke warned him, the camp's secretly trained commando unit, plus the nearly 9,000 combat-trained airmen in Stalag Luft 1, would rush guards and take over the prison. An alternate solution, Zemke suggested—one requiring less bloodshed—would be for the commandant to relinquish the camp to him and then flee with his guards to the west before the Russians arrived. Von Warstedt made no commitments and excused Zemke without further discussion.

On Sunday, April 29, we learned the Red Army was less than 25 miles away and marching directly toward the camp. Late that morning Zemke received a telephone call ordering him to report to Von Warnstedt's office immediately. Upon his arrival, Von Warnstedt asked Zemke to take a walk outside the camp.

"The war is over for us," he began once they were out of earshot of prisoners and guards. Would Zemke consider taking over command of Stalag Luft 1 and allow the Germans to leave without violence? Zemke gladly accepted, but he was apprehensive about the German exodus. All guards must leave as a group, take only small arms and not destroy the camp's facilities, he demanded. Von Warnstadt consented. The two commanders agreed not to inform the POWs of the change in leadership until after the Germans had left. They set the departure time for midnight May 1, shook hands, and parted company.

Early on Monday, April 30, we woke to loud discharges at the Flak School and at the aerodrome. As we stood by the fence nearest the anti-aircraft school to watch the explosions, a guard in the tower called down and politely asked us to please not lay a hand on the fence, a sharp contrast to the old reaction, which would have been to shoot without warning any prisoner who touched the guard wire.

As we watched a building burn, a large explosion very near to us blew out the windows of the nearby sergeants' barracks. Men dropped flat to the ground and we crawled toward the newly dug trenches. Another explosion shot straight up in the air like an inverted bolt of lightning, making my ears ring for hours. It took even longer for my hair to lay flat again and for me to quit shaking.

From the airfield we saw FW 190s, Ju 88s and Me 109s taking off in rapid succession. All were headed west, possibly to Norway, to the Western Front, or to war-wary, neutral Sweden. That evening, Hitler prepared his last will and testament, recording in his journal he blamed Jews for the war, then he shot himself in the head. The Thousand Year Reich had ended.

Tuesday, May 1, we awoke to find the guard towers occupied by Americans. Our barracks were surrounded by a band of POWs acting as military policemen (MPs), who informed us Colonel Zemke had confined everyone to quarters. The sun was out and the weather, considerably warmer. Excitement and relief swept the camp. Suddenly, a wonderful feeling overwhelmed me and I nearly cried from joy. Ten days short of thirteen months in captivity, I was free. I was going home.

We still felt like prisoners, but now we were in Allied hands. We couldn't leave camp. We were thirsty because the main water supply was *kaput*. Everyone grumbled, "What's up?" But our leaders — or the *Wheels* as we referred to them — seemed sworn to secrecy. To appease us Colonel Zemke promised that we would be allowed to roam the peninsula to the north of the stalag.

Even as we rejoiced, we distrusted the news of our liberation, terrified the Germans would return in force. Colonel Zemke sent out scouting patrols, and when they returned in early afternoon, they told him the Red Army was twenty miles away. Requisitioning a jeep, Zemke, the journalist Lowell Bennett, and a translator drove to the 65th Soviet Army headquarters and were warmly welcomed by Colonel T.D. Zhovanik, regimental commander.

Zemke asked for help for an immediate evacuation of all the POWs by air. Zhovanik explained he couldn't comply because the Germans had left eighteen fused 250 kg HE bombs, 38 booby trapped planes, including four Ju 88s in flyable condition, on the airfield and a couple of un-assembled Arado 234 Jets in the hangers. "Would you remove the fuses, drag the bombs out of the way, disarm the booby traps from the planes, and clear the runway?" Zhovanik asked. Anxious to speed up the evacuation, Zemke readily agreed.

On their return to camp Zemke's party passed the Red Army — a disorderly mob of wild-looking men, singing folk songs, drinking vodka straight from the bottle, and cursing the shuttered windows of the local residences—marching toward Berlin.

Back at the camp, drunken German guards that hadn't fled made us nervous. One Kraut was so drunk that it took two soldiers to keep him in line while he checked out. He was flashing Red Cross rations and bragging about it. As another guard reached out to steady himself, the guard gave him a "Heil Hitler" salute and fell flat on his stomach. We felt nothing but contempt for these prime examples of Hitler's super race.

German refugees, including former guards, soldiers, and civilians, broke into the storehouse of Red Cross rations intended for us and we saw them eating our rations all around the camp. After chasing the intruders away, Colonel Zemke sent us in details of one hundred men to the Flak School to claim our rations from the storehouse. As we walked into the storeroom, German civilians gathered around us offering Luftwaffe boots in trade for cigarettes.

The children appeared hungry and their parents, depressed. It was a pitiful sight to see, but I didn't feel too much pity because the Germans showed us no such consideration when we were eating nothing but dehydrated vegetables and black, sawdust-diluted bread. Bennett, who had seen Paris when the Germans invaded at the start of the war, said French citizens exhibited the same confusion, drunkenness, and panic. Hunger and fear make us all desperate.

When the POWs heard the Soviet Army was only three miles away from camp, everyone ran to the fences and stood on the incinerators trying to spot the incoming Russians. We watched all day but never saw so much as a Russian tank. As night fell, we felt neglected and somewhat downcast, in contrast to the elation of the day before. The Colonel continued to confine us to the camp and kept things the same; we still had air raid drills. Every so often the Colonel, or one of his appointed men, ordered us to hit our foxholes and remain in them until an "All clear!" sounded. On one of these practices, Commander Brown who had lathered up for a shave and under the impression that the air raid was the real McCoy, plunged in headfirst, bringing a load of dirt with him and almost filling our trench.

The Germans had left us without water or electricity, and the water shortage made it hard for us to cook. Just before leaving, they had moved us to a new barracks with old-fashioned wooden outhouses, and we worried our fourteen holes would fill up.

Someone sprung the locks between North 1 and North 2 Compounds. I had no earthly reason for leaving North 1, but after a year in North 1, I decided I could stand a change of scenery. Consequently, I was in North 2 when the gates were re-locked and I had to stay there until official orders reopened them.

CHAPTER 17

Chaos Reigns

Rumors ran rampant in the camp. One rumor claimed the Russian colonel planned to send us home via Odessa, Ukraine, on the Black Sea. I returned to my quarters and was told the Russians wanted us to march to the American lines and we had six hours to be ready to move. I packed my clothes, toilet articles, and rations from the Red Cross parcel, but the order to move out never came. That evening we listened to our first BBC news broadcast on the battery-powered radio and thrilled to hear the sweet rendition of "The Star Spangled Banner."

The next day a drunken Russian soldier rode into camp on a white horse, fired his long barreled pistol into the air and demanded to know why we were still behind barbed wire fences. When Colonel Zemke tried to calm the man, the Russian pointed his gun at the Colonel's head and cocked the hammer. Zemke diffused the situation by asking the man to tell the POWs that they were free. As he talked with the soldier, Zemke sent a runner to the North 1 Compound to assemble a welcoming committee at the gate to cheer when the Russian spoke to them. A couple hundred kriegies complied and the ploy worked. Gratified by the welcome, the Russian holstered his pistol and was overpowered by the MPs, ending the crisis peacefully.

Many of the POWs agreed in principle with the Russian and took matters into their own hands, tearing down the fences and guard towers. That evening a wave of POWs swept out of camp to blow off steam tearing up the Flak School. I agreed it was long past due and got caught in the tumult.

We rushed into the school seeking souvenirs, breaking windows, slamming doors, and looting, although there was little of value to loot. Once a beautiful, large, modern building, it had evidently been the scene of a German farewell party. We found empty liquor bottles in all of the rooms, beds ripped apart, radios destroyed, wastebaskets tipped upside down, maps and papers scattered about, light bulbs broken, and vomit and feces on the floors in a scene of total disorder. Mob action ruled as we finished the job the Germans had started.

One of my buddies, William H. Ritzema, a big man from Greenville, Michigan, crashed through several doors and threw chairs through the windows. As I stepped into one room a brick came flying through the window from below, barely missing me, so I decided to leave the building by the nearest exit.

My plunder included German fur caps, insignia, pictures, maps, and a haversack. A couple of other men salvaged hastily abandoned German uniforms for their souvenirs. K. C. Reimer, one of my roommates, came into the barracks with a long German saber and a wine bottle. Harold L. Cooke, another of my roommates originally from Elkhart, Indiana, claimed a luger. Amid this chaos I even saw a chaplain securing his share of the booty.

While I was plundering the Flak School, I assumed the whole camp was there, but when I got back to my barracks, I saw several men returning from Barth, riding bicycles and horses, or in cars, carrying liquor and souvenirs. They told wild stories of Russians sacking the town en masse, often referring to the Red Army as the *Mongol horde*, and since the Russians usually rode horses or drove horse drawn vehicles, the description seemed appropriate. One kriegie joined them and drove a team of horses through a barbed wire fence. Another kriegie arrived at camp doing a good imitation of rodeo champion Hoot Gibson, riding a big bay mare and rending the air with his high pitched, "Ki yay yippie yi yos." My friend

Mike Malerba returned sporting a black eye and a goose egg on his head, injuries sustained in a fall from a horse.

The Barth visitors shocked us with tales of Russian atrocities. Russians would kill anyone who got in their way, whether civilian or soldier; they would take everything they wanted and would steal anything for an American, they said. Most of the Russians the kriegies met were either drunk or were trying to get that way, as they raided houses and stole food, jewelry, bicycles, and automobiles. My roommate Frank G. Pringle, Oakland, California, spent the afternoon eating, drinking their liquor, and celebrating with a group of Russian soldiers.

That evening, we visited the storehouse where the Germans had hoarded supplies sent to POWs by the Red Cross, and we were issued new shirts, clean sheets, and I would have received new shoes, but my size was gone. One building was full of wooden bowls, light bulbs, brushes, and other articles the Germans claimed they had been scouring the countryside to get for us. We seethed, knowing they willfully withheld such mundane articles from us. In revenge, several kriegies smashed wooden bowls with a vengeance, which availed them nothing but a release of a little tension.

On May 3, our first full day unrestrained by barbed wire, rumors ran hot and heavy about our departure date and ranged from predictions we'd be flown home immediately, to claims we'd leave in a month.

In the morning Zemke talked to the camp, reporting that in yesterday's mêlée, a land mine killed one AWOL prisoner and Russian guards shot four others. Three POWs had discovered a supply of liquor and died when the "borrowed" car they were speeding in smashed into an irrigation ditch.

Zemke said he had sent men to our lines for help the day before and warned us the Russian generals wanted us to stay in camp. He called for us to maintain order, organized us into flights, and instituted roll calls and bed checks. Zemke insisted the Russians were very hostile to us. This conflicted with the stories I had heard the day before from the POWs who visited Barth. The POWs said Russians were kissing Americans and drinking with them.

A Russian general had promised Zemke, "I will provide you with food. I will clear the airfield. My men will take care of everything." Zemke assured us the Russians would help us, and to reduce the possibility of more men slipping away into dangerous circumstances, he confined us to the camp and issued 90 passes per day to allow authorized visits to Barth.

The POWs would have none of it. They were fed up with forced isolation and imprisonment, some having been locked up for as long as five years, and most of the men blatantly disobeyed. Our roommate Frank S. Rzatkowski, Wyandotte, Michigan, sent us a note conveying the news he had caught a wagon and was on his way to Poland.

In the afternoon, roommate Jacob R. Brown, Harlingen, Texas, and I went on a walk around the peninsula and came across the bodies of three women, a child, and a baby in a carriage, all shot through the temple except the baby who had been shot through an eye. We surmised the women were terrified of being taken by the Russians and one killed the others before taking her own life. I was sickened by the senselessness and evil of war; not that I sympathized with Germany's adults, the Hitler youth, or their armies; but it was a pity to see a year-old baby murdered in his crib.

That morning, MPs patrolling near camp discovered the bodies of nearly two-dozen women, strangled or shot. In the days that followed, frightened women and children from Barth appeared often at the gates of the camp and begged to be allowed in. Zemke, fearing the diseases they might introduce to our isolated camp, refused to allow them in. Disappointed but not dissuaded, the terrified citizens camped in the nearby fields for whatever protection proximity to the camp might provide.

The German people were more frightened than anyone I had ever before seen. Al Strom reported seeing several German families hiding in the woods near camp with no food or shelter, afraid to go back to town where Russians were occupying their homes. A few Germans, including former Stalag Luft 1 guards, tried to give themselves up to the Americans in order to avoid being taken prisoner by the Russians. Other Germans asked Americans to sleep in their homes to prevent the Russians from moving in. At Barth the burgomeister administered poison to his family before ingesting it himself.

Some drunken American POWs were nearly as unruly as the Russians, stealing horses and carriages and driving them wildly through villages, shooting their pistols into the air. Other POWs behaved more civilly and bartered cigarettes and Red Cross soap for fresh eggs from townspeople.

I wondered what the Germans were eating, because the kriegies and the Russians were devouring all the looted food they found in the countryside. In North 3 Compound kriegies captured and butchered a sheep. Chicken feathers floated all over the place. On our walk, Brown and I saw a buck deer running around like a frantic German. Kriegies herded him into the bay, and as the animal tried to swim across, they pursued him in a boat, caught him, and ate venison that night for supper.

By Friday, May 4, the week nearly over, we still had received no word about our release or when planes would arrive to take us home. Unwilling to wait, many men went "over the hill" and most of us contemplated following them. Despite our impatience to leave, we had to admit life in the camp had improved markedly. With access to the storage areas, we now had plenty of food. Each man received three Red Cross parcels with orders to make them last three days, at least. It felt good to eat until I was full, and then eat some more.

With restored order in the camp came restoration of utilities: water, for drinking, cleaning, and bathing, and electricity, for lights and for the radio. We eagerly listened to the latest programs, greatly appreciating the music after not hearing a radio since we were captured.

Early Friday morning I went to the South Compound to visit Fred Pratt. He was in bed but I woke him up and we walked to the police barracks to find Ely, now an MP, and found him playing with a wicked-looking machine gun. Ely told us a horror story about a Russian who was riding a bicycle, stopped and entered a house. Upon making his exit, he saw an Englishman commandeering his bike. Angry, the Russian shot and killed the Englishman in cold blood.

As an MP, Ely helped clear the airfield and reported it was about ready for use. "The Germans did a fine job of mining it," he said. "They are experts at demolition." He had seen how effectively they had blown up the Flak School equipment inside the buildings without harming the structure, except for powder burns on the interior walls.

Ely told us MPs had discovered three two-story barracks, encircled by barbed electrical fencing, nestled between the Luftwaffe mess hall and the workshops at the airfield. Inside this small compound there were 2,000 emaciated and dying Greek and French civilian prisoners, forced by the Germans to do factory work.

The SS guards who watched over them departed weeks before leaving the prisoners to fend for themselves. Many had slowly starved, and others had died from typhus and tuberculosis, incubated in the close confinement of the quarters and exacerbated by malnutrition. Some of the prisoners had been in a dungeon for four years without seeing daylight. Already 300 were dead.

With medical supplies provided by the Russians, the camp doctor hospitalized the sickest prisoners but couldn't save them. American POWs started to clean the place, but were so sickened by the stench that they abandoned the job. Colonel Zemke recruited Germans to bury the dead in mass graves.

Rocky invited me to go with him at seven o'clock in the evening to visit a couple of Frenchmen he had met earlier in the day. The Frenchmen had spent five years in Barth, forced to work twelve-hour shifts in a munitions factory, where if one of them showed signs of slacking, he was shot without question, they said. Their food was very poor and scarce so Rocky gave them a couple of Red Cross parcels to tide them over. However, at the specified hour, we waited at the designated location, but they never showed up. We supposed the Russians confined them to their labor camp.

We went instead to the South compound, arriving just as a Soviet car drove up carrying two soldiers and a Russian woman doctor, who inspected one of the barracks. The doctor was very young but nothing much to look at, being about as well fleshed as a corn-fed steer. The Russian soldiers with her, unlike the soldiers I had seen wandering around Barth, were very clean and tidy, though far from handsome. A Canadian soldier fluent in Russian spoke to the two soldiers and later told us of his conversation.

One of the Russians soldiers had said, "Americans good."

The Canadian answered, "I'm Canadian."

The Russian answered, "Canadians are good, but Americans are better." We had a good laugh.

In our wanderings we recognized several of our former German guards roaming the streets of Barth in civilian clothes. Major von Muller, the former head of the Intelligence Section at Stalag Luft 1 and the most reviled man in camp, tried to surrender to the Americans, but was turned away. The Russians later picked him up.

On the morning of Saturday, May 5, Zhovanik's supervisor, Major General V.A. Borisov, visited the camp but provided little assistance. With the British and Canadian advance at Wismar, Germany, on the Elbe River, seventy miles south of Barth, he was too busy fighting Germans to deal with the POW evacuation, he told Zemke.

Nonetheless, Borisov gave Zemke permission to communicate with the Russian Army as long as he didn't use the radio to do so. He also allowed Zemke to send four officers to the British lines to report what was happening at the camp and he gave him permission to do whatever he wanted in the Barth area, including looting the town or shooting its inhabitants.

Borisov then brazenly requested Zemke to provide men to help assault Rugen, an island north of Stralsund where he suspected a garrison of German SS troops were protecting a V1 rocket test site. Very gingerly Zemke declined, saying his men would be willing to provide support, but since they were nearly all airmen they lacked infantry combat training. Ironically, Borisov never followed up and the conversation changed to other topics.

When Zemke brought up the subject of evacuation, Borisov informed him the Allies had agreed all liberated POWs would travel by train eastward to the port of Odessa, Ukraine. "Why not evacuate the POWs by plane?" Zemke asked. Borisov replied that an agreement signed by Churchill and Roosevelt at Yalta prohibited Anglo-Americans from flying over Russian-held territory.

Transporting 9,000 POWs by rail further from the Allies lines seemed ludicrous to Zemke, especially since the British lines were so close. Immediately after meeting with Borisov, Zemke returned to his office and wrote letters to General Spatz and Marshal Rokosoffski of the Soviet Army requesting air evacuation using the Barth airfield. Captain Ginger Weir, the SBO, did the same.

That afternoon we cheered as a British officer accompanied by a Russian-speaking noncommissioned officer arrived from Wismar. We cheered even louder when two jeeps loaded with American GIs of the 82nd Airborne Division drove into camp, coming as a result of Zemke's reconnaissance mission to report on our situation. Major Nelander, one of the envoys from our camp, had directed the colonel and his escort back to Stalag Luft 1. When a higher-ranking officer took Nelander's spot for the jeep ride back to our lines, the major balked at being left in camp. It did seem cruel since the other envoy that went with Nelander had gone on to England. Adding insult to injury, a kriegie, AWOL from our camp—who was dead drunk—had beat Zemke's envoys to the American lines, even though Major Nelander and his companion had been the first men Zemke officially released from camp.

Meanwhile, despite progress of ground troops closing in on German positions, morale at Stalag Luft 1 ebbed, and men continued to leave, most with designs to join up with the British Army. Zemke and his officers attempted to entertain the POWs, but ball games and educational pursuits no longer motivated us. Everyone simply wanted to go home. When Zemke ordered popular swing music broadcast over the camp loudspeaker system to pacify the POWs, it backfired. The music only made us more homesick.

That afternoon we received a message over the radio from General Eisenhower, addressed to all Allied prisoners of war. We expected words of advice, encouragement, and direction. He simply said, "Stand by." We felt more neglected than before and yearned for information about our removal from Germany.

After the general's message, Pratt and I received orders to inventory the motor pool of confiscated cars, bicycles, and motorcycles reserved for use by officers above major in rank—or terrific brown nosers. At the motor pool we heard another hair-raising story from the night before. A POW had met a Russian officer in Stralsund for dinner. As they conversed, a German woman at an adjoining table continually hurled insults at the two Allied officers. Finally, the Russian blew up and shoved his plate of food into the woman's face. A German man at an adjoining table jumped up and advanced on the Russky, a bad mistake, because the Russian pulled out his pistol and shot him dead. The American, unused to such ruthlessness, began to cry, and then laugh hysterically. The Russian mistook his hysteria for pleasure and slapped him on the back, kissed both of his cheeks, yelled, "Comrade," and went on eating his dinner as if nothing had happened.

CHAPTER 18

Disquiet in Camp

On Sunday, May 6, the former SAO, Colonel Byerly and two British officers flew to England and reported on the conditions of our camp to the 8th Air Force headquarters. Concerned that the Russians might march the men to the Soviet Union, headquarters initiated evacuation of the liberated POWs by air.

Mid-morning I joined other men of the LDS faith in a testimony meeting at South Compound chapel, our first combined church meeting of the entire camp. It turned out, we of North 1 Sunday School held the record for the longest running LDS group—almost a year. Men of North 3 had held services since February. I met Bert Clifton, of Magrath, Alberta, Canada, who knew my Canadian Ririe relatives, and he also had mutual acquaintances with Rocky.

After church, Clifton told us he had been a tank driver when his Canadian commando regiment had been captured as they struggled to climb some cliffs and capture a particular town. When their supporting P-51s fighter planes arrived, the Germans mistook the planes for their own Me 109s and allowed the P-51s to fly in and out of the area unmolested. The P-51s blew the German positions to smithereens. The second wave of planes met a little opposition but lost no aircraft. The third wave of planes was actually German ME 109s responding to the Allied attack and twenty of them were shot down by friendly fire. This mistake of aircraft identity spooked the Krauts, and when a German plane flew over the column of Canadian POWs on their way to prison camp, German guards ordered everyone to jump over a fence and into a ditch. In the skirmish the Canadians grabbed the guards' swords and bayonets and stabbed the nearest German. After that, the Germans remained behind the column whenever they ran for a ditch.

When the Canadians arrived at the prisoner of war camp near Breslau, the guards tied their wrists together, only giving them freedom to move their hands about 12 inches apart, and kept them bound for a month. Then they replaced cords with handcuffs for about another month. Later, the Germans marched the men to labor camps called *Arbeit Commandos* and forced them to load ammunition into railroad boxcars for long hours with very little to eat. Overseers with bullwhips lashed anyone who slacked his pace. Clifton said life improved when the Krauts assigned them to much easier farm work, where they received better treatment.

After a year or so on the farm, the Germans transferred the Breslau POWs to *straff*—or punishment—camps. These installations had no parade or sports grounds, only barracks. Worse yet, the men had no shoes, no heat in the barracks, and their clothes were taken away in the evenings. If they spoke to anyone outside the prison, the guards silenced them with a burst of deadly machine gun fire.

Ironically, Clifton said, none of the prisoners knew why they were being punished. Besides Canadians, the camps held thousands of Poles, Italians, Frenchmen, and Russians—all equally baffled by the undeserved punishment. "I have no sympathy for Germans," Clifton said. "Even little kids threw bricks at us. I have no pity, none at all."

Clifton's final camp was Greifswald, near the marshalling yards at Barth. The day the Jerries abandoned Stalag Luft 1, Major Von Muller, the stalag's former head of security, marched the Greifswald POWs to Barth in hopes that the Americans would take him prisoner and keep him out of Russian hands, Clifton said. The night after Clifton's group left Greifswald, a wave of British planes bombed a carload of ammunition and the ensuing explosion demolished the camp. If not for the evacuation, the POWs would have perished.

Late in the day I planned to visit Ellis, but he had gone over the hill in an attempt to reach the American lines. He left me a pair of German Luftwaffe boots he bought from a German kid for the price of a bar of soap. When I returned to the barracks, the Russians had delivered several pigs and about forty Holstein cows, plus some flour for our food supply.

Just before lights out, our roommate who never failed to promote fun, John M. Coppinger, Denver, Colorado, came in with a loudspeaker that he planned to hook on to the compound sound system. He abandoned the project when the *Wheels* outlawed it to prevent overloading the power supply.

In an effort to appease the restless ranks, Zemke provided 250 daily passes to men, formed into marching parties, for a walking tour of the Barth area. Once beyond the gates, however, the men broke ranks and ran into the woods to explore the area on their own. Predictably, several POWs ran into trouble; the following day the Red Army found a couple of them dead in a ditch and another with his head caved in. MPs suspected Germans seeking final revenge had murdered them.

Apprehensive about our unsettled future and bored with confinement in camp, Joe (whose last name I can't remember), Cooke, and I went AWOL for the following day. Missing the ferry from the north end of the peninsula, we found an old boat in the rushes, jumped in, and using its one oar, a shovel, and a board, paddled across the bay. I rowed the oar, the only locked-in device on the boat; Cooke sat in the front end, nearly drowning in the spray from the makeshift oars he and Joe manned. Our wake meandered like the wake of a freighter in sub-infested waters.

When we came to the shore, Cooke jumped out and sank about a foot into the mud. No sooner had we disembarked, than two men who had been AWOL overnight climbed into the boat and rowed back to the peninsula where another group of men were waiting for our boat and its makeshift paddles to cross the bay.

We walked to the nearest village where we found Germans moving out, Russians billeted in every house, and Americans trying to converse with Russian soldiers and dodging MPs. A sergeant passed us on a bicycle with two flat tires. We started walking to Zingst, but a Russian soldier stopped us at a bridge. We would need a special pass from his commander to cross, he said. The soldier had three looted watches but refused to trade any of them with us.

Turning back from Zingst we visited the village of Pruchten. We talked to a couple of German boys, about ten or eleven years old, who spoke English they said they had learned in school. They told us the Russians had taken everything and the people had nothing to eat but a little bread. Cooke took pity on them and gave them a half dozen dried prunes, which they devoured ravenously. As we talked, camp mates Frank G. Pringle, of Oakland, California, and Ritzema came strolling along. Pringle slumped down beside us and said, "I'm bushed." As he sat watching the kids he suddenly blurted out, "Hell, no wonder that kid looks queer. He only has three fingers." It was true; the boy had lost his index finger to the last joint. We didn't ask the boy for details, because just then a passing soldier warned us of MPs headed our way. We parted company with Pringle and Ritzema and walked back up the street.

Along the road we saw wrecked bicycles, carriages, and cars, one that someone had driven into a tree. We'd heard an American captain had been in a wreck the previous night, possibly in one of these cars. Little wonder wrecked vehicles lined the road because Russians rushed passed us on all sides at top speed no matter what vehicle they were driving. More than a few times we leaped aside as a team of horses raced by at full gallop pulling an iron-wheeled wagon filled with dirty Russian soldiers, laughing, bouncing, or sleeping. Usually, the party included Russian women who were as filthy as the troops.

We hadn't gone far when a Russian soldier, dressed in a drab green uniform so blotched with dirt and grime it looked like camouflage, hailed us. Joe asked him if he spoke Polish and he said he did, launching into a conversation Cooke and I couldn't follow. Joe later told us, the Russian switched from Russian to German to Slavic, anything but Polish, in an accent he couldn't understand. The Russian declared to Joe that the Germans had burned his mother, father and three sisters to death, but he told the story with a grin, and we wondered if he was telling the truth.

We stopped at a Russian field kitchen thinking it would be an interesting experience to eat with our allies. However, after inspecting the setup and seeing the scum on the kettles and a Mongol cook's grime caked hands, we lost our appetite.

On the road back to camp, we surprised a big, friendly Russian guard, who was bouncing a naked German child on his knee. We had to laugh at his embarrassment. Generously, he gave us milk to drink and directed us to a nearby German home where Cooke traded a bar of soap for two eggs.

Back on the road, we turned a corner and ran headlong into an army detail sent out from camp to canvass every house in the area and secure liquor for the troops. We doubted that the kriegies in camp ever saw any of the liquor, as these men seemed to surpass the acquisition rate with their own consumption. The major in charge of the detail asked for our passes. Finding we had none, he flaunted his rank and ordered us to use our brains and stay in camp. I thought, I'm sure we have as much right to be out of the camp as he, considering his drunken condition, but I kept quiet.

As luck would have it, we got a ride back across the bay with a Russian boatman. And although a group of MPs spotted us, they quickly realized the boat we were in belonged to the Russky and allowed us to cross unmolested. Ritzema and Pringle weren't as lucky. On their way back to camp, they met a soldier who assured them they could enter the camp through the main gate and not be questioned. The two naïve POWs believed the lie, and the MPs led them off to the guard house where a major gave them a fine bawling out and confined them to quarters until we were evacuated.

After our foray in the countryside, we heard refreshing news. The BBC had announced over the radio that the Russian Army had liberated Stalag Luft 1, thus notifying our next of kin of our liberation. Colonel Zemke ordered us to cover our foxholes, which we had dug just a week before. Despite the waste of effort, I was thankful we hadn't needed to use the trenches for anything but drills.

> **AT 2:40 A.M.** on the morning of May 8, 1945, *Victory in Europe* Day, the German unconditional surrender became official as Colonel General Gustaf Jodl, chief of staff of the German Army, signed paperwork in a brick schoolhouse in Reims, France, Eisenhower's command center. The five-year war in Europe, the most costly, the most murderous conflict in history, was over.
>
> Churchill wanted to make the announcement of Germany's capitulation as soon as General Jodl signed the paperwork but Stalin, with the situation at the Russian front still uncertain, demanded that he and Truman wait. By unanimous agreement, all three allies made the announcement at the same time, at 9:00 a.m., Washington time. Truman broadcast the announcement over live radio from the diplomatic reception room, where Roosevelt had often held his Fireside Chats. The broadcast broke the record for the largest listening audience ever. New York, London, Paris, Moscow, and many other major cities around the world erupted in wild celebration.
>
> In a separate statement, Truman called on Japan to surrender, warning them that "the striking power and intensity of our blows will steadily increase," and that the longer the war lasted, the greater the suffering of the Japanese people would be.

Through the BBC we knew Germany would surrender May 8, 1945, and at one minute past midnight we built a huge bonfire with our hated window shutters, fence posts, and any other flammable materials we could find. Somebody shot flares obtained at the airport into the dark sky. After the fireworks, we sang songs around the fire until our voices gave out. We went to bed in high spirits, but even so complaints leaked out. We ached to be home in the States, celebrating with our families and girlfriends.

That night I slept well and didn't stir until about ten o'clock the next morning, long after the sun was up. Anxious for news about our release, I declined another invitation to go over the hill, ate a large breakfast, shaved, and hung around camp listening to commandeered German radios for an announcement of when we would be rescued. None was forthcoming, so I decided to wash clothes. Washing was much easier now than before, because Block 3 stole a field kitchen, which we used exclusively for heating laundry water, eliminating a trip to the mess hall for hot water. I turned out my wash, which I hoped was the last one I would ever have to do at Stalag Luft 1. For some reason—perhaps it was too much food all at once—I came down with what the Army calls the screaming GIs.

While I stuck close to the lavatories, Brown went out on a walking tour with one hundred other men under the leadership of a captain. In town Brown tried to barter for eggs, but the impatient captain forced him on before he could close the deal. Ironically, he saw Schubert, another of our former guards who was walking about town in civilian clothes. Many of the German soldiers tried to prevent the Russians from making POWs of them. Few succeeded in avoiding capture; the Russians had their names, and in most cases, eventually took them into custody. Brown was tired and vowed, "Never again will I sign up for a walking tour."

Around noon, two American majors from the Medics arrived in camp, but all they could tell us about our evacuation was, "Hold on." They bragged up our camp, saying it was the best they had seen. Someone in the crowd yelled, "Do you want to move in, Major?" When the major observed we had plenty of food, clothes, medical supplies, and water, another POW yelled, "You should have been here last March." By this time the major was flustered. He sat down in the jeep and didn't say another word. After the majors left, we worried that our visitors had taken back such glowing reports of our well-equipped camp that headquarters placed us last on the list to evacuate.

After lunch, Joe, Francis P. Smith, and Cooke tried to get to the ferry to escape off our peninsula, but the MPs stopped them and confiscated their boat, forcing them to abandon the idea of sailing to freedom. Adding salt to their wounds, Cooke stepped off the boat onto some floating sod and came back to camp with his clothing soaked.

A fellow named Grass, whom we affectionately called *The Gay Caballero*, came into our barracks that afternoon with bullets that he wanted Cooke to shoot from his luger. The only trouble was the bullets were meant for a larger cannon. Being the bright boy he was, the Caballero placed the bullets in a bucket and set fire to them. The explosions demolished the bucket, much to the indignation of Captain Smith, who owned the pail.

That evening after a troupe of Russian singers and dancers entertained us, more than 300 POWs, miserable and annoyed by the forced inactivity, abandoned camp using any conveyance they could lay hands on. They rode bicycles, horses, cars, trucks, or walked the 400 miles to the American lines. Included in the exodus was journalist Lowell Bennett, who with three of his friends had commandeered a small two-cylinder car from the camp motor pool. "Complete indescribable chaos existed everywhere," he later wrote in an article about the conditions he saw on the journey.

CHAPTER 19

Final Days

Late in the afternoon, two British soldiers of the 6th Airborne Division arrived at camp with news that Marshal Rokosoffski had promised Field Marshal Montgomery that all 9,000 POWs would be delivered to the British at Wismar within two days. Zemke immediately informed the camp, and then he learned that none of the local Soviet commanders knew of the decision.

Nonetheless, Zemke began making plans to move the POWs to Wismar. With motorized vehicles in short supply, Zemke planned to commandeer whatever he could find to transport the sick POWs, while the healthy men would cover the seventy miles to Wismar on foot. Zhovanik agreed with Zemke's plan, but when they presented it to Borisov, the general exploded, furious that the two officers had devised evacuation plans without first consulting Moscow.

Meanwhile, POWs continued to revolt. Russians began jailing all American and British airmen caught without passes. On May 9, the Russians turned over seventy noncompliant men to Zemke. Afterwards, Colonel Zemke gave us a severe tongue lashing. It was the usual line, "Stand by, men. We're asking for your cooperation. I'll be the last man to leave here." Zemke must have made quite an impression on General Borisov, because he appointed Zemke to take charge of all POWs in this section of Germany. Colonel Spicer took Zemke's place as camp commanding officer.

After Zemke's lecture, I tagged onto a North 2 walking tour and went into town. The captain instructed us to stay in formation, but upon arriving in Barth, he cut us loose, saying that we could do as we pleased until three o'clock. About half of us broke ranks immediately. Smith and I headed to the airfield, still littered with airplanes the Germans didn't have time to fly away. We saw Ju 88s, Ju 52s, FW 190s, and several other types of planes I couldn't identify, all purposely burned, wrecked, and loaded with booby traps. Live bombs lay all over the field as we walked aimlessly about. When we stumbled onto the Field Force, or MP, headquarters, we knew we were out of bounds and beat a hasty retreat.

Smitty had a can of sardines, which we decided to eat to stave off hunger pangs until we returned to camp. Searching for a place sufficiently private and free of *kinder* to eat unmolested, we passed through a camp filled with refugees from the Stettin area. Scores of kids milled hopelessly about and we tried to talk to them in our meager German, finding them very polite and pretty in contrast to German youths we had seen before. As we talked to the kids, two women jumped over a fence and made eyes at us a little too brazenly for our comfort, and we retreated to the road.

Finally, we reached a place far enough from hungry people that we could eat the sardines in peace. We sat down and prepared to eat, only to find that Smith had forgotten his knife and I didn't own one. Smitty was a little sheepish. We decided we didn't want to eat fish anyway and headed back to camp for dinner.

As we walked along the street we suddenly heard a shot ring out. Rounding a corner we came upon two grinning Russians. One of them had accidentally fired his gun. The Russians were still as dirty as they had been when I met my first one a few days earlier. Except for the officers, Russians made a poor impression hygienically. I also observed that most Russian officers had a flunky with him to do all the dirty work, quite a contrast to America's wartime army.

That evening Big Jim Geary came back with a wild tale after being AWOL for a couple of days. He was visiting in a room at the French laborers' camp when an MP came to the window and looked in. The MP started around toward the front door to capture Geary when Big Jim made his escape via the window and ducked into a Russian camp. When he told the Russians he was an American officer, they gave him food to eat and prepared a bed, making one of their privates sleep on the floor.

The following morning, Thursday, May 10, found our five-man combine (Joe, Smitty, Thompson, Rocky, and me) seated around our rickety table, eating steak and fried potatoes, thanks to the Russians. After breakfast I wrote a letter home, sent out through the lines by the Russians. How pleasant it felt, writing in longhand again on a full sheet of paper, rather than on a German writing form.

Colonel Zemke, disturbed by POWs still leaving camp without passes, canceled all marching parties for the next day and ordered head counts and calisthenics to resume, after we'd totally neglected them in the excitement of the past few days. The calisthenics were a joke because they were too easy to be of value but at roll call, Zemke discovered 730 Americans missing of the 7,725 supposed to be in camp. Meanwhile, only 31 British POWs were AWOL of the 1,458 listed in the camp on their rolls.

A while after the revealing census, two American officers arrived at camp stating that the U.S. 7th Airborne Corps had been ordered to organize air transport to evacuate Stalag Luft 1, but the division had never received the order. Complicating the situation, the Russians still refused to give permission for aircraft to fly over the Soviet-held combat zone. Captain Weir, the senior British officer, his patience frazzled over the impasse, jumped into a jeep and called on Colonel General Pavel Batov, commander of the 65th Red Army, demanding the Russians permit an air evacuation.

Meanwhile, negotiating secretly with the Americans near the Elbe River, the Russians agreed to a POW airlift if the Americans surrendered former Red Army commander Andrei Vlasov, a traitor who had helped the Germans form an army of Russian prisoners to fight against Stalin.

With no chance to go on any more walking tours, Bernard J. "Doc" Gillespie, Fort Dodge, Iowa, and I joined three fast basketball games of *Twenty-One*, playing some very adept men. Afterwards, I took a nice long shower. With Americans running the hot water, they gave us showers like the Jerries had never dreamed of taking, much less giving to us. No more of their get wet, soap up, rinse inadequately showers.

With plenty of food coming into the camp from the Russians, that evening I cooked a real supper of salmon loaf, cabbage slaw, mashed potatoes, and toast. Some of the men wanted me to be the permanent cook, but I declined all such suggestions. Smitty and I finished the day playing bridge with Doc and Joe and were soundly trounced.

The next day, Friday, May 11, **1945,** a wave of pessimism swept through camp. After experiencing freedom outside camp, we felt stifled by having to remain in the compound not knowing when we would be let out again. With the guard ring tightened and the countryside cleared of souvenirs, few men were eager to go AWOL. Rumors began to float that we would leave for sure in ten days. Our Red Cross rations were running low, but thanks to the Russians we had steaks every day. With nothing to do, Basil D. Morris, Otsego, Michigan, and I broke down and scrubbed the floor in our room, rinsing it afterwards with a hose, a pleasure since it saved us having to carry water.

At breakfast that morning a POW was shot in the shoulder while sitting in his barracks by a kriegie shooting at a deer. The bullet went through the barracks wall and wounded the man. The injury wasn't severe, but the accident struck me as senseless. That evening, at 6:30 p.m., Zemke received a letter from Borisov's headquarters at Tribses, a small town 25 miles south of Barth, reporting Moscow had cleared a 20-kilometer wide flight path for the evacuation planes to follow — as long as routes and times were approved in advance. Weir flew into action and cleared evacuation plans with

Montgomery. Late that night Weir returned to camp with news the POWs could expect the first planes to arrive the following day.

Zemke immediately wrote a letter to General Borisov informing him of the evacuation plans and thanking him for his assistance—but he postponed delivering the letter until after the first plane landed, when it was too late for Borisov to cancel the agreement. The Soviets provided release forms in English and Russian for each POW, burying a crew of clerks in paperwork for two full days.

Group 1 planned to have an open ranks inspection on Saturday, May 12, 1945. In preparation, I shaved, shined my shoes, made my bed in the regulation manner, and was waiting for another crew to finish the last room in the barracks when at a little before 2:00 p.m., the first B-17 came over the horizon.

The airplanes circled overhead as pandemonium reigned among thousands of cheering POWs. Some men shot flares, others shouted, and one group scaled a building—which caved in when too many men clambered onto the roof. Men of my barracks shook hands and everyone agreed that this was obviously the most significant day in the history of Stalag Luft 1.

The planes came in by squadrons of six. After the first two landed, one of which carried Brigadier General William Gross, commander of the 8th Air Force's 1st Air Division, the other four planes peeled off from the formation. We thrilled at the sight, our love of flying rising in us again. At 2:30 p.m.—the very moment the traitor Vlasov was being handed over to the Russians—the first B-17 landed on the tarmac at Barth airfield.

The first POWs evacuated were the hospital cases. Soon two more B-17s and a C-46 landed, carrying radio operators who established links with England and other B-17s due to arrive that afternoon. Second on the list to leave were the British, including several hundred who had been captured at Dunkirk and other early battle areas. By nightfall they were talking to their folks on telephones.

I spent the afternoon until 4:00 p.m. getting ready to move. Packing was easy because I had so very little in my possession and a large portion of what I did have was worn out and not worth carrying. We could only take a portion of the Red Cross parcels with us, because our weight limit was forty pounds, and besides, I wanted to travel light. Yet, I almost cried when I left a can of powdered milk behind. Food had been scarce for too long.

The rest of the afternoon Joe and I played ping-pong in North 1's new recreation room, the former German barracks, which had been converted into a club with card tables, sofas, a ping-pong table, pictures on the walls, and other luxuries. That evening morale spun 180 degrees. Barbecue fires burned late into the night as we sat around singing, laughing, and remembering friends who didn't make it. Most of us felt too excited to think about sleep.

Early the next morning, Sunday, May 13, 1945, planes again swept down from the sky, their engines never stopping. They remained on the tarmac only long enough for 25 to 30 men to cram into the B-17s' before lifting off. Men practically danced to the awaiting planes, carrying shaggy pillowcases on their backs or Red Cross boxes stuffed with belongings.

Planes continued to fly and fill up until Monday, May 14, when around 3:00 p.m. the last plane lifted off. In all, forty-one planes, including thirty-five B-17 Flying Fortresses and six C-46 transports, evacuated 8,498 ex-POWs. We were free men at last.

CHAPTER 20

Camp Lucky Strike

Sunday, May 13, 1945, we arose on farmer time. By 8:00 a.m. we had dressed, shaved, eaten, finished packing, marched about five kilometers to the Barth airfield, and lined up ready to board evacuation planes and leave Germany. Our march through Barth bore little resemblance to that sad day just over a year earlier, on Hitler's birthday, when citizens hurled jeers and taunts as we trudged dejectedly through town. On this march people kept silent, looking out from windows or doorways, or from their place in a long breadline. I felt privileged to be going home to America.

On the tarmac, we loaded into the B-17s of the 1st Division as quickly as possible. I squeezed into a seat behind the copilot where I could see well. As we took off we assured our pilot, First Lieutenant Dowler, a 44F man who graduated from training after I went down, that this was the best mission he had ever flown.

During the peaceful passage over Germany's beautiful green countryside, Dowler allowed the pilots in our group to take short turns flying the airplane. The serenity of the country transformed as we flew over the Ruhr Valley, where we saw the ruined towns of Munster and Duisburg, Germany, and Cologne,

Cologne, with only its shell-blasted cathedral standing, was a ravished ruin. Having seen Frankfurt and Leipzig on the train ride to Dulag Luft the year before, I thought I was prepared for the destruction of Cologne, but nothing could have prepared me. It was so thoroughly demolished that it is difficult to describe. Partially submerged bridges lay broken in the Rhine River and buildings were reduced to piles of loose bricks and chunks of concrete.

In the brisk cool air of the spring afternoon, we landed at Laon airport, near Reims, France. We were met by olive-drab GI trucks and driven to a troop carrier regimental base at Reims, another scene of devastation. On the way to the base, the driver became lost, driving us around for about an hour before finding our destination.

At Reims, we waited in a long line for chow, but it was a tasty dinner of spaghetti, asparagus, peaches, and bread and butter. After over a year of coarse black German bread, GI bread tasted as good as cake. German POWs washed our mess kits, peeled our potatoes, and dug slit trenches and urinals, but I felt no sympathy for them.

A voice over the loudspeaker told us returning soldiers were required to have a typhus inoculation before boarding a boat for home. The voice invited us to a nearby tent where medics administered the immunizations. Getting that injection put me one step closer to going home.

French civilians lined up along the base fence waving and smiling at us, asking for souvenirs and making us feel welcome, a pleasant contrast to the Germans' scowls. I didn't know whether I'd been in a POW camp too long to know a pretty girl when I saw one or if the slim, trim French girls really were cute, but they looked pretty to me. They weren't husky like the German and Russian women I was accustomed to seeing.

Later, I went to an outdoor movie with a sound system so poor the voices blew away in the wind before they reached our ears. Even without sound, the American movie and a short film showing skiers shooting down Ecker Hill just out of Salt Lake City, Utah, thrilled me.

The next morning I knew I was back in the Army when they woke us up before dawn. At 6:00 a.m. we breakfasted on eggs, pineapple juice, and oatmeal mush, then boarded a flight to Le Havre, France, 178 miles (287 km) to the west. We rode on a C47 transport plane, built expressly for troop transport, equipped with good seats, magazines to read, and windows for viewing the world below. On my seat I found February's "Outdoor Life" magazine. I thumbed through it and discovered a well written article about fishing with a grey nymph fly, written by Clyde Ormond, one of my grade school teachers. What a coincidence that I should find an article written by someone from home in the first magazine I came across.

After reading Clyde's article I tried to relax, but the rough ride upset my stomach. Evidently I wasn't ready for the rich food I had eaten the past few days, because just as we touched down at Le Havre, I deposited my eggs and pineapple juice into a pail at the rear of the plane, pulling another airman's head out of the bucket to get access. Ironically, about half of the men, all of us ex-aerial combat POWs, became sick on the flight.

At Le Havre, Red Cross women served us doughnuts and coffee. I ate one doughnut, hoping to remove the sour taste in my throat before boarding GI trucks bound for Camp Lucky Strike, the POW processing center, fifty-seven kilometers (35 miles) north. Named after a brand of American cigarettes to confuse the enemy into thinking men were discussing cigarettes in overheard radio transmissions and keep its precise location secret, the camp was built on a former German airfield near the small town of Saint-Sylvain, situated five kilometers southwest of Saint-Valery-en Caux.

The France passing outside my window was an appalling spectacle. Shattered bridges and railroads, the wreckage of factories and entire villages, battle-destroyed war machines, and marked mine fields on scarred, burned lands lay on both sides of the road. In the villages, French men, women, and children waved and smiled cheerfully, scrambling like starved chickens chasing after a handful of wheat when we tossed them cigarettes.

The trucks stopped at Camp Lucky Strike in the warmth of mid-afternoon. Managed by the 89th Infantry Division, the camp was one of eight staging-area camps the army established around the harbor of Le Havre on the Bay of the Seine in Northern France, the only liberated port big enough to handle large ships. A key V-1 rocket launch site while in German hands, the RAF bombed the airfield heavily, eventually capturing it in June 1944. Soon after, American Engineer Corps troops arrived and repaired the 164 foot (50 meter) by 5,906 foot (1800 meter) landing strip and hastily set up a reception camp for transient soldiers.

Extending over 1,500 acres, the camp, composed mainly of canvas tents and wooden huts, was segmented into four sub-camps— A, B, C, and D—with each sub-camp containing 2,900 five-man tents to house 14,500 men. Each sub-camp maintained its own theater, cinema, chapel, hospital, post office, police station, barbershop, and PX where soldiers could buy toothbrushes, chocolate, watches, cigarettes, and knives for themselves, and perfume, lace, and jewelry from Paris to send to mothers, wives, and girlfriends.

Camp Lucky Strike originally served as the compulsory port of entry for American soldiers on their way to assembly camps before going to the front. After Germany surrendered, the camp became the primary departure point for repatriated and furloughed soldiers, liberated POWs, and soldiers leaving for the Pacific Theater. Built for a capacity of 58,000, the actual number of American soldiers in camp depended on the ebb and flow of men and machines required for combat. Some soldiers stayed for a couple of days of rest; others took up residence for months. Some days the number of men in camp surged to 100,000. The day after I arrived, 20,000 POWs showed up and they kept coming.

Army personnel assigned POWs to a packet of Recovered Allied Military Personnel (RAMP), containing 200 men, before processing them as a group to the States. Ritzema and I were assigned to Group 12, and after we provided our names and serial numbers, and designated where we intended to go on leave, personnel ushered us through a shower line, gave us a thorough delousing, issued us clean clothes and led us to trucks waiting to haul us to our tent. We stowed our gear, then feeling clean and tidy in fresh uniforms, we rushed over to the mess hall only to stand in a very slow moving, quarter mile long chow line. From then on, due to the influx of incoming soldiers, long lines were the norm all over camp—for chow, movies, and Red Cross tents.

Despite our return to the civilized world with all its comforts and luxuries, Ritzema and I nearly froze to death in bed that night. Trucks hadn't arrived with sufficient blanket supplies, so the only bedding issued was an unlined sleeping bag. The following afternoon Rocky and my former POW roommates arrived at the camp from Reims, tired and hungry after riding for thirty-six hours in a cramped train without sleeping accommodations or food. Conditions were so miserable on the journey, they said, that when the train stopped at one rail station a couple of soldiers slipped off, looted a wine car, and became intoxicated on the next leg of the journey.

Desperate to sleep warmer that night, I lined up in the bedding queue with Rocky and his group and received a blanket. The night was still cold but I slept in relative comfort.

Early the next morning I walked to the airfield to see a new night fighter plane and stumbled into Sergeants John Russell and Vincent Muffoletto, my former *Expectant Father* crew mates. I believed for thirteen months they were dead and was overjoyed to see them. A fisherman had picked them up from the Baltic Sea after they bailed out of the plane and turned them over to the German authorities. As luck would have it, they were processed through Dulag Luft the day before I arrived.

Displaced airmen continued to arrive at the camp in droves. The green-capped soldiers were everywhere, clogging streets and bunched around the landing strip, at every corner, and in all the stores. In the chow line I waited three hours and seven minutes for a breakfast of eggs, oatmeal mush, jam, toast and butter, and a can of milk. My appetite was destroyed by frustration after standing in line for such a long time, yet we had little else to do.

The enlisted men from Rocky's flight crew were in the same RAMP group as I, so with Muffoletto's help I tried to locate the rest of Rocky's crew. We searched the camp records for a couple of hours, finally finding their names, but two of the men had already shipped out, and we couldn't locate the other two. I felt exhausted by the effort, but at least Rocky knew his men were out of Germany.

A Negro band gave a concert one night, and it seemed ever so good to see music being made, and hear their swinging sound. It was so much better than hearing a recording.

Meanwhile, conditions at the camp improved. The Red Cross came to our aid and issued us pencils, notebooks, soap, shoe polish, razor blades, gum, and other comforts. I got plenty of rest with so little to do, and every time I sat on my bunk, I dozed. New packets were formed, and we moved to a new area, which was much better. The chow line shortened and the kitchen provided us plenty of clean hot water to scour our old mess kits. The only cloud on the horizon came from rumors that more troops would soon descend on the camp. I hoped they were just rumors, since camp was already overcrowded.

Before retiring that night, I visited Doc and Rocky at their tent. They had a fire cooking a supplement to their supper, because they only received half enough food to eat. Their mess staff claimed they didn't want to make POWs sick by giving them too much to eat. Pringle became so disgruntled by the lack of food that he had gone over the hill that afternoon, and Doc and Rocky expected he would stumble in late in the evening—drunk. I was glad our mess kitchen prepared plenty for everyone to eat till they were full, and we never went hungry.

A damp cold fog enveloped the area during the night and cold temperatures forced me out of bed early the next morning. After breakfast a big black staff sergeant led a ragged group of despondent and frightened German POWs through our area, marching them at a brisk double time. They looked as bewildered as I once felt. The sergeant bawled out a command, made a circular motion over his head with his hand, and the POWs did an about face so fast that it must have set their brains spinning. Perhaps the sergeant felt they deserved a little rough treatment after all they put other nations through, and close order drill certainly is punishment. Generally, the German prisoners rode in trucks and received plenty to eat.

After breakfast Rocky and I went for a stroll in the countryside. We saw mined beaches, strewn with barbed wire entanglements, and a French town the Germans had demolished and looted, and mined the surrounding area before they evacuated. Generally spared from destruction, beautiful churches dominated nearly every hamlet, ornamented with chandeliers, altars, and stained glass windows. One church, I judged, was several hundred years old.

Though desperately poor, the villagers treated us kindly and, thanks to Rocky's French, eagerly engaged us in conversation. The people we met insisted we tell them our horror stories and they related theirs, reluctant to let us leave once we became acquainted. We spoke with several French ex-POWs who sang the praises of General Patton and the American Army.

A couple of old ladies invited us into their home and gave us bread, eggs, onions, and apple cider. In return we gave them tea and cans of C rations, and Rocky promised to send them shoes when we got home. The villagers either wore cumbersome wooden shoes or rough shoes woven from manila rope.

I slept very well that night, my bed feeling so cozy I slept in until 9:30 a.m., making up for so many nights I couldn't sleep because of the cold. Ritzema and I took showers; they were "primo." I still felt a good bath was something to cheer about after being dirty all the time as a POW.

Fred Pratt and I met up and I took him to visit Russell and Muffoletto for a joyous reunion. After much hand shaking and back-slapping, we tried to locate Ely, our pilot. We found him listed in the files at the Air Corps liaison office, but the area he was reported to be in didn't exist.

On Sunday, May 20, 1945, one week after we flew out of Barth, Rocky and I were soaked to the skin in a rainstorm as we waited in line for lunch. Ironically, the majority of rainstorms hit while we stood in chow line. It was dreadful to stand there while the downpour nearly washed away the mess tent. Rocky generally ate his meals in our camp where food was plentiful. I had no dry clothes so I returned to my tent and got into bed after lunch, napping until my clothes dried.

We read an account in the *Stars and Stripes* newspaper reporting that in March, while we were sweating out the famine, Hitler ordered all Allied prisoners executed. Fortunately, the Wehrmacht refused to carry out the order. Had we known what Hitler planned to do with us, we would have sweated about much more than our next meal. The newspaper also ran the story of Colonel Spicer's pep talk that nearly cost him his life.

Rocky, Doc, and I took another walk in the country in the evening and were cordially invited into a French home. During our conversation, the family complained heatedly about Pierre Laval, the French politician who served twice as head of government in the Vichy Regime, following France's Armistice with Germany in 1940. They said Laval signed orders deporting foreign Jews from French soil, in effect condemning them to the death camps. Apparently, most French citizens agreed with the assessment, because Laval was executed for his treason a month or so after our conversation. Ironically, the family could not understand why the U.S. bombed their village, as if they didn't notice German installations under their very noses.

On the fifth consecutive day of rain the weather turned colder and I exploded in rage over spending another night freezing. Tentmate Fred Rector took pity and gave me one of his many blankets. For some reason some men had as many as seven blankets while others received one or none. When we complained to the officers, they said, "Tough luck. See the Chaplain." I began to feel like going over the fence to Paris.

The Allies' Supreme Commander General Eisenhower visited Camp Lucky Strike on Tuesday, May 22; the same day I received my first military ribbon, the European Theater of Operations (ETO) campaign ribbon, emblazoned with a bronze battle star. The General thanked us for the part we played in winning the war and assured us that everything possible was being done to get us home, explaining the delay was primarily caused by an over-taxed transportation system, plus the increased tempo of the war in the Pacific.

On Wednesday, our CO and packet commander, Captain Douglas, fed up with the lack of supplies, charged up to B Block headquarters and demanded action. As a result, we had a clothing formation in which the U.S. Government issued me a good fitting blouse and a pair of pants, which didn't fit as well. I had them altered a few days later.

About midmorning the following day I bumped into Ely, our long lost pilot. He rejoiced to hear of Muffoletto and Russel's miraculous resurrection from the dead. I learned he was a packet leader and he expected his group would be leaving in a couple of days.

Impatient with my group's slow progress toward departing, I signed up for a pass to spend seven days in the United Kingdom before heading for home, which would change my departure point to Southampton instead of Le Havre. Truth of the matter was, I wanted out of the camp, and if I could to visit London for seven days without it affecting my sixty-day leave in the States, so much the better.

At breakfast I learned the night before MPs had shot and killed two drunken Negro soldiers as they attempted to crash the Red Cross eggnog line, set up for RAMP soldiers only. In the melee, the two men tried to disarm an MP and he shot them. A bullet passed through one of the Negroes, ricocheted, and struck an ex-POW. Both Negroes died but the ex-POW survived. That afternoon I walked over to see Pratt, but he had escaped to Paris, fed up with five years of army restrictions.

I attended a USO show with F. Peter Smith, who went wild when the beautiful Mistress of Ceremonies announced she was from Denver, his hometown. She introduced a variety show featuring a pianist, a dancer, a violinist, and a baritone, who sang, "On the Road to Mandalay" and "Believe Me If All Those Endearing Young Charms," both old favorites of mine. The violinist, a beautiful young girl, held us spellbound with her "Ipana" smile as she skillfully played several difficult numbers.

The next day the boredom continued, and I craved progress of almost any kind. The day was saved when Chuck Curtiss and I went to a movie in the afternoon, "Rhapsody in Blue," dramatizing George Gershwin's life. Unfortunately, we couldn't see the movie because the wind kept blowing the tent door open, letting light hit the screen, and when the wind whistled through, it was also hard to hear, but what music I could hear was wonderful.

A furor at breakfast on Saturday over a write up in the *Stars and Stripes* kept our minds off of our frustrations with Camp Lucky Strike. The newspaper article featured interviews with Lieutenant Colonel Gabreski and Colonel Zemke and annoyed us by giving the fighter pilots thick praise, but not mentioning the POW majority, the bomber boys. In general, Zemke's statements met with our approval, but Gabreski, the leading ETO fighter ace, who spent only six months in Stalag Luft 1 and was already home on a sixty-day leave, had the gall to say, "Give those men thirty days and they will be ready to pit their skills against the Japanese." Perhaps it didn't occur to him that some of the men weren't anxious to go to the Pacific Theater. When asked why so many fighter planes were shot down, a sore subject with fighter pilots, Gabreski stated that freak accidents and flak brought down most of our fighter planes, not enemy planes.

CHAPTER 21

Days of Frustration

On Sunday, May 27, 1945, our two-week anniversary of leaving Barth, my patience at an all time low, rumors flew thick as ducks on a flooded seed pea field about our passes to England. Some wags said the seven days would count against our promised sixty-day leave. Others insisted getting passage out of England would take ten to fourteen days, and still others claimed we would have to sign another list before we could go home if we went to England. Personally, if the chance had come, I would have gone, but I was a little leery of the deal since no one knew anything about it.

In the middle of the night, long after we had retired to bed, Captain Douglas burst into our tent with a lantern and asked us our names, ranks, months overseas, months of service, number of children, and our decorations—all factors in the U.S. Army Demobilization Plan point system for determining discharge dates. The army awarded points for months of service overseas (one point per month), commendations (five points per award), campaign battle stars earned (five points per star), number of children (12 points per child), and other aspects. Eighty-five was the magic number for discharge. Soldiers with 80 to 84 points transferred to other ETO units. Those with fewer than eighty received furloughs home for a couple of months before being retrained for an assignment in the Pacific.

My tally added up to a grand total of forty-seven points. Douglas insisted the information gathered didn't affect officers and was merely obtained for a survey, but most of us knew our lot was cast. At any rate, what a heck of a time to come around with a questionnaire when we sat around all day with nothing to do!

The next morning was bright and cheery, so I rose early, ate a hearty breakfast, took a hot shower, shaved, changed clothes, and even sang a little. Two hours of sunshine did a lot to liven and cheer me up. But a totally cloudless day would probably have made me turn somersaults and go crazy by evening. Camp Lucky Strike had the worst weather I had ever experienced in my life. We received so much rain that in the interior of our tent, moss grew on the legs of my cot, water dripped from the roof, and the two men with me, who weren't over twenty-five, complained of rheumatism. True to form it rained all that afternoon.

When a Douglas A-26 Invader attack bomber, the fastest bomber in the war with top speed of 355 mph, crashed after the right landing gear collapsed, I went out to see the plane. I barely caught a glimpse of it before a colonel made me leave the scene of the accident. When I returned to the tent the captain told me our packet had been divided by U.S. states and I had been moved to D Area with Blaine Harris. Later, Rocky announced he received seven days leave to England before his sixty-day furlough started. I rushed to the bulletin board but my name wasn't on the list.

To assuage my disappointment, I went to a USO show in the evening, presented by Stubby Kaye, a comedian who must have weighed 300 pounds. Stubby cracked some jokes about himself and I laughed heartily for the first time since arriving at Camp Lucky Strike.

The next morning I presented myself at the clinic for a required physical examination and filled out a health questionnaire, our next-to-the-last-step in processing before departure from the camp. The physical checkup wasn't very thorough. We were asked if we felt well, checked for teeth and eye problems (I had 20-30 vision), given blood pressure and urinalysis tests, and weighed. Due to plentiful eggnog and copious amounts of food I had been eating, I weighed three pounds more than I had when I was shot down. The doctors could have used data from my last 64 physicals and been accurate on my current state of health.

On Thursday, May 31, pay formation was postponed but par for the course, no one notified us. So we waited around all afternoon, relating combat stories with the airmen, infantrymen, and guys from other branches of the service.

THE HIGHLY SECRET COMMITTEE on the Manhattan Project meeting in U.S. Secretary of Defense Henry Stimson's office at the Pentagon reached three recommendations:

1. Drop the bomb on Japan as soon as possible;
2. Drop the bomb on industrial targets surrounded by workers homes and cause as much psychological damage to the population as possible;
3. Drop the bomb without forewarning.

Secretary of State Jimmy Byrnes went directly to the White House afterward and reported the proceedings of the meeting to President Truman. None of the scientists had a clear idea of what power the weapon might have, Byrnes told Truman. The scientific panel's estimates of the explosive force ranged widely, from 2000 to 20,000 tons of TNT. Despite the uncertainty, Truman responded he could think of no alternative and reluctantly gave the committee his approval to go ahead with the project.

Meanwhile, I took one more step toward my departure for home—I registered my souvenirs with a Lieutenant Mayfield at the booty tent. The soldier next to me registered knives, saddlebags, gun sights, flags, and pictures. How he managed to carry so much loot is a mystery to me. My Luftwaffe boots gave me such a struggle I eventually abandoned them.

In the evening Rocky and I slipped out of camp and visited Cany-Barville, a village of 10,000 people, about five miles away. We edged around the MP at the gate, only to run squarely into another MP about a mile from camp. To our relief, the MP only grinned when he discovered we didn't have passes and instead of booking us, hailed a jeep and asked the driver to take two passengers to town.

As we left the jeep, the fragrance of colognes of the townspeople nearly overwhelmed us. The French men slicked down their hair with fragrant dressings. The women, who painted their faces with thick makeup, doused themselves liberally with strong perfume.

Mingling with the natives, Rocky and I attended a stage show with live music and dancing. I liked it, even though I could only understand one word in a hundred. Rocky turned to speak to an elderly man seated next to him to practice his French, but to his surprise, the old man spoke only Spanish. He had fled his homeland during the Spanish revolution and had established himself as a funeral monument maker in Cany. We tried speaking Spanish, but I hadn't learned much in my Stalag Luft 1 class.

During the intermission we walked outside the theater and saw men answering the call of nature at every corner. Apparently, as long as your back was turned to the street it was acceptable to urinate anywhere you wished. Women walked by as if the men weren't there and nothing was amiss. Frankly, I have no idea where the women relieved themselves.

In the second half of the show, instead of offering a regular bank night at the theater, like I was accustomed to in Rigby, Idaho, the stage manager drew numbers from a hat and presented cigars to the men and ten-cent earrings to the women in the audience with winning numbers. As grand prizes, he presented the lucky winners with photographs of General Eisenhower and General De Gaulle.

After the show Rocky and I thought about asking a couple of the pretty mademoiselles to let us walk them home but decided against it, as it was already one o'clock in the morning and we were afraid the girls might live two or three miles out in the country. In any case, we were pleased to see so many good-looking girls—at least they looked good after dark.

Back on the road to camp we walked about two miles before catching a ride in a very crowded truck filled with drunken soldiers. When we unloaded, one of the soldiers fell over the side of the truck and hit the ground with a loud thud, but stood up and walked away. He was too drunk to feel any pain.

The paymaster came through with our wages the following morning and I received approximately one hundred dollars in five hundred French franc notes, the first money I had received in over a year. Frankly, I had managed pretty well without money, and in most places I couldn't have used it anyway.

With money in our pockets, Harris and I obtained twenty-four-hour passes, and early Saturday morning we headed out of camp to visit the surrounding towns. At the edge of camp, a friendly driver in a jeep picked us up and we rode in relative comfort to Yvetot, where we caught a truck to Rouen. At heavily bombed Rouen, it took a while, but eventually another Frenchman gave us a ride in the back of his truck to Paris. Since the bed had a cover over it, we missed seeing the countryside, but at 9:00 P.M. we arrived in "Gay Paree."

The driver dropped us off at Pont de Neuilly, a station of the Paris Metro in the community of Neuilly-sur-Seine, where we caught a subway into the heart of Paris. Neither Harris nor I had ridden a subway before, but by deciphering the maps we made our way to the station near Boulevard de l'Opera, the closest stop to the Rainbow Center, a luxury hotel run by the Red Cross to provide billets for soldiers and entertainers. To our dismay, the Red Cross couldn't billet us for the night because we only had twenty-four-hour passes. An MP gave us directions to a hotel, without asking probing questions. An hour later we were in soft beds in a hotel in a section of Paris called Invalides.

Despite the comfort of the bed, I slept poorly. After our kriegie beds and army cots, the hotel bed was too soft. We arose early, cleaned up, and walked to the Red Cross Center where we obtained directions to Hotel Louvais, where LDS servicemen held Sunday School services. We located the place, but we arrived hours before the meeting would begin, so we set out to see the sights until time for the meeting.

On Champs de Elysses, we admired colorful flowerbeds, gardens, and parks, bubbling fountains, statues, and grand buildings. We studied an Egyptian obelisk covered with ancient hieroglyphics and strolled beneath the Arc de Triomphe, with its bas-relief sculptures depicting Napoleonic French wars. We saluted the tomb of the Unknown Soldier before catching a subway to Trocadero Station and riding the lift to the top of the Eiffel Tower. From that vantage the beautiful city lay glistening around us in the morning sun.

Sunday School, meanwhile, was starting without us. Rushing back to Trocadero, we climbed aboard a subway and made a mad dash to Hotel Louvais, where we slipped in just after the meeting started and enjoyed a lively Sunday School lesson on the subject of peace planning, the changed social conditions, and their effect on the Church. It felt great to attend an organized church meeting again.

As soon as Sunday School ended, we grabbed a bite to eat, rode the subway back to Pont de Neuilly and hitchhiked back to Camp Lucky Strike, catching rides on four trucks. Thankfully, the good weather held until we reached Cany-Barville, when three thundershowers drenched us in the five miles between the town and camp. We arrived looking like drowned ground squirrels, our passes eight hours overspent, but luckily no one asked to see them. Weary to the bone, we dropped onto our cots, contented that we had been to Paris.

Later that evening Captain Douglas told us the commander of the Normandy Base Section, General Lee, had visited the camp on an inspection tour and was miffed because when he walked through camp no one saluted him. In retribution, he scheduled us for calisthenics, close order drill, a military courtesy hike, and a formal retreat ceremony. Needless to say the GIs were complaining bitterly. "I didn't believe the Army would punish me for being a POW," said one disgruntled soldier. Another said, "I guess they are trying to force us to volunteer for the Pacific Theater so we can leave." We all went to sleep laughing. It was Sunday, June 3, 1945, exactly three weeks after we'd left Barth.

General Lee's orders were never carried out because, predictably, the following morning it rained pitchforks. Instead, Harris and I, exhausted from our marathon trip to Paris, spent the day in the sack. Meanwhile, tongues were wagging as the camp rumor mill ground out fresh gossip that by the ninth of June every soldier in the camp except two thousand men would be on their way home. By the sixteenth of June, the remaining soldiers would leave.

Rain fell almost all day. In the evening the sky had cleared sufficiently for Harris and me to see a movie, exclusively *for* the Air Corps, entitled "Casanova Brown", a hilarious comedy starring Gary Cooper. Well rested after spending Monday in the sack, I arose early the next morning and walked to Area D determined to get a haircut from an American barber. Generally, German barbers shaved the sides so my ears stuck out like telephone poles, and left a mop on top, only cutting every other hair. I had never seen anything like it since Red, the barber back home, got drunk and gave Dad a similar haircut.

Postponed but not forgotten, General Lee's inspection day fell on the first anniversary of D Day. Determined to straighten us up or be damned, the general ordered that we couldn't leave our tents unless we wore Class A uniforms. Why a whole camp ought to dress up and police the grounds for one solitary man stumped me. At least our chow had improved; the night before we had pork chops and fresh tomatoes. Captain Douglas alerted us that the officers in our packet were filling up empty packets and we would move soon.

ONE-MISSION MAN

On Thursday, June 7, 1945, we finally received the glorious news we'd awaited since leaving Germany: my group was alerted we would leave at noon the following day. We packed and changed our French currency to American dollars. In the evening Harris and

> **SECRETARY OF WAR STIMSON** again met with President Truman in Washington, D.C., to discuss the atomic bomb. Unsettled by reports describing the destruction in Japan caused by the B–29 firebombs, Stimson attempted to convince the President that precision bombing was a better strategy than the A-bomb. Earlier in the year, in February, in three high-altitude strategic bombing raids, British and American forces dropped incendiary bombs on Dresden, Germany, setting off a fire storm in which an estimated 135,000 people died. A month later in bombing raids on Tokyo, American incendiary bombs killed more than 100,000 people. On May 14, 1945, five hundred B-29s dropped the largest concentration of firebombs ever delivered on Nagoya, Japan's third largest industrial city. Nine days later, on May 23, 1945, firebombs obliterated five square miles of Tokyo. A day and a half later, firebombs destroyed 16 square miles.
>
> Japan had as much as admitted defeat but vowed to fight to the finish, so why not continue to wear them down with similar raids? Stimson argued. The Air Force contended that precision bombing no longer worked in Japan, because unlike Germany, Japan built cottage industry resistance, and rather than concentrate its industrial plants, it disbursed them in residential neighborhoods. This demanded a new war strategy, they insisted.

I decided to attend a movie and for the second time since our arrival in Camp Lucky Strike, we went early and occupied some very good seats. When the movie started we were disappointed as it was, "Abroad with Two Yanks," which we had just seen and laughed at the previous night. We couldn't justify seeing it again, despite our great seats no matter how funny it was so we left.

Even though I had exchanged most of my French money, I had a couple of francs remaining, so after breakfast the next morning, I went to the gift shop and bought a bracelet for my sister Carma. At noon an anxious Group 12 loaded into, and out of, several different vehicles before finding the right truck headed for Le Havre, our port of embarkation. Our driver took a wrong turn at Fecamp and drove us about five miles (eight kilometers) out into the country before he checked his maps and discovered his error. We were late but we made it, and the ship looked mighty good as we pulled in next to it. After twenty-six days in despicable Camp Lucky Strike, we were looking forward to going home.

CHAPTER 22

Over the Ocean Blue

On Saturday, June 9, 1945, I boarded the SS *Excelsior*, a Type C3-S-A3 troop transporter steamship, built by the Bethlehem Sparrows Point Shipyard and used by the army to convey troops during D-Day, a year earlier. Officers' quarters on the upper deck were clean and comfortable, but the enlisted men slept on five-decker bunk beds in the hold.

The food the Navy cooks prepared was as good as we dreamed about last March during the famine: beef, pork, or fish, three vegetables, two desserts, olives, pickles, and bread and butter. Eating from plates again, instead of mess kits, enhanced the gastronomic experience further.

The men with me received assignments to serve as loading officers for the embarkation and departure from Le Havre. Thanks to the alphabetical organization of the officer list, I was the next to the last man assigned and missed the detail by a hair's breadth. The next morning while my fellow officers supervised loading operations, the Commanding Officer (CO) called a mandatory meeting for second lieutenants, and I, like a dumb rabbit, showed up early. Consequently, the CO assigned me to be Officer of the Day (OD) over Compartment 2, giving me overall responsibility over the hold daily for a four-hour watch for the duration of the voyage.

At 9:00 p.m. Sunday, June 10, French tugboats hauled the *Excelsior* out into the English Channel, and as we bid goodbye to war battered Le Havre, I told myself, "If I ever see Europe again, it will be too soon." Later that night in my quarters I wrote in my journal, "My first trip abroad has been enlightening. I have learned that Europeans are a disgusting lot who look to the United States to police the world and pay for their wars."

The following day, June 11, our first full day at sea, the water was rough, pitching my bunk and my stomach to and fro all day. At noon I reported for my first watch as OD and I had only been in the hold about an hour when I had to run up two flights of stairs, cut through a chow line like a fullback, and burst into an open latrine, where I urped away to my heart's content. By evening I was able to eat again, although my stomach still stood in the way of the so-called pleasure cruise.

For the next few days I didn't know who was rocking the boat, but whoever it was did a good job. Swells as tall as the Rocky Mountains lifted and tossed us as the ship bucked over the top of each wave like a teeter totter. I was so sick I hoped the Army would issue me a new stomach or at least transfer me to the Pacific where I could die honorably. Even seeing a sailor high on a mast fixing an antenna made my stomach turn.

A couple of days out of Le Havre, the ocean calmed down as we moved away from land, and the sun shone brilliantly all day long. From my deathbed I began to view my surroundings with a brighter outlook. Out on deck I watched a porpoise bounding through the waves beside the ship and saw my first albatross. Toward evening a fifteen-foot shark was caught across the bow of the ship, unable to release itself from the force of the waves, which eventually battered it to pieces against the ship.

Many former POWs went nuts with money in their pockets, buying candy at the PX. Major Hale had boasted the PX had an unlimited supply of everything except cigarettes. He obviously didn't understand POW psychology. Only three days after leaving Le Havre, the PX's supply of candy had been exhausted, some of the men admitting to buying as many as five cartons of candy bars.

Actually, it was no wonder that men who had gone for months with nothing but the bare essentials of life were now going hog wild.

The ship reached the Gulf Stream and the weather turned warmer, which made my stomach turn more revolutions. Just as I became used to the ship rolling, it began pitching. Fortunately, we'd reached the halfway point, according to the steward.

On Thursday morning, June 14, I began OD duty at midnight. Lieutenant Beckham, who preceded me as OD for Compartment 2, awakened me. I dressed, grabbed a book to read, and was briefed on my duties. In the hold, enlisted men were still playing poker when I arrived, so I drew up a chair and watched them.

It was a good thing smoking was banned everywhere but on deck, because I would have been sick all the time if I had had to work in a smokehouse, which it would have been, had the men been free to do as they pleased. One of my duties was to make sure the rules were obeyed. As it was, the early morning shift nearly did me in and I spent the rest of the day sick.

Later in the day we were informed our debarkation port would be Hampton Roads, Virginia, instead of New York City. I was disappointed because I wanted to see the Big City, and that meant I wouldn't see it until after the War. But I was not on a pleasure cruise, I reminded myself.

Most of the time my OD duties were fairly light. I read James Hilton's *Random Harvest* during down time while on duty and wrote in my journal later that the book was as fine as *Goodbye Mr. Chips* and *Lost Horizon*. The hold was hot and crowded, and I was always glad when my shift ended.

The Captain was quite the speed demon, bent on passing every ship we came upon, and whenever he opened up the engines full throttle, the ship vibrated wildly. Since the Captain pushed the old boat hard and fast as he could, it quivered all the time, and I thought she would probably fall apart about fifty miles from the coast. Only one ship ever passed us, the *West Point* sailed by as if we were standing still, leaving us in her wake on the last day of our journey.

Eating like kings and getting very little exercise, all us ex-POWs put on weight once we got used to the pitch and roll of the ship. One evening the cooks served us chicken, rice, soup, spinach, potatoes and gravy, fruit salad, apples, pickles, onions, bread and butter, chocolate layer cake, ice cream, tea, coffee or cocoa, and assorted cold cuts, for those who could hold them. Three months before, such a feast would have brought tears to my eyes as I beheld it. Needless to say, I expected by the time we docked my pants would be the tightest fit I had ever worn.

One morning the fellow in the bunk above me told me his candy supply was getting low; he only had four boxes left. About every five minutes he remarked, "Get ready stomach, start squirming and rolling, because I'm going to eat another candy bar."

Besides our obsession with food, we thought constantly of home and what lay ahead for us. Peter Smith and I sat on the deck one evening and swapped yarns for about two hours. Peter felt he was unable to get far with the ladies and was always doing something embarrassing. On a dare, he had once written a dashing letter to a nurse, then he spent the rest of the time until he joined the Army avoiding her. He told me he hoped that she had never received his POW notice and still believed he was missing or killed in action.

I entered the hold the next morning in a state of dread, because the enlisted men were required to give their quarters a GI clean. To my surprise and relief, the men had already begun to clean the hold for inspection, and within a few minutes, they had swept the place, mopped the floor, and made the beds. I ordered the sergeant in charge to have his detail clean up the landing above the hold, and when he ordered the men do the extra duty, they did it without grumbling. When it came to cleaning the latrines, the detail was not so eager. The sergeant couldn't locate men assigned to do the task, so he came to me to assign someone to help. I promptly made friends with six men sitting on deck and drafted them to do the job.

As I walked away it dawned on me that on a ship the difference of treatment between officers and enlisted personnel is more pronounced than in any other place in the service. Enlisted men's quarters were crowded, hot, and they ate out of mess kits, while we officers had clean, comfortable, relatively private quarters. I wondered if I would take orders as well as they did. In any case, we passed the major's inspection with flying colors.

The transportation major in charge of the Army men on board was an older man quite meticulous and he seemed to think all of us wanted to be model soldiers. *The Voice*, as we dubbed him, almost drove us into insanity by constantly yelling "At ease" over the loudspeaker system. He then asked us to be cooperative obey orders be good soldiers and keep our quarters clean. All this pleading came across as nagging. He annoyed us until we felt like telling him to jump overboard. We managed to put up with him, since we knew it was only for a few more days.

One evening as I sat on deck, the sea was as calm as a swimming pool at closing time. My seasickness had finally passed, and I almost enjoyed the voyage. Another day I took a sunbath on deck, my skin turning crimson red, I looked out to sea as a whale spouted off the port bow. We weren't able to see much of the animal, but I concluded that it was even larger than I had imagined, considering its wake which was about as large as the one the ship made. A few days later I saw a whale flash its tail completely out of the water just as the captain was passing another ship. To my consternation, the captain didn't deviate course but headed directly for the whale, which sputtered and spouted, moving to one side as the ship passed between it and the other vessel.

Viewing marine life was very interesting to me. Seaweed beds reminded me of the green moss floating on fresh water streams in Idaho but seaweed was more yellow. During the voyage I saw numerous flying fish jump out of the water several feet above the surface, sail twenty or thirty feet in silver flashes, and then dive back into the sea with a splash. Since the deck was about forty feet above the water level, the fish were hard to see in any detail, but I was convinced they did fly.

As the days passed the weather became hotter and more humid as the summer heat bore down upon us. One hot afternoon near the end of the voyage, the captain ordered everyone on the vessel to undergo an inspection for fleas, lice, and communicable diseases. The enlisted men were all sent to the hold to line up for the parade. As two hundred steaming bodies joined me in the hold, sweating like proverbial butchers, I almost roasted. Worse yet, the enlisted men hadn't had the advantage of facilities for frequent bathing, and the hold stunk. Needless to say, I was overjoyed when eight bells rang and my tour of duty ended.

One night it was so hot that I slept without blankets. I woke up in the middle of the night to see one of my roommates wandering about the room. He was so uncomfortable in the heat, he had taken a cold shower, changed his steamy bedding, and was just going back to bed. I found it very oppressive, too. About an hour after my shower, my skin became damp and then felt prickly as a gunnysack. My motto became, "Give the sea to those who can stand it, and let me have a little chunk of solid land."

At 9:00 p.m. on Sunday evening, June 17, 1945, I saw a flashing light on a buoy guiding us into Hampton Roads harbor. It was the most beautiful light I have ever seen. It was exactly one week after tugboats pushed us out into the English Channel. I thought I knew how Columbus felt when he spotted the New World. As we stood on deck and looked at the shore, nearly every man could admit to himself that, at some point, he never expected to see the United States again.

To Henry Valera, Ogden, Utah, it was even more of a thrill, because he guessed the time of arrival to the exact moment and won seventy-five dollars the men had pooled at a buck a guess. Shore lights surrounded us on three sides as we entered the harbor. That night when I hit the sea sack for the last time I was the most contented man in the world.

CHAPTER 23

Overland Trek

At about 1:00 a.m. on Monday, June 18, 1945, a rumbling noise jerked me awake. I sat bolt upright, frozen in fear, and strained to hear, "Abandon Ship!" ringing over the intercom. Mines, submarines, and torpedoes raced through my flak-happy brain. One of my roommates rolled over in his bed and said, "It's nothing but the anchor being cast overboard." Relieved, I fell back onto my pillow and into a sleeping stupor.

Morning light found the *SS Excelsior* in port at Hampton Roads, Virginia, surrounded by land on three sides—it looked good to me. An enormous Essex class aircraft carrier sat on the other side of the harbor, and Navy cadets buzzed our ship every time they shot a landing in their BB3C Seagull seaplanes. They were show offs, just like Army cadets.

The debarkation began at 3:30 p.m. The major confined us to quarters until then, and I almost suffocated during my last duty in the hold. At the bottom of the gangplank, smiling WACs directed us to waiting trains. Either WACs turned gorgeous while I was gone, or they just looked good by comparison, because when I left I thought WACs looked awful. On the pier a group of Red Cross girls handed us cold lemonade and doughnuts, which we welcomed, since we were sweltering.

Onlookers waved and cheered us on the train ride to Camp Patrick Henry and in the station, where a military band met us, playing while we marched into a theatre. A major spoke to us, telling us we would be well fed, processed quickly, and leave for home in forty-eight hours. While on base, he said, military courtesy and discipline were for the permanent personnel. Then he added a rather peculiar statement. He said the German POWs on the base would receive less food, of lower quality, than we would receive. After his speech, everybody cheered, and as we marched to our quarters, I smiled when the band played, "Way Beyond the Hills of Idaho."

We dropped off our gear outside the barracks and raced to the mess hall for a supper of steak, with cold milk to drink, and ice cream and cake for dessert. It even surpassed the meals we had eaten on the ship. After mess, Lieutenant Barber and I walked over to the telegraph office and sent wires home to our parents with news of our arrival in the States. On the way back to the barracks a thundershower drenched us with good American rain, warmed and softened by the southern sun. When I returned to quarters, I discovered that some kind soul had covered my duffel bag with a tarpaulin so that it wasn't soaked, as I had expected. I took a hot shower, grateful to wash off all that perspiration from the day.

Camp Patrick Henry did its best to please us, processing us quickly and smoothly, issuing us B-4 bags, the military's answer to the suitcase, and passes for our 60 day furloughs. They made stencils for us to mark our bags, loaded our luggage for us, and helped us send our baggage home. They gave us rides all over the base. At the PX we encountered the usual very long lines, but when we got to the end of it, we found clothing, candy, toilet articles, writing supplies, gifts, tobacco, and most anything a man could want. I bought enough additional changes of clothing to get me to Salt Lake City, at least.

We were scheduled to ship out the next morning, Wednesday, June 20, but our departure was postponed. I supposed it was because the trains were busy hauling the essentials of war to the West Coast for shipment to the Pacific Theater, but no one ever told us a reason.

As we waited for the order to leave, I finished reading Norman Hall's *Lost Island*, the story of a Pacific atoll the Americans turned into a base for Pacific defenses. The destruction of the beautiful island, removal and deterioration of its people, and the loss of the island's tranquility and wildlife was the underlying theme. As I pondered the book, I realized the war had affected every section of the world. In fact, America seemed to be about the least affected of any nation. I wondered when, or if, the U.S. would realize that the way to prevent war is not to assume a laissez-faire attitude of selling oil to Italy, arms to Germany, and scrap metal to Japan. It seemed to me industrialists' profits were no guarantee of peace.

In the evening we saw a funny movie and I laughed till tears ran down my face. It felt good to laugh again. We also heard that the Japanese on Okinawa were exterminated. That meant there wasn't much more than the Japanese mainland and China to invade. I hoped the end would come soon so all the men could have the thrill of turning homeward.

With no chance to adjust to Virginia's hot, humid weather, many of us broke out with heat rashes. My buddy J. Wyley Hansen had splotches all over his stomach, and my crotch became so sore that I could hardly walk. The infirmary insisted there was nothing for us to worry about and gave us cans of talcum powder, sending us to the barracks with orders to take a cold shower. After taking three showers and emptying my can of talcum powder, I was still sore.

At 4:00 a.m. on Saturday, June 23, I called home, and a cheerful telephone operator kept me laughing as she insisted a dim-witted operator along the line was wreaking havoc with the connection. After an hour she discovered my folks had changed their phone number during my absence and in the confusion Central called my parents' next-door neighbors. Finally, a sweet voice said, "Here's yo father." I talked with Dad, Mother and Carma and it was wonderful to hear their voices again. I learned that both Clive and Max were in the military, but neither one was in a combat zone thank goodness. Carma spoke up clearly and I could understand every word she said. Hearing them made me more homesick than ever.

At noon we marched two abreast out of the gates at Camp Patrick Henry, hiked down to the station, and climbed aboard an old, outmoded, uncomfortable passenger car belonging to the New York Central Railway. Rolling toward Richmond, Virginia, the train moved very slowly, but I'd gladly have ridden in a *40 by 8* to be on my way home. That's the Germans' name for a boxcar, in which they crammed 40 people or eight horses.

After we passed through Richmond and through a gap in the Appalachian Mountains, I expected at every turn to see a tattered house with Daisy, Lil' Abner, and Lonesome Polecat sitting under a tree in the front yard. We traveled alongside a stream jumping with fish and past a lake full of people boating on that summer Saturday afternoon, and I remembered the last year's wasted Saturday nights, our loneliest night of the week.

East of Lynchburg, Virginia, while the train filled up its water supply, a crowd of enthusiastic villagers greeted us and answered our questions in a most pleasant manner. I noticed all the children in the town under the age of fourteen ran around barefoot.

On the morning of Sunday, June 24, 1945, I awoke with a combination of seasickness, airsickness, and rheumatism, feeling more tired than I was when I fell asleep, my stomach rolling and every limb aching. No matter what I did to make myself comfortable during the night, I just couldn't sleep in a sitting position.

At Huntington, West Virginia, the train stopped and almost everyone got off the train to stretch their legs. It looked like everyone had as poor a night as I. Passengers' hair was flying, their faces were dirty, eyes were bleary, their clothes disheveled and everyone was covered with coal soot from the smoke blowing in through windows opened for ventilation.

We traveled along the big muddy Ohio River for many miles with fine scenery on both banks, though not as fine as the Snake River scenery, mind you. Fog settled over Kentucky, but it cleared when we crossed the river into Cincinnati, Ohio. Our porter promised to take on water for us to drink at Cincinnati, but he forgot, so we figured we were doomed to be thirsty all the way to Chicago. I jested that the train was only a slight improvement over Germany's boxcars, but compared to the train I rode to Barth, this train seemed like the world's best. Passing through Ohio, Indiana, and Illinois with their tidy fields of headed-out wheat and knee-high corn standing in weed-free fields impressed me.

At 6:00 p.m. the train puffed into Chicago, and as we climbed down onto the platform, every passer-by stopped to speak to us or shake our hands, and they gave beer to all the men who wanted it. In fact, Chicago's hospitality was so warm that when we pulled out of the station, thirty men were missing, including Stanley Cooper, who was so disgusted with our accommodations that he flew like a big bird as soon as the train doors opened. We also lost our packet commander, Lieutenant Banks, who evidently received a bum steer as to the length of our stay. Ironically, just after Cooper bolted, we were transferred to a Pullman car with a bed for every passenger and plenty of cold water to drink. Our packet of ex-POWs occupied half of the train while the other half held Pacific-bound troops.

On Monday morning, June 25, **1945,** the train was rolling across the rich farmlands of Iowa when I awoke from a deep, restful slumber. We passed through the hometowns of two of my kriegie roommates, Doc Gillespie, of Fort Dodge, and Bob Johnson, of Wall Lake. At Council Bluffs, Iowa, swarms of kids—the healthiest looking kids I had seen in a long time—lined up beside our train and gave us nickels and candy bars. At Lincoln, Nebraska, a carload of pilots en route to Roswell, New Mexico, for B-29 Phase Training were attached to our train, and they reported the country's supply of pilots was still unlimited.

At about 9:00 a.m. the following morning the train stopped just out of Denver and released the boys from Wyoming and Colorado, shuttling them to a reception center at Fort Logan. My buddy J. Wyley Hansen called home from Denver and learned his father had died the previous October. Meantime, we continued to lose men at every stop. As the train pulled out of Denver, a GI sprinted about a mile to catch it.

High up in the mountains west of Denver the train stopped for water at a small station. I watched a drama across the street as a girl of about fourteen years of age tried to lead a cow through a gate. She became entangled in the rope, fell down, lost her temper, and finally allowed the cow to go its own way, reminding me of something I learned on the farm: cows are as stubborn as mules.

At Grand Junction, Colorado, we were handed the biggest insult of my Army career—the Rio Grande lunchroom locked its doors in the faces of a trainload of hungry servicemen. When a woman unlocked the door long enough to let a civilian enter and then slammed it on us again, my temper swelled to the boiling point. I expected to be mistreated by the Nazis, but I didn't expect it from my own countrymen.

The train was standing silently in front of the Denver and Rio Grande Railroad Station in Salt Lake City when I awoke on the morning of June 27. I jumped out of bed, shaved, washed, and went into the station to call my folks. I told them to expect me in a few days, but Jimmy couldn't wait that long to tell me Max, who was stationed in Hawaii, had sent him a genuine Hawaiian coconut.

GI trucks shuttled us to Fort Douglas on the foothills east of the city for processing. Sitting on pins and needles as an Air Corps captain droned on about our processing, I just wanted to be on my way. The base's medical examination didn't amount to much, thank goodness. Nearby, a group of recruits, mostly young kids in high school sweaters, with a few older men the army had either finally caught up with or had deferred and taken as a last resort, were being examined by army doctors. At day's end I again saw the new recruits out on the lawn wearing ill-fitting uniforms and tossing rifles around.

In the last formation for partial pay, I could have withdrawn up to one thousand dollars if I had wished, but I only took two hundred dollars. My pockets stuffed with folding money, I killed a couple of hours in the PX, waiting for my orders to be printed, and bought new pants, a hat, and a pair of shoes. At 4:00 p.m. they cut us loose and I rode the bus to Beth Hamblin's house. She was prettier than I remembered and I amazed myself by telling her so. Mrs. Hamblin invited me to dinner, which was delicious even though I couldn't eat much. My stomach seemed full all the time and I could survive on practically nothing. Afterwards Beth and I had a long walk and she told me my friend, and her cousin, Ellsworth Brown, had finished his fifty combat missions the previous fall and qualified for pilot's school in Arizona.

The next morning at Aunt Melba's place, I visited my cousin Fred Hardin, home after twenty-seven months overseas, and his half-sister Florence, whose husband Wally was still in Europe. Aunt Melba told me that another cousin, George Boyes, was killed when the plane he piloted was shot down while fighting the Japanese at Midway. He was the family's only wartime fatality, a remarkable fact since we had many members in the service.

The visit primarily focused on the family's war-related activities, but as I asked about my family, Aunt Melba let it slip that Mother had given birth to a baby girl while I was in the POW camp. When she realized I didn't know about the blessed event, she begged me, "Please don't tell your mother you learned the news from me." I took the request to heart.

After visiting the Barneses, I dropped in on MarDean Dalley Ririe, my new sister-in-law, and learned Max was stationed at the Hawaiian headquarters of the U.S. Army Forces in the Middle Pacific (MidPac) where he claimed he was "replacing a WAC for active duty." As a Tech Sergeant he prepared messages for the high command staff, including a certain urgent top-secret communiqué regarding a major new weapon yet to be released against Japan. MarDean, a petite, sweet-tempered schoolteacher, was grateful that the army liked Max for talents other than his fighting ability. "I didn't have to worry about him being shot," MarDean would later recall.

I returned to base, packed up my clothes, bought my bus ticket for the next day, and cleaned up before tripping back up to J Street to see one of Salt Lake City's sweetest girls. Beth and I went to a Humphrey Bogart movie entitled, *Conflicts*. When I fell into bed late that night, I found myself wishing my home were closer to Salt Lake City.

Early the next morning, Friday, June 29, 1945, I caught a bus to Idaho Falls. On the way I sat by a young man about thirteen years old who was traveling to Ashton and Yellowstone National Park. He told me about his experiences in the Boy Scouts and in the Aaronic Priesthood of the Church.

At Pocatello, the bus stopped for the passengers to stretch their legs and I called home to ask my parents to pick me up in Idaho Falls. As we passed through Blackfoot the woman sitting across the aisle from me asked if I were a Latter-day Saint. "Yes," I replied. She beamed and confessed she could tell. I took her observation as a compliment.

My family met me at the bus station, Dad, Mother, Carma, Wayne, Jim, and my new sister Verna Elaine, who looked more like Mother than anyone else and was the prettiest baby I had ever seen. As Aunt Melba requested, I feigned surprise when Mother introduced Elaine to me and, try as I might, I never gathered the courage to tell her differently before she died twelve years later.

In Ririe, the car pulled into the driveway of our newly remodeled home and I barely recognized it. In my absence Mother had designed several additions and supervised their construction. That afternoon Wayne, Jim, and Carma took me for a ride on the new tractor, and I was impressed with Wayne's driving ability. While my life had come to a complete stop the past year, my family's hadn't and it surprised me.

That evening I crossed the street and dropped in on our longtime neighbors, the Bush family, and learned that Alf, the father, had been killed in a gun accident near his farm a few months earlier. His son Dean was seriously wounded in military action in France.

Vivian, Alf's wife, was heartbroken and had aged considerably but was as hospitable and thoughtful as I remembered from my youth. As I returned home, I felt extremely blessed to have found both my parents still alive and well. The day had been one of the happiest days of my entire life.

During the war the army sent captured German POWs to the Snake River valley to work on farms. A branch of Camp Rupert, a POW camp near Paul, Idaho, was only ten miles from Ririe. The POWs lived in tents and were trucked to and from the fields morning and night in crews of 15 men to farmers who requested help harvesting their crops.

Being short handed, my father often requested crews. One hot afternoon the guard sat in the cool shade of a large tree on the edge of the ditch bank and fell fast asleep. He awoke to find a German POW sighting down the barrel of his rifle. When the POW realized the guard was awake, he smiled and handed him the gun. "Why didn't he escape?" Wayne asked Dad when he heard about the incident. "Why would he?" Dad replied. "He is getting better treatment here than he would receive in the war in Europe."

Like a great many of their neighbors, my family acquired a decided bias against the German POWs. They thought most of them were pompous and lazy, and that the government had coddled them. One POW, assigned to thin sugar beets, a miserable, backbreaking job, said to my uncle Hy Lovell as he stood up to stretch, "Hitler told us we would cross the United States, but he didn't say it would be on our hands and knees."

The Relief Society sisters of the Ririe Ward often baked bread for the POW camp, my mother included, but Mother fought back anger when she saw a neighbor woman carrying refreshments to German prisoners working on her farm. As it turned out, Americans' kindness to the German POWs didn't go unappreciated. Years later the *Improvement Era*, the Church's magazine for members, published a letter of gratitude written by one of the German ex-POWs who had later joined the Church. Undoubtedly, having German POWs in close proximity kept alive my family's concern for me.

Saturday, June 30, 1945, Dad and I drove to Rigby to get our driver's licenses renewed. Hanging on the wall in the waiting area, I saw a wanted poster seeking a German POW who had escaped from Camp Rupert the prior December. A woman next to me in line noticed I was reading the poster and said, "The authorities should leave him alone, now that he's been gone so long." Instantly my blood boiled. Without saying a word I pivoted on my heels and exited the building to cool off. I was so angry I hardly knew how to contain myself. "People must think we were on a picnic," I steamed to Dad as we drove back to Ririe.

In Sunday School the next morning, I was asked to speak briefly about my POW experiences. It was the hardest talk I'd ever given because I was so happy to be home that I became choked up. I stumbled through it some way. When church was over, Uncle Hy and Aunt Velda invited my family to dinner. It was delicious; I only wished I could have eaten more of it. Afterwards, while our folks attended a funeral, my cousin Gayl and I washed the dirty dishes. As we chatted about Gayl's husband and the new baby she was expecting, I felt that I ought to be married myself.

When we got home after dinner, in a spur of the moment decision, my parents decided we should spend a couple of days fishing in Yellowstone National Park, since I was home on leave. The Park was 125 miles away and we arrived too late in the day to enter. As a rule, we camped in tents, but my folks splurged and we stayed in cabins. I didn't complain that we weren't sleeping in a leaky tent on the cold, hard ground.

Tuesday, July 2, we arose early and arrived at the entrance gate as soon as the Park opened. When the ranger saw I was a serviceman on leave, he admitted us free of charge. Intent on fishing, we only stopped once—to watch Old Faithful Geyser spout off—before heading directly to Fishing Bridge on Yellowstone Lake. As soon as we had rented cabins, Dad and I grabbed our tackle, ran to

ONE-MISSION MAN

the marina and checked out a boat. I hooked my first fat rainbow trout on the bridge while we waited for a boat. Within an hour we had nine beautiful trout lying in the hull.

> **ON JULY 4, 1945,** the U.S. government signed a secret agreement with England to use the atomic bomb on Japan. The following day General McArthur announced the Philippine Islands were liberated.
>
> On Sunday, July 15, 1945, President Truman joined British Prime Minister Winston Churchill and Soviet leader Josef Stalin in Potsdam, Germany, beginning a 17-day conference to discuss the administration of defeated Germany and devise plans for continuing the war against Japan. Gone was the goodwill of former wartime conferences as each nation, now suspicious of the others' motives, brazenly sought to promote its own interests.
>
> Late on the afternoon of Tuesday, July 24, 1945, following a particularly controversial session, Truman casually mentioned to Stalin that the U.S. had a new weapon of "unusual destructive force." Two days later, Friday, July 26, 1945, a half a world away, the cruiser, *Indianapolis*, delivered Little Boy, the U-235 section of the atomic bomb to the island of Tinian in the Pacific. That afternoon, President Truman issued a statement outlining the Potsdam Declaration as a basis for Japan's surrender and threatened stronger air attacks unless Japan complied. At 7:48 A.M. Berlin time, Monday, July 31, 1945, Truman sent an urgent top-secret cable to Secretary of War Stimson giving him final go-ahead to drop the bomb.

By 1:00 p.m. the next day, we had caught 71 fish, not counting the ones we'd eaten, which was one over our combined limit. Dad gave away a couple of fish to Uncle Joe, who hadn't filled his limit. It was a good thing he had because when the ranger checked us out, Dad had trouble convincing him that six-year-old Jimmy had caught his limit. We didn't tell the ranger that I had helped him reel some of them in. At one point we were reeling two lines in at once.

Mother took the prize when she reeled in a fish that had another angler's spinner dangling from its lip.

On the way home from Yellowstone, we stopped at Rosie Powell's service station in Rexburg and were drinking cold soda pop when a man rushed in and yelled, "Rosie, my car's on fire." Rosie ran to the car and threw a bomb-like extinguisher on the fire. As I watched the smoke pouring out of the burned engine, I wished to myself the fire extinguisher in our B-17 on April 11, 1944, could have been as effective.

CHAPTER 24

Citizen Ririe

At 7:15 the evening of August 5, 1945, the flight crew of the *Enola Gay,* flying high above Hiroshima, Japan, opened its bay doors and dropped *Little Boy,* a single atomic bomb. The results were instantaneous: 80,000 people killed and sixty percent of Hiroshima leveled. Another 50,000 people died over the next few months.

Sixteen hours after the bomb hit, Truman released a statement to the world, indicating the U.S. was "prepared to obliterate" every Japanese enterprise unless they capitulated in complete unconditional surrender. No surrender was forthcoming. Four days later, on August 9, 1945, the U.S. dropped a second atomic bomb, code named *Fat Man,* on Nagasaki. On Tuesday, August 14, 1945, the Japanese government abruptly surrendered unconditionally.

Feelings of relief and excitement swept the country. The war was essentially over, but few young people my age were around town with whom I could celebrate. Anxious to mark the occasion, I borrowed the family car, picked up the first available girlfriends I could find, and we honked the horn long and loud as we drove through Ririe and on to Idaho Falls. Surprisingly, both towns were unbelievably quiet. I suppose residents had worked so hard to do their part in the war that they were content to just kneel and pray in thanks to God for its beneficent end.

A couple of days later, I ran into two women from church, Myrtle Ker and Jessie Moss. Myrtle had taught me in Primary. Gene, her son, was seriously wounded but Myrtle expressed no bitterness as she spoke jubilantly about the end of the war. "You just had to come home, because all of the children prayed so earnestly for your safe return," Myrtle said. Jessie, a young war bride whose husband Johnny was listed as missing in action, made an effort to congratulate me on my survival but broke down in tears while Sister Ker and I tried unsuccessfully to console her.

Late that afternoon Johnny's father, Alma Moss, called me on the telephone to welcome me home. He asked if I knew anything about Johnny's combat missions or his disappearance over Germany. Of course, I knew nothing. All I could do for that grieving father was tell him how sorry I was for his loss. I felt guilty that when I returned home on leave as a newly commissioned second lieutenant I had encouraged Johnny, who was about to be drafted, to join the Army Air Corps. I spoke enthusiastically about my exciting career, and I suspect Johnny may have opted for gunnery school in the Army Air Corps because of my glowing account, a thought that grieves me whenever it crosses my mind.

My leave about over, I asked the army for an extension to help Dad with the wheat harvest that was just getting underway and was granted three more days. Rocky drove up from Nevada and spent a couple of days with me in Ririe. We had a great time hunting, fishing, and double dating girls.

Rocky thought I was pretty nervy to ask for additional days of leave to help Dad. In retrospect, he was probably right, especially since I was so well treated while in the military, but when I considered how incredibly hard my father worked to produce crops during the war, I felt entirely justified. Hired help for farmers during the war was not the best, being mostly high school boys, and Dad couldn't begin to replace the work output of his three sons who had entered the military with hired hands. Any sacrifice I could bear was small in comparison to what Dad was doing.

During harvest, the farm was a buzz of activity. After a year of forced inactivity in Stalag Luft 1, longing to get on with life, hard work healed me deeply. Even physically demanding jobs such as irrigating and putting up hay were pleasures to perform. I would have paid the uttermost farthing during that wasted year if the Germans had given us honest work to keep us busy.

On September 2, 1945, the official end of the war came quietly on the deck of the battleship Missouri, docked in Tokyo Bay, when Japanese foreign minister Mamoru Shigemitsu ceremoniously signed the document of capitulation. Until the Japanese surrender I fully expected to finish my leave, be reassigned to another crew, and be deployed to the Pacific Theatre.

After my restful and much appreciated leave, the army sent me to Santa Monica, California, where they leased beach front hotels to provide rest and recuperation billets for soldiers returning from combat. For a couple of weeks we lazed in the sand and enjoyed Army sponsored excursions to the Hayden Planetarium, Chinatown, and Los Angeles. My favorite excursion was a deep sea fishing trip on the Pacific Ocean.

One weekend Clive came up from San Diego where the Navy had stationed him. He complained bitterly that several detachments had been assigned to ships and sent to exciting places in the world but he wasn't part of any of them. What he had envisioned as a great adventure turned out to be boring duty on a training ship, scarcely out of sight of the San Diego harbor. That he was dissatisfied with Navy life was no surprise to me, given we had grown up landlubbers. Unsympathetic of his angst, my parents rejoiced that the only battle he fought was against San Diego traffic.

After the rest camp—which I enjoyed but really didn't need—the army again sent me to Santa Ana Army Air Force Base. After a few months I was asked if I wanted to pursue a career in the Army, and when I politely declined, preparations for my release kicked into high gear. Following the requisite physical examinations, record updates, and explanations of veterans' benefits, including the educational benefits provided by the GI Bill of Rights, my contingent separated from the service and I was placed on inactive reserve on December 16, 1945.

Shortly before departing Santa Ana, I ran into Thorland Summers, a soldier from my hometown who was also leaving the service. Learning I was heading home, Thorland invited me to ride home with him in the used car he had purchased a day earlier. As this would save me the trouble and expense of taking the train or bus home, I accepted the invitation.

We began the one-thousand-mile trip in the early afternoon and had no sooner gotten underway when Thorland proposed I drive his car. Within minutes I realized the used car dealer had taken Thorland for a sucker. The steering was loose and the car meandered wildly. To avoid over correcting I fought the monster from the moment I sat in the driver's seat. In fact, I couldn't have been busier if I had been in a race car on the Laguna Seca racetrack.

Thorland had fought in several battles in the European Theatre. As we drove along we shared war experiences, but he must have stayed awake the night before. After an hour conversing with me he crawled into the back seat and fell asleep. After driving about three hundred miles I pulled over, woke Thorland, and asked him to relieve me, but I was too tense to sleep. After tossing and turning for about thirty minutes, Thorland again asked me to drive, and I finished the journey in the driver's seat.

After my release from the Army, I had enough savings to pay cash for an automobile. With checkbook in hand, I walked into the Swager Motor Company in Rigby, expecting to buy a used vehicle. As I entered the showroom, Mr. Swager greeted me. He was standing by two brand new Fords. "I'm glad you came in," he said. "I am between the proverbial hard place and a rock." He explained the cars were the first he had been able to buy for several months, because the Ford Motor Company's output had been devoted to the military effort during the war. "I have hundreds of applicants wanting to purchase a new automobile," he explained, "but I don't dare offer these cars to any of them, for fear of infuriating the others. But I can sell a car to you since you are an ex-POW, and no one will get mad at me." So I bought a new car.

While waiting for my academic training under the GI Bill, I worked on my family's farm and initiated an active search for a wife. My first flame, Beth Hamblin, married shortly after my return from Germany, and broke my heart. Next, my attention turned to Joanne Heileson, a petite and very attractive girl from Tetonia, Idaho. I felt deeply in love with her and we became engaged.

While teaching school during our courtship Joanne boarded with a family from Ammon, Idaho, who had a son approximately Joanne's age. Not long after I proposed, Joanne broke off the engagement and returned my ring, but not my jacket on which the Russians had written "American" across the back—I expect it must have made her husband happy whenever she wore it. I was devastated. And to add insult to injury, Ammon was our high school rival and always seemed to beat Ririe High teams.

Demoralized and depressed about my lost love, one night I had a forceful impression that I shouldn't worry because I was to marry a girl named Ruth. At the time I knew only one eligible girl named Ruth. Ruth Rowan was a pretty girl from Ririe, attending the University of Utah. Would she become my Ruth?

Meanwhile, I began to consider a profession. Dad would have taken me into the farming business with him, but I decided to seek a college degree before choosing a vocation. Prior to the war I thought I might become a teacher and studied in the Department of Education at Ricks College. The study of chemistry also appealed to me.

Incentives tempted me to consider enrolling in several universities in Utah. My army friend Rocky attended the University of Utah, as did Ruth Rowan and her sister Peggy. Utah State University was the happy home of a high school buddy, Wendell Harris. Brigham Young University was the choice of my cousin, Ray Lovell. Filled with indecision, I armed myself with college catalogues from all three universities and drove to Utah determined to visit each school and choose one of them.

I first drove to BYU, the furthest school, planning to visit the other two on my return to Idaho. As I walked down a hall in one of the campus buildings, an attractive blonde hailed me with a very friendly, "Hello, Dave Ririe." At first I didn't remember her, but after a few moments I recalled she was Jody Irwin, from San Bernardino, whom I had met briefly at church while stationed at Victorville. She was gorgeous and I was smitten. I didn't need to stop at the other two universities. I walked directly to the registration area feeling like the Prophet Brigham Young had when he first surveyed the Salt Lake Valley and said, "This is the right place."

In the registration area, I approached the chemistry department table, introduced myself to Professor Nicholes, the head of the department, and announced my desire to register. Since I was starting in the middle of the school year, some classes were already full, others required pre-requisites I hadn't taken or that were only offered in the first quarter. Therefore, Professor Nicholes suggested I take a class entitled "Soil Fertility" and referred me to Dr. Thomas L. Martin, head of the agronomy department.

I could not know then how much influence Dr. Martin would have on my life. In his energetic, high-pitched voice, with a trace of a British accent, Dr. Martin visited with me briefly, signed me up for his class, then asked, "What kind of grades did you make at Ricks College?"

"All As and Bs," I answered.

"Good," he said. "We'll send you East to graduate school when you finish here."

During the spring of 1946, I began to court Jody earnestly and in one of our many conversations I learned her full name was Ruth Joanne Irwin. I had found my Ruth! On September 6, 1946, we were married in the Idaho Falls LDS Temple for time and all eternity. A year and a half later, on January 5, 1948, our first son James Irwin was born. Over the next few years, four more children joined our family: John Thomas in 1949, Nancy in 1952, Marianne in 1957, and David Wendell in 1961.

In June of 1948 I graduated from Brigham Young University with a Bachelor of Science degree in agronomy. True to his word, Dr. Martin obtained a fellowship for me to study for a PhD degree in the Soils Department of Rutgers University, the land grant college of New Jersey.

When I consider my life, including my military career which culminated in an honorable discharge and my education which led to a doctorate in soil science, made possible by the generosity of the United States Government and a great support team composed of a beautiful wife, my family, teachers, associates, and the grace of a merciful God, I regard myself to be a very blessed man. Life has a way of working out if you work hard, stay on course, and have faith.

AFTERWORD

My original flight crew and POW friend, Rocky Matheson, established themselves in meaningful careers. Edd Ely finished a career in the Army Air Corps and flew with the Strategic Air Force, obtaining the rank of colonel. Bill Ellis enrolled in flight training, received his pilot's wings, served a tour in Italy, and became a successful lawyer and the mayor of Aransas Pass, Texas. Fred Pratt started his own used car business in Los Angeles, California. John Russell completed a successful career with the Pacific Telephone Company in Redding, California. Vincent Muffoletto owned an accounting firm in Buffalo, New York. Rocky became a medical doctor and practiced in Salt Lake City.

Of the four lost enlisted men of *The Expectant Father* crew, Leo K. Kornoely, Constantine G. Scourbys, Harvey L. Ringer and Thomas Neill, only Ringer's body was recovered. His remains washed up on the shore near a town on the Baltic Sea, and thoughtful Germans buried him. Years later his relatives became aware of his fate and his body was returned in 1995 to Philmont, New York, and placed in a final resting place. To commemorate the occasion, Governor George Pataki signed a resolution praising him.

SOURCE NOTES

Chapter 1

1. Flight was lengthy: Freeman, *The Mighty Eighth*, 133.; "Missing Air Crew Report, 3776,"122472.
2. Posen, headquarters of Germany's 21st Wehrkreise (Military Region): *Atlas of Nazi Germany*, 69.
3. Crucial time for Allies: Miller, *Masters of the Air*, 5.
4. Brits resorted to high-altitude strategic bombing: Ibid, 6.
5. Daylight bombings…so disastrous Royal Air Force resorted to night bombings: Ibid, 7.
6. Precision bombing abandoned: Ibid, 8.
7. United States Army Air Corps held to different strategy: Ibid, 8.
8. Both British and American philosophies proved disastrous: Neillands, *The Bomber War*, 133.
9. The Eighth Air Force was an elite outfit: Miller, 4.
10. Roosevelt's 1943 order ended voluntary enlistments: Ibid, 4.
11. We were in the left wing position of element one of Group A: "Missing Air Crew Report of the U.S. Army Air Forces, 3776," 12240.
12. Over 900 B-17s and B-24s from the Eighth Air Force were to annihilate Focke-Wulf and Junkers aircraft production centers in Eastern Germany: Freeman, *The Mighty Eighth*, 133.
13. Two hundred and seventy-four B-17s from the Third Bombardment Division formed the strike force: Hammel, *Air War Europa Chronology*, 278.
14. When we reached Danish Peninsula, our P-51 fighter escort, Mission 92: www.388bg.org.
15. Twenty-five ME 109 twin-engine fighter planes attacked: Ibid, 92.
16. Weather conditions prevented us from bombing Posen: David Ririe, *The Life Story of David Ririe (cited hereafter as LSDR)*, 68.
17. Rostock's anti-aircraft batteries saw us: Ibid, 68.
18. Third shot hit with a jolt: Ibid, 68.
19. The tail was riddled: Ibid, 68.
20. Minutes later we lost an engine: Ibid, 68.
21. Ten or twelve FW 190 German fighter planes, Mission 92: www.388bg.org.
22. *Shoo Shoo Baby*, serial number 42-32003: Ibid, 92.
23. An FW 190 suddenly flew up from below: *LSDR*, 68.
24. Flames engulfed entire plane behind the radio compartment, Mission 92: "Missing Air Crew Report, 3776,"12240.
25. Crash-landed on the Anti Aircraft Gunner Training School, Defense Unit Two military reservation at Bad Doberan, near Rerik in Mecklenburg, Germany: Ibid, 12240.

26. Ellis, in confused terror . . . kicked and stomped on the object that lay beneath him: Ellis, *Wartime Memories*, stalagluft1.html.
27. Norden bombsight: Charles Hudson, Quoted in Neillands, 169.
28. Serial number 42-97241, Mission 92: Krepinki, Quoted in www.388bg.org.
29. Ellis was still bleeding from the gash on the forehead, Ellis, *Wartime Memories*, stalagluft1.html.
30. In the middle of the night I awoke: Ririe, *LSDR*, 69.
31. You will return home rejoicing: Call, *David Ririe Patriarchal Blessing*, (cited hereafter as *DRPB*), 2.

Chapter 2

1. Warren G. Harding, White House: www.whitehouse.gov/about/presidents/warrenharding.
2. Impressive two-story stone house: *Post Register*, Quoted by Hoggan in *Life Story of David Ririe, 1860-1919*, 9.
3. Idaho birth certificate shows my birthday as March, 19, 1922: *Certificate of Birth*, State Registrar of Vital Statistics, State of Idaho, 1922.
4. Granite Creek, a sparsely populated farming area twenty-miles to the east of Ririe: N48° 0.6276′, W116° 40.2286′.
5. Low rolling hills known as Antelope Flats: N43° 42.1794′, W110° 38.8958′.
6. Conant Valley: N43° 28.9783′, W111° 26.0304′.
7. Clive Perry joined the family April 4, 1927: Ririe, Clive, *Notable Dates*, 1; Certificate of Birth, State Registrar of Vital Statistics, State of Idaho, 1927.
8. Anne Ririe, July 12, 1929- July 15, 1929: buried in Ririe-Shelton Cemetery, Ririe, Idaho, Certificate of Birth, State Registrar of Vital Statistics, State of Idaho, 1929.
9. Six-month proselyting mission in Trenton, New Jersey, and Allentown, Pennsylvania: Ririe, James E., *My Life Story*, 3.
10. I was baptized in a ditch flowing from the Farmer's Friend Canal: *LSRD*, 14.
11. The Ririe Ward at the end of 1930 had 719 members, 196 of which were children: Jensen, *Encyclopedic History of the Church*, 710.
12. Andrew Young, ran out of feed and persuaded Dad to buy his 100-head ewe flock: Ririe, Max, *My Life Story*, 1.
13. Hyrum T. Moss, Ririe Ward bishop: Jensen, 710.
14. President of the Ririe Lions Club, Ririe Grain Growers, and Potato Cooperative: *Post Register*, obituary, October 15, 1973.
15. Mutual Improvement Association (MIA): youth organization of Church of Jesus Christ of Latter-day Saints.
16. Aaronic Priesthood. In the LDS Church a young man who has been baptized and confirmed a member and is worthy may be ordained to the office of a deacon when he is 12 years old and assigned to a quorum of deacons. Duties include passing sacrament, maintain church grounds and collect fast offerings. Each quorum is presided over by a president: *Gospel Principles*, 75.
17. Carma Ririe Fillmore, born May 22, 1931: Certificate of Birth, State Registrar of Vital Statistics, State of Idaho, 1931.
18. Wayne J. Ririe, born August 1, 1933: Certificate of Birth, State Registrar of Vital Statistics, State of Idaho, 1933.
19. James A. Ririe, born November 30, 1939: Certificate of Birth, State Registrar of Vital Statistics, State of Idaho, 1939.

Chapter 3

1. Bishop of the Ririe Ward in 1935, James E. Ririe: *Post Register*, obituary, October 15, 1973.
2. Ward Teaching program of LDS Church, now known as Home Teaching program; a home teacher is "a priesthood holder who, with a companion, visits assigned homes each month to assist and support the visited family in their efforts to live the principles taught by Jesus Christ" : Quoted on http://newsroom.lds.org/article/home-teacher.
3. Little boy stopped breathing after inhaling carbon monoxide: Verna Ririe, *History of Verna Fanny Perry Ririe*, 4.
4. Ricks College in Rexburg, Idaho, now Brigham Young University-Idaho: N43° 49.3833', W111° 47.1167'.
5. Hyrum Manwaring (1877-1956) was a member of the Ricks College, now Brigham Young University-Idaho, staff from 1914 to 1930. From 1930 to 1944 he served as the school's president: www.byui.edu/aboutbyui/legacy.htm.
6. Oswald Christensen (1881-1960), Professor, Ricks College; LDS stake patriarch; counselor, LDS stake presidency: www.wikipedia.org.
7. Leslie Thomas Perry (1885-1966), son of Henry Morgan Perry and Fannie Young: Perry Family records.
8. Sunday, December 7, 1941, Japan attacked U.S. military forces at Pearl Harbor, Hawaii; Philippine, Midway Islands: Hammel, 37.
9. The LDS Church only called older men as missionaries during World War II: *The Deseret News 2011 Church News Almanac*, 292.
10. James E. Ririe served in the Rigby Stake, counselor to President George Christensen: *Post Register*, obituary, October 15, 1973.

Chapter 4

1. "Wayne, my little pal": Wayne Ririe, *Times and Seasons of My Life*, 14.
2. "I sure hate to see you go": *LSDR*, 54.
3. "Don't Get Around Much Anymore," Lyrics by Sidney Russell: www.wikipeia.org.

Chapter 5

1. British and American troops landed on the island of Sicily: Hammel, 150.

Chapter 6

1. Norden bomb sight, a top-secret analog computer: Neillands, 169.
2. Automatic Flight Control Equipment (AFCE): Ibid, 169.
3. A similar name mix-up: "Notable Dates," Clive Ririe, 2.

Chapter 7

1. U.S. 7th Army captured Palermo: Hammel, 156.
2. Operation Gomorrah: Ibid, 158.
3. Ill-fated air raid on Ploesti, Romania: Ibid, 163.
4. Italy signs armistice, Ibid, 179.
5. Mussolini escapes from prison in daring raid: www.ww2timeline.info
6. Thirteen Articles of Faith: *History of the Church*, Vol. 4, 535-541.

Chapter 8

1. 246 B-17 and B-24 bombers attacked Gdynia and Danzig: Hammel, 194.
2. Black Thursday: Ibid, 196.
3. Battle of Berlin approved: www.ww2timeline.info.
4. British bombers attacked Mannheim and Ludwigshafen, Germany: Ibid.
5. Churchill and Roosevelt were meeting with Chinese President Chiang Kai-shek in Cairo, Egypt: Hammel, 209.
6. British bombers attacked Berlin: www.ww2timeline.info.

Chapter 9

1. Built at a cost of $204,370 each: Ethell, *Bombers of World War II*, 45.
2. A normal average bomb load: Neillands, 175.
3. 12,677 B-17s sent to Europe: Ethell, *Bombers of World War II*, 45.
4. U.S. organized 29,370 bombardment crews: Ibid.
5. B-17 required ten men to operate: Neillands, , 174.
6. B-17G came equipped with chin turret: Ibid, 175.
7. Tours extended: Ibid, 174.
8. Bombers attacked Brunswick: Hammel, 237.
9. Bombers attacked Emden: Ibid, 241.
10. Bombers attack Frankfurt am Main: Ibid, 241.
11. Eight Air Force B-17s attacked Frankfurt: Ibid, 243.
12. 1st Bombardment Division B-17s attack Bruswick: Ibid, 243.
13. Bombers attack, Frankfurt am Main: Ibid, 243.
14. 1st Bombardment Division B-17s attack Frankfurt am Main: Ibid, 244.
15. The *Big Week* bombing offensive: Ibid, 248.
16. Coordinated attack by Eighth and Fifteenth divisions: Ibid, 250.
17. Coordinated attack by Eighth and Third: Ibid, 252.
18. Twenty-four percent loss: Ibid, 254.
19. Two hundred fifteen B-17s from Third division attacked Brunswick: Ibid, 255.
20. Five hundred and twenty American bombers attack Berlin: Ibid, 258.

Chapter 10

1. Serial number 42-97241, MACR 3776, *The 388th at War*, Improvements of B-17G: Neillands, 175 .
2. Unpainted planes attracted enemy's attention: Freeman, *The Mighty Eighth*, 132.
3. Of airfields: Ibid, 54.
4. The location of the 388th bomb group: Ibid, 154.
5. Colonel William B. David, CO from February 1, 1943 – October 6, 1944: Freeman, *The Mighty Eighth*, 255.
6. British suffer *operational defeat* and called bombing of Berlin quits: www.ww2timeline.info

Chapter 11

1. Met Dad three miles from Ririe: Wayne Ririe, *Times and Seasons of My Life*, 15.
2. "My whole world collapsed": Ibid, 15.
3. Each had a lucid dream: Ibid, 15.
4. Return home rejoicing: *DRPB*, 2; Wayne Ririe, *Times and Seasons of My Life*, 16; Wayne Ririe, *Growing Up in a Spud Town*, 111.

5. Our faith was tested and family ties welded together: Carma Filmore, "The Life Story of Carma Ririe Filmore,"6.
6. *Post Register* newspaper clipping: Wayne Ririe, *Times and Seasons of My Life*, 16.
7. Transfer to Dulag Luft, Oberusel: "Missing Air Crew Report, 3776", 122468.
8. Dulag Luft existed to extract information: Simmons, Kriegie.
9. Number of captured airmen escalated: Ibid.

Chapter 12

1. Hitler's birthday is April 20: Giblin, *The Life and Death of Adolf Hitler*, 4.
2. Stalag Luft 1, a camp for U.S. Army Air Force and Royal Air Force officers: Miller, 511.
3. L-shape configuration: Zemke/Freeman, *Zemke's Stalag*, 20.
4. Luftwaffe maintained an antiaircraft artillery school: Ibid, 20.
5. Polish slave laborers: Ibid, 20.
6. Trigger-happy guards: Hatton, 2.
7. North 1 built for Hitler Youth activities: Hatton, "American Prisoners of War in Germany," 1.
8. Frame buildings built of rough-hewn lumber: Ibid, 1.
9. In the beginning, Rocky and I were assigned to Room 5 of Barrack 11 in the North 1 Compound with Gordon L. Anderson, California; Herbert J. Bunde, Minnesota; J.P. Downey, Michigan; Robert H. Johnson, Iowa; Albert R. Johnson, Georgia; Reginald R. Miner, New Jersey; J.B. Patterson, Kansas; Kenneth C. Reimer, Ilinois; A.I I. Strom, Ilinois; Fernando A. Tellez, California; Garold D. Tessman, Michigan; and Fred D. Veal, Florida www.merkki.com.
10. In late 1944 we were transferred to Room 6, Barrack 1, with 16 men: Henry T. Bengis, New York; Francis J. Brodzik, New York; Jacob R. Brown, Texas; Harold L. Cooke, Indiana; John M. Coppinger, Colorado; Tom F. Ganno, New Jersey; Bernard J. Gillespie, Iowa; Paul W. Mattox, Florida; Basil D. Morris, Michigan; Charles F. Popken, New Jersey; Frank G. Pringle, California; William H. Ritzema, Michigan; John J. Ryczek, New York; Francis P. Smith, Colorado; William B. Snead, Texas; and Frank B. Thompson, Utah: www.merkki.com.
11. Colonel Byerly, Senior American Officer: Hatton, 1.
12. Provisional Wing maintained order: Zemke/Freeman, 15.
13. Swiss government, the camp's *Protecting Power:* Hatton, 3.
14. Swiss government inspected camp every four months, Ibid, 3.
15. YMCA inspected Stalag Luft 1 every four months: Ibid, 3.
16. Red Cross supplied food, blankets, clothing: Ibid, 3.
17. YMCA supplied sports equipment and requested supplies: Ibid, 3.
18. Red Cross food distributed at rate of one parcel per POW per week: Ibid, 3.
19. Provisional Wing administration divisions: Zemke/Freeman, 23.
20. Compounds organized internally: Ibid, 24.

Chapter 13

1. The war got serious: Brinkley, *World War II The Allied Counteroffensive*, 187.
2. Unauthorized secret newssheet, the *Pow-Wow*: Zemke/Freeman, 32.
3. A copy of *Pow-Wow* found in Llowell Bennett's room: Ibid, 33.
4. Secret radios, Morse code keyer: Ibid, 33.
5. RAF radiomen built radio: Ibid, 33.
6. Concealed receiver between wall panels: Ibid, 33.
7. Two barely discernible holes: Ibid, 33.
8. D.J. Kilgallen transcribed the news: Ibid, 34.

9. Warrant Officer R.R. Drummond' watch: Ibid, 35.
10. Sent a copy to each compound: Ibid.
11. POWs read the news silently in groups of three: Ibid.
12. None of the guards were charged: Ibid.
13. Two days in a small lifeboat: *Stars and Stripes*, May 1945.
14. Before the guards finished their count: www.merkki.com
15. Spicer recalled the men to his barracks: Ibid.
16. Only required to salute officers of higher rank: Ibid.
17. "Don't let them fool you": Ibid.
18. Defaming the German character: Ibid.
19. Execution by a firing squad: Zemke/Freeman, 44.
20. The Germans didn't issue clothing: Hatton, 3.
21. Germans confiscated clothing resembling civilian attire: Ibid.
22. Redistribution of uniforms in February 1945: Ibid.

Chapter 14

1. Central Security Committee: Zemke/Freeman, 35.
2. Guard to prisoner ratio: Ibid, 26, 40.
3. Tunneling the only logical way of escaping: Ibid, 35.
4. The barracks were built about eighteen inches above the ground: Richard, *Kriegie*, 67.
5. Stooging system: Durand, *Stalag Luft III*, 272.
6. "Goon's up": Miller, 397.
7. "Goon," German Officer or Noncom: Durand, 89.
8. Moles: Miller, 397.
9. 19 ½ in the air and 10 ½ on the ground: Freeman, *The Mighty Eighth*, 278.
10. P-51 Mustang lost a wing: Zemke/Freeman, 2.
11. Gabreski, an air ace who shot down 28 enemy fighters: Freeman, *The Mighty Eighth*, 272.
12. Major Gerald Johnson, an ace with 18 kills: Freeman, *The Mighty Eighth*, 278.
13. Gabreski and Johnson served with Zemke in the 56th Fighter Group's Thunderbolt outfit: Miller, 511.
14. Major Cyrus E. Manierre, OSS agent: www.specialforcesroh.com/awards-9432.html.
15. Battle of Bulge: Brinkley, 247.
16. Gnawing hunger: Zemke/Freeman, 21.
17. Meals: Ibid, 21.
18. Germans seldom gave us meat: Ibid, 21.
19. Weevils: Miller, 498.
20. Red Cross food parcels: Spiller, *Prisoners of Nazis*, 116.
21. Christmas 1944: Richardson, 87; Miller, 408.
22. Cigarettes valuable units of exchange: Richard, 63.
23. Roosevelt spoke to my family over the radio: Wayne Ririe, *Growing Up*, 103.
24. Ririe residents abandoned their farms and moved to California: Ibid, 103.
25. Wore tires until they were bald and slick: Ibid, 103.
26. "Everything was scarce": Ibid, 103.

27. Mother would give me one little cube of chocolate: James A Ririe, "The Life Story of James A Ririe," 1964.
28. Bomb dangling from a balloon: Ibid, 115.
29. Dean had been severely wounded at the Battle of the Bulge: Ibid, 116.
30. Small flag hanging in our living room window: Ibid, 102.
31. Mother was cheerful and optimistic: Ibid, 103.
32. Ririe had sent an unusually high number of young men to fight in the war: Ibid, 102.
33. Mother's life when she wasn't thinking and praying for her prisoner son: Clive Ririe, 3.
34. Oberst von Warnstedt replaced the commandant Oberst Sherer: Zemke/Freeman, 26.
35. Von Warnstedt installed a single wire fence: Ibid, 28.
36. Limit on the amount of food an individual could save from his Red Cross parcels: Ibid, 28

Chapter 15

1. Germans segregated the Jewish prisoners: Ibid.
2. British Roman Catholic priest allowed 100 Jewish men to worship: Hatch, *American Ex-POW*.
3. Ferrets, guards assigned to prevent escapes: Durand, 89.
4. British Bomber Command sent 659 bombers to attack Hanover: http://www.ww-2timeline.info.
5. Seventy divisions of the 1st Ukrainian Front crossed the Vistula River: Ibid.
6. The Soviets liberated Warsaw: Ibid.
7. Red Army reached the Oder River: Gilbert, *The Second World War*, 635.
8. Russians had the advantage: Brinkley, 319.
9. Became evident Germans were using seismographic equipment: Zemke/Freeman, 36.
10. Finish the tunnel before caving it in was a ploy: Ibid, 36.
11. 90 attempts to escape: Ibid, 35.
12. Legalized the shooting of escaped POWs without warning: Ibid, 28.
13. Oberst von Warnstadt was particularly liberal in his "shoot to kill" regulations: Ibid, 62.
14. British eventually forbidden from attempting escape: Ibid, 38.
15. Hitler planned to execute the Jewish POWs: Bussel, *My Private War*, 156.
16. Russian Advance created chaos: Zemke/Freeman, 65.
17. Dresden was hit by two massive air blows of firebombs: Miller, 434.
18. German turnip crop had failed: LSDR, 87.
19. We tended to sleep more and care less: Richard, 90.
20. Stopped talking about food: Ibid, 90.
21. Power lines were down: Zemke/Freeman, 91.
22. Cutting the daily loaf of bread became a revered ceremony: LSDR, 87.
23. Collection runs on Swedish Red Cross trucks: Zemke/Freeman, 65.
24. It was made known to me: Ririe, Verna. "History of Verna Fanny Perry Ririe.", 9.

Chapter 16

1. Red Cross parcels arrived: Zemke/Freeman, 65.
2. 90,000 parcels: Richard, 90.
3. Roosevelt died of a cerebral hemorrhage: McCullough, *Truman*, 345.
4. Stone administered the presidential oath to Harry S. Truman: Ibid, 347.
5. Nazi death camp, Ohrdruf-Nord: Ibid, 350.
6. 512 British bombers pummeled Potsdam: http://www.ww2timeline.info.
7. Truman gave his first address to Congress: McCullough, 358.
8. American troops reached Nuremburg: http://www.ww2timeline.info.
9. American bombers attacked Dresden: http://www.ww2timeline.info.
10. British and American troops met Soviet forces at Torgau: http://www.ww2timeline.info.
11. Eisenhower orders the U.S. 9th Army to suspend its march: Ibid.
12. United Nations Conference opened in San Francisco: McCullough, 376.
13. Himmler offers to surrender to western Allies: Ibid, 379.
14. British bombers and one hundred U.S. Mustang fighter planes destroyed Hitler's residence at Berchtesgaden: Gilbert, 672.
15. Younger guards disappeared from the camp: *LSDR*, 88.
16. American and British bombers flew overhead day and night: Ibid, 88.
17. Constant roar of Russian cannons: Richard, 91.
18. Dig slit trenches and foxholes near the barracks: Richard, 92.
19. Red Army was less than 25 miles away from Stalag Luft 1: Ibid, 92.
20. Allies captured Milan, Italy: Gilbert, 673.
21. Mussolini killed by Italian partisans: Ibid 676.
22. Oberst von Warnstedt receives orders to move the POWs to Hamburg: Zemke/Freeman, 75.
23. 150 mile Forced march: Ibid, 75.
24. Explosions at the Flak School and at the aerodrome: Richard, 93.
25. Hitler prepared his last will and testament, blamed Jews for the war: Gilbert, 677.
26. Soviet forces attacked Berlin and captured the Reichstag: Ibid, 681.
27. Hitler commits suicide: Gilbert, 681.
28. Germans left us without water or electricity: Zemke/Freeman, 91.

Chapter 17

1. Stalin officially announced the fall of Berlin: Gilbert, 683.
2. Zemke talked to the camp: Richard, 97.
3. Bodies of three women, a child, and a baby: Spiller, 119.
4. Two-dozen women strangled or shot: Miller, 513.
5. Frightened women and children appeared often at the gates: Zemke/Freeman, 90.
6. Barth's burgomeister administered poison to his family before ingesting it: Ibid: 86.
7. 2,000 emaciated and dying Greek and French civilian prisoners: Ibid, 102; Spiller, 120.
8. One million land, sea and air troops in Holland, Denmark, and northern Germany surrender: http://www.ww2timeline.info.
9. British and Canadian advance at Wismar, Germany, on the Elbe River: Zemke/Freeman, 104.

10. Allies had agreed all liberated POWs would travel by train eastward to the port of Odessa: Ibid, 106.
11. Agreement signed by Churchill and Roosevelt at Yalta prohibited Anglo-Americans from flying over Russian-held territory: Richard, 97.

Chapter 18

1. Colonel Byerly and two British officers flew to England: Zemke/Freeman, 107.
2. Zemke provided 250 daily passes to men: Zemke/Freeman, 107.
3. Colonel General Gustaf Jodl, Chief of Staff of the German Army, signed German unconditional surrender paperwork in Reims, France: Miller, 506; Gilbert, 689.
4. A troupe of Russian singers and dancers entertained us: Zemke/Freeman, 106.
5. 300 POWs, miserable and annoyed by the forced inactivity, abandoned camp: Miller, 514.
6. Churchill wanted to make the announcement of Germany's capitulation at once: McCullough, 381.
7. All three allies announce end of war in Europe at the same time: Ibid.
8. Truman called on Japan to surrender: Ibid, 382.

Chapter 19

1. 9,000 POWs delivered to the British at Wismar within two days: Zemke/Freeman, 107.
2. Borisov was furious the two officers devised evacuation plans without first consulting Moscow: Ibid, 108.
3. Russians began jailing all American and British airmen caught without passes: Ibid, 110.
4. Zemke gave us a severe tongue-lashing. It was the usual line, "Stand by, men": Ibid, 110.
5. Borisov appointed Zemke to take charge of all POWs: Ibid, 105.
6. Zemke, disturbed that POWs were leaving camp without passes, canceled all marching parties: Ibid, 110.
7. Zemke discovered 730 Americans missing of the 7,725 in camp: Ibid, 110.
8. U.S. 7th Airborne Corps had been ordered to organize air transport to evacuate Stalag Luft 1: Ibid, 111.
9. Russians still refused to give permission for aircraft to fly over the Soviet-held combat zone: Ibid, 111.
10. Weir called on Colonel General Pavel Batov, commander of the 65th Red Army: Ibid, 111.
11. Russians agreed to a POW airlift if the Americans surrender former Red Army commander Andrei Vlasov: Miller, 515.
12. Borisov cleared 20-kilometer wide flight path: Zemke/Freeman, 111.
13. First evacuation planes arrive May 12: Ibid.

Chapter 20

1. Cologne a ravished ruin: Wheal, *A Dictionary of the Second World War*, 103.
2. Camp Lucky Strike: www.skylighters.org/special/cigcamps/cmplstrk.html.
3. Hitler ordered all Allied prisoners executed: *Stars and Stripes*, May 1945.
4. Colonel Spicer sentenced to death for pep talk: *Stars and Stripes*, May 1945.

5. French Foreign Minister Pierre Laval: Wheal, 271.
6. "On the Road to Mandalay," Lyrics by Oley Speaks, popularized by Peter Dawson: www.wikipedia.org.
7. "Believe Me If All Those Endearing Young Charms," a 19th century Irish folk song, lyrics by Thomas Moore: www.wikipedia.org.
8. Overseas Motion Picture Service: Brinkley, 475.
9. Newspaper article featured interviews with Gabrieski and Zemke: *Stars and Stripes*, May 1945.

Chapter 21

1. Demobilization Plan point system: Sharp, "Bring the Boys Home," Chapter 4, UA917U5S5.
2. Douglas A-26 Invader: Ethell, *Air Command*, 153.
3. United Service Organization shows: Brinkley, 475.
4. "One hundred dollars." In 1944 a second lieutenant received $1,800 per year: Ethell, *Air Command*, 6.

Chapter 22

1. SS Excelsior: Charles, *Troopships of World War II*, 24.

Chapter 23

1. Committee on the S-1 Manhattan Project included Stimpson; James Conant Bryant, president, Harvard and chairman, National Defense Research Committee; Karl T. Compton, president, MIT; Vannevar Bush, president, Carnegie Institute and director of Office of Scientific Research and Development; Ralph A. Bard, Under Secretary of the Navy; George L. Harrison, president, New York Life Insurance; Jimmy Byrnes represented President Truman. Joining the committee members was an advisory panel of four physicists charged with developing the atomic bomb: Enrico Fermi and Arthur H Compton, of the University of Chicago; Ernest O. Lawrence, of the radiation laboratory at the University of California at Berkeley; and J. Robert Oppenheimer, head of the Los Alamos laboratory, where the bomb was being created. Listed by McCullough, 390.
2. Three recommendations on atomic bomb: Ibid, 391.
3. Estimates of the explosive force of atomic bomb: Ibid, 392.
4. Booty tent, name of location where returning soldiers registered contraband: www.skylighters.org/special/cigcamps/cmplstrk.html.
5. Obliteration by firebombs: McCullough, 393.
6. Dresden firebombing: Brinkley, 266.
7. Precision bombing wouldn't work in Japan: McCullough, 393.
8. Japs on Okinawa were exterminated: Gilbert, 700.
9. Philippine Islands liberated: Gilbert, 702.
10. Camp Rupert: Jaehn, *Unlikely Harvestors*, 46.
11. Ririe Ward often baked bread for POW camp: Wayne Ririe, *Growing Up*, 111.
12. A crew of German POWs arrived at my parent's farm: Ibid, 112.
13. Letter of gratitude written by one of the ex-POWs: Ibid.
14. Truman joined Churchill and Stalin in Potsdam, Germany: McCullough, 449.
15. Truman casually mentioned to Stalin that the U.S. has a new weapon of "unusual destructive force": Ibid, 449.

16. *Indianapolis*, delivered *Little Boy*, the U-235 section of the atomic bomb to the island of Tinian in the Pacific: Ibid, 460.
17. Truman threatened stronger air attacks unless complied: Ibid, 447.

Chapter 24

1. *Enola Gay* dropped *Little Boy*, a single atomic bomb: Gilbert, 712.
2. 80,000 people killed and 60 percent of Hiroshima leveled, Ibid, 712.
3. U.S. was "prepared to obliterate" every Japanese enterprise: McCullough, 455.
4. U.S. dropped a second atomic bomb, code named *Fat Man*, on Nagasaki: Ibid, 457.
5. The Japanese government abruptly surrendered unconditionally: Ibid, 458.
6. Shigemitsu ceremoniously signed the document of capitulation: Gilbert, 722.

BIBLIOGRAPHY

BOOKS

Anderson, Barbara Louise Ririe. Ririe Memories. *The Life Histories and Genealogy of the Families of James and Ann Boyack Ririe 1750-1964*. Provo, Utah: Brigham Young University Press, 1964.

Bowman, Martin. *The Mighty Eighth at War. The USAAF 8th Air Force Bombers Versus the Luftwaffe, 1943-1945*. Barnsley, England: Pen and Sword, 2010.

Brinkley, Douglas. *World War II. The Allied Counteroffensive, 1942-1945*. New York: Times Books, 2003.

Bussel, Norman. *My Private War*. New York: Pegasus Books, 2008

Charles, Roland, W. *Troopships of World War II*. Washington D.C.: Army Transportation Association, 1947.

Deseret News 2011 Church News Almanac. Salt Lake City, UT: Deseret News, 2011.

Dugan, James. *The Great Iron Ship*. Kingsport, Tennessee: Kingsport Press, 1953.

Durand, Arthur A. *Stalag Luft III. The Secret Story*. Baton Rouge, Louisiana: Louisiana State University Press, 1988.

Ethell, Jeffery L. *Air Command. Fighters and Bombers of World War II*. Ann Arbor, Michigan: Lowell & B. Hould Publishers, 1997.

Ethell, Jeffery L. *Bombers of World War II*. Ann Arbor, Michigan: Lowell & B. Hould Publishers, 1996.

Ethell, Jeffery L., and Robert Sand. *World War II Fighters*. ST. Paul, Minnesota: MBI Publishing Company, 1991, 2002.

Freeman, Michael. *Atlas of Nazi Germany*. New York, New York: Macmillan Publishing Company, 1987.

Freeman, Roger A. *The Mighty Eighth. A History of the U.S. 8th Army Air Force*. Garden City, New York: Doubleday, 1970.

Giblin, James Cross. *The Life and Death of Adolph Hitler*. New York, New York: Clarion, 2002.

Gilbert, Martin. *The Second World War. A Complete History*. New York: Henry Holt and company, 1989

Gill, Anton. *The Great Escape*. London, England: Headline Book Publishing, 2001.

Gospel Principles, Church of Jesus Christ of Latter-day Saints. Salt Lake City, Utah: Intellectual Reserve, Inc., 2009.

Hammel, Eric. *Air War Europa Chronology. America's Air War Against Germany in Europe and North Africa 1942-1945*. Pacifica, California: Pacifica Press, 1994.

Harding, Stephen. *Great Liners at War*. Osceola, Wisconsin: Motorbooks, International, 1997.

Hatch, Gardner N., and John S. Edwards. *American Ex-POW*; Volume IV. Paduca, Pennsylvania: Turner Publishing Co., 2000.

Hitler, Adolf. *Mein Kampf*; Translated by Ralph Manheim. Boston, Massachusetts: Houghton Mifflin, 1925, 1971.

Huntzinger, Edward J. *The 388th at War*. San Angelo, Texas: Newsfoto Yearbooks, 1979.

Jenson, Andrew. *Encyclopedic History of the Church*. Salt Lake City, Utah: Church of Jesus Christ of Latter-day Saints, 1930.

Kaufman, Mozart. *Fighter Pilot. Aleutians to Normandy to Stalag Luft 1*. St. Simons Island, Georgia: M & A Kaufmann Publishing, 1993.

Keegan, John. *The Second World War*. New York, New York: Viking, 1989.

McCullough, David. *Truman*. New York, New York: Simon & Schuster, 1992.

Lovell, Travis, *Ririe – You Just Thought You Were Lost*, Provo, Utah, Travis Lovell, 2003

Miller, Donald L. *Masters of the Air*. New York, New York: Simon & Schuster, 2006.

Newell, Gordon. *Ocean Liners of the 20th Century*. New York, New York: Bonanza Books, 1963.

Nichol, John, and Tony Rennell. *The Last Escape*. New York, New York: Penguin Books, 2002.

Neillands, Robin. *The Bomber War: The Allied Offensive Against Nazi Germany*, Overlook Press, New York, 2001.

Parker, Ray. *Down in Flames*. Minneapolis, Minnesota: Mill City Press, 2009.

Richard, Oscar G. III. *Kriegie. An American POW in Germany*. Baton Rouge, Louisiana: Louisiana State University Press, 2000.

Rolf, David. *Prisoners of the Reich. Germany's Captives 1939-1945*. London, England: Leo Cooper Ltd, 1988.

Simmons, Kenneth W. *Kriegie*. Nashville, Tennessee: Thomas Nelson Publishers, 1960.

Spiller, Harry. *Prisoners of Nazis, Accounts by American POWs in World War II*. Jefferson, North Carolina: McFarland & Company, 1998.

Spinelli, Angelo M., and Lewis H. Carolson. *Life Behind Barbed Wire. The Secret World War II Photographs of Prisoners of War*, Bronx, New York: Fordham University Press, 2004.

Smith, Joseph, Jr. *History of the Church*, Salt Lake City, Utah: Shadow Mountain, 1991.

Wheal, Elizabeth-Anne, Stephen Pope and James Taylor. *A Dictionary of the Second World War*. New York, New York: Peter Bedrick Books, 1989.

Zemke, Hubert, and Roger A. Freeman. *Zemke's Stalag*. Washington, D.C.: Smithsonian Institution, 1991.

PUBLISHED PAPERS/ARTICLES/REPORTS

Breitman, Richard, and Norman J.W. Goda. "Hitler's Shadow: Nazi War Criminals, U.S. Intelligence, and the Cold War." Washington, D.C.: National Archives, 10 December 2010.

Hatton, Greg. "American Prisoners of War in Germany." Washington, D.C.: Military Intelligence Service War Department, 1 November 1945.

"Missing Air Crew Report, 3776." Washington, D.C.: U.S. Army Air Forces, 1943.

Sharp, Bert M. "Bring the Boys Home. Demobilization of the United States Armed Forces After World War II." PhD dss. Michigan State University, 1976.

Jaehn, Tomas. "Unlikely Harvesters: German Prisoners of War as Agricultural Workers in the Northwest," Helena, Montana: The Magazine of Western History, Vol. 50, No. 3, Autumn, 2000.

UNPUBLISHED MANUSCRIPTS

Call, Josiah. "David Ririe, Patriarchal Blessing." Salt Lake City, Utah: The Church of Jesus Christ of Latter-day Saints, 1936.

Filmore, Carma Ririe. "The Life Story of Carma Ririe Filmore," 1964.

Hoggan, Elizabeth Ririe. "The Life Story of David Ririe, 1860-1919."

Ririe, Clive Perry. "Notable Dates," 2001.
Ririe, David. *The Life Story of David Ririe*, 1920-, 2009.
Ririe, James A. "The Life Story of James A Ririe," 1964.
Ririe, James E. "Life Story of James E. Ririe."
Ririe, Max Henry. "My Life Story." 2009.
Ririe, Verna Fanny Perry. "History of Verna Fanny Perry Ririe." 1957.
Ririe, Wayne J. *Growing up in A Spud Town. Memories of Ririe, Idaho, 1933 to 1953*. 2003.
Ririe, Wayne J. *Times and Seasons of My Life*. 1997.

ORAL HISTORY TRANSCRIPTS

Ririe, Max H.
Ririe, MarDean Dalley

SELECTED WEBSITES CONSULTED

www.airpowermuseum.org
armyairforces.com
www.atomicmuseum.com
www.b24.net
www.behindbarbedwire.org
dadswar.com
www.fleetairarm.com
www.merkki.com
www.ww2timeline.info
www.wartimememories.co.uk
www.388bg.org
www.whitehouse.org
www.skylighters.org/special/cigcamps/cmplstrk.html
www.specialforcesroh.com
www.thedropzone.org
www.tailside.firelight.dynip.com
www.wikipedia.org

MAGAZINES, NEWSPAPERS AND JOURNALS CONSULTED

Church News (Utah)
Deseret News (Utah)
Post Register (Idaho)
Stars and Stripes
Salt Lake Tribune (Utah)

INDEX

A

Aachen 73
Aaronic Priesthood 17, 20, 218
"Abroad with Two Yanks" 202
"A child could have written ..." 100
ack-ack 3-4, 119
Adamcik 44
Allied Armed Forces 63
Ammon, Idaho 227
Anderson 115
Antelope Flats 11
Anoxia 43-44
appell 107, 114, 120, 181
Arado 234 jets 157
Arbeit Commandos 172
Ardennes-Alsace campaign 127
Ardmore Air Force Base 75, 77, 80, 85, 87
Army Air Corps 23-4, 36, 42, 71, 75, 85, 106, 136, 140, 224
Arrowhead Lake 52
Articles of Faith, 67
AT11 training planes 50
atomic bomb 141, 202, 221, 223
Augsburg, Germany 83
Austin, Texas 83-4
Automatic Flight Control Equipment (AFCE) 54
AWOL 168, 173, 180-2

B

B-17 bomber 2, 73, 77-8, 83, 87, 183-5, 222
B-24 Liberator bomber 110
ball 3, 73, 114-15
Baltic Sea 3-4, 105, 121, 136, 139, 141, 189
Banjo 15
barbed wire fences 106, 139, 161-2
Barber, Lieutenant 212
barbers 31, 70, 201
Barley Bashers 115
Barnes, Fred 71
Barnes, Florence 71
Barnes, Jeanne 71
Barnes, Joe 75
Barnes, Melba 71, 73, 75, 217-18

Barth, Germany 105, 155, 162, 164-7, 172, 180, 182, 185, 191, 195, 215
Barth airfield 154, 168, 183, 185
Batov, General Pavel 181
Bayer 44
BB3C Seagull seaplanes 211
BBC 153, 176
Beckham, Lieutenant 207
Belfast 91
Bennett, Lowell 117, 157-8, 178
Berchtesgaden, Germany 155
Berlin 74, 105, 118, 139, 149, 153-5, 158, 221
Betenson, F. H. 110
Bethlehem Sparrows Point Shipyard 205
bicycles 62, 92, 162-3, 166, 169, 174
Big Bear Lake 52
Big Red 39
Big Springs, Texas 49
Big Timers 115
birth 11, 217
Blackfoot, Idaho 218
Bogart, Humphrey 218
Bombardment Division, Third 2
Bomber Group, 388th 1-2
Bomber Group, 96th 2
bombing, precision 202
bombsight, Norden 53-4, 66, 78, 80, 82-3
Book of Mormon 111-12
Borisov, General V. A. 167-8, 179, 182-83
Boyes, George 217
bread 97, 150-1, 186, 191, 205, 208
Breslau, Germany 172
Brigham Young University 28, 227, 229
Bright, Ruth 70
British Bomber Command 59
British bombers 74-5, 117, 155
British POWs 107, 181
Brooks, Lieutenant 65
Brown, Elsworth 41, 59-61, 69, 71, 217
Brown, Jacob R. 164, 177
Brunswick, Germany 83
Buck, Frank 65
Bulge, Battle of 127, 149
bull 17, 56, 70
Bunde, Herbert 114
Bush, Alf 218
Bush, Dean 218
Bush, Vivian 219
Byerly, Colonel Jean R. 109, 114-15, 125-6, 171
Byrnes, U. S. Secretary of State Jimmy 197

C

C3-S-A3 troop transporter 205
Call, Josiah 21

camp cooks 128
camp doctor 166
Camp Hahn 60
camp library 113
Camp Lucky Strike 185, 187-8, 194, 196, 200, 202
Camp Patrick Henry 211-12, 214
Camp Rupert 219-20
Campo Imperatore Hotel 64
Canada 62, 87, 89, 171
candy bars 206, 208, 215
Cany-Barville, France 198, 200
Captain Bell 42
captivity 112, 135, 140, 142, 157
Carlsbad, New Mexico 66-7
Carson, Captain John Paul 109
Cassibile, Sicily 64
Castellano, General Guiseppe 63
catwalk 79
cave-ins 124-5
Central Security Committee 123
Champs de Elysses 200
Chandler, Arizona 49
Challenger, The 28
Chaing Kai-shek 75
Charlson, Father Michael 145
Chicago 16, 215
chilblains 108, 121
children 158, 164, 187, 214, 224
Chinese Red Cross 150
chocolate 128, 130, 188
chorus girls 63
Christ, Jesus 67
Christmas 128, 131, 135
Christensen, George 24
Christensen, Oswald 22
Churchill, Winston 74-5, 77, 120, 168, 176
Church of Jesus Christ of LDS, 14
cigarettes 98-9, 116, 128, 150, 158, 187-8
Cincinnati, Ohio 214
Clark, Idaho 17
Clark, Newell (Stan) 28-30
"Clear the runway, you Irishmen." 90
Clifton, Bert 171-2
CO (Commanding Officer) 71, 84, 179, 193, 205
coffee addiction, POW's 128
Cologne, France 185-86
Colorado 173, 215-16
Combat Wings, three and four 2
Commander Brown 158
Conant Valley 11
confinement, solitary 96, 99, 120-1, 126, 147
Cooper, Gary 201
Cooper, Stanley 215
Cooke, Harold L. 173-5, 178
cookhouse 129
cooler 120, 126, 147-8

copilot 1, 75, 78, 136, 185
Coppinger, John M. 173
Council Bluffs, Iowa 215
crew, bomber 93, 143
crewmen, missing 83
cursing 15, 52, 158
Curtiss, Chuck 194

D

Dammtor Gate 105
D-Day 201, 205
Danish Peninsula 3
Davis, Dayle 61
Deacon's Quorum 17
De Gaulle, General 198
demerits 46
Demobilization Plan 195
Demming, New Mexico 49
Denver 173, 193, 215-16
Denver and Rio Grande Railroad 216
digging 124-6, 148
dimes 37, 45
doctors 14, 35-6, 38, 58, 167, 197
Douglas A-26 Invader 196
Douglas, Captain 193, 195, 200-201
Dowler, Lieutenant 185
Dresden, Germany 149, 153
drills, close order 38, 72-3, 191, 201
Drummond, Warrant Officer R. R. 118
Dublin, Ireland 90
Duisburg, Germany 185
Dulag Luft 99-100, 185, 189

E

Eastern War Time (EWT) 153
Eighth Air Force 1-2, 92-3, 171, 183
89th Infantry Division 187
Eisenhower, General 155, 169, 192, 198
Elbe River 155, 167
Elegantes 115
Ecker Hill 186
Ellis, William L. 2, 4-6, 75, 78-79, 81, 84-5, 88-90, 101-2, 113, 173
Ely, Edmund J. 2-7, 75, 77, 80-3, 85, 88-89, 90, 100, 166, 191, 193
England 1, 71, 87-8, 91-2, 136, 168, 183, 195-6, 221
Enola Gay 223
error, circle of 51-2, 55, 64, 67
Escape Committee 124, 146
escape hatch 3, 5
European Theater of Operations (ETO) 192
Expectant Father, The 7, 136-8, 143
Excelsior, SS 205-206, 211

ONE-MISSION MAN

F

Faith   21, 67, 96, 145, 229
Farmers Equity Elevator Company   10
Farmers Friend Canal Company   10
Farmers Friend canal   14
farm, dry   11, 13, 15, 19, 134
Fast Sunday   61
Fat Man   223
Fecamp, France   203
ferrets   145-7
Field, Lieutenant   53-6, 67
Filmore, Carma Ririe   18, 23, 26, 95-6, 135, 203, 213, 218
First National Bank of Ririe   10
Flak School   156, 158, 162
Flinch   114
Flying Fortress   77-78, 87
Focke-Wulf aircraft   2, 71
Fort Dodge, Iowa   215
Fort Worth, Texas   84
40 by 8   214
Foster, Lieutenant   42
Freeman, Cleo   24
Freeman, Josephine   24
funeral procession   21, 93
Fugo balloons   130
FW 190 fighter plane   4

G

Gabreski, Colonel F. "Gabby"   126-7, 194
Gardner, Jay   25
gas masks   41-2
gasoline tank   82
Geary, Jim   180-81
Geneva Conventions   109
German guards   147, 158, 171
German guards, former   167
German POWs   186, 212, 219-20
Gershwin, George   194
GI Bill   225, 227
Gibson, Hoot   162
gigs   46, 53
Gillespie, Bernard J. "Doc"   182, 215
God   67, 110-11, 223
Goodbye Mr. Chips   207
"Good show, men."   125
"Goon's up"   124-5
Gordon Creek   11
Gotha   83
Grand Council of Fascism   59
Grand Island   87-8, 90, 136
Grand Junction, Colorado   216
Granite Creek   11, 16
Grass, *The Gay Caballero*   178

Greening, Colonel Charles Ross   109, 126
Greenland   88
Greifswald   172
Griego, Lieutenant   56
Gross, General William   183
Group 12   108, 203
guard towers   106, 124, 157, 161
guards, former   158, 177
guns   2-3, 5-6, 41, 62, 78, 161, 180, 219
gyro   54-5, 63

H

Hamblin, Beth   74, 217-18, 227
Hampton Roads, Virginia   207, 210-11
Hall, Norman   212
Harbaugh, Lieutenant   50, 53, 65
Hansen, J. Wiley   215
Harden, Fred   217
Harris, Blaine   110-11, 196, 199, 201-202
Harris, Marshal Arthur   74
Harris, Wendell   227
Has Beens   115
Heath, Lieutenant   30-2, 38, 42
Heileson, Joanne   227
Helendale, California   65
Herr Hauptman   108
High Holy Days   145
Hilton, James   207
Himmler, Heinrich   155
Hinky dinky parlez   45-6
Hiroshima, Japan   223
Hitler, Adolph   64, 92, 126, 149, 155-6, 158, 192, 219
Hollingshead, Lieutenant   60
Hollywood   96
Holy Ghost   67
horses   11-13, 59, 127, 162-3, 178, 214
hose   43, 129, 182
Hotel Louvais   200
hungry   127, 189-90
Huntington, West Virginia   214
House of Adolph   115

I

Iceland   89
Idaho Falls, Idaho   12, 26, 69, 218, 223
Idaho Falls LDS Temple   228
Improvement Era   219
index finger   114, 174
Inspector-General   40
Inspector Hawkshaw   50
Invalides   199
Iowa   63, 182, 215
Irwin, Ruth Joanne   61, 228

235

ONE-MISSION MAN

J

Jackson, Verna Elaine Ririe 131, 135, 218
Jascyk, Lieutenant 53
Jefferson County Fair 16
Jews 145
Jodl, Colonel General Gustaf 176
Johnson 115-16
Johnson, Bob 215
Johnson, Major Gerald 127
Ju 88 fighter planes 156
"Jump story" 119
Junkers aircraft 2
"Just aim over your toe" 83

K

Kassel, Germany 103
Kaye, Stubby 196
Ker, Gene 223-224
Ker, Myrtle 223-4
Kigallen, D. J. 118
Kimball, Spencer W. 131
Knettishall 1, 92-3
Koldewyn, Brother 60
Konev, General Ivan Stepanovich 149
Kornoely, Sergeant Leo K. 3, 75, 84
KP 40, 50, 129
Krauts 127, 158, 171-2
Kreising 83
kriegies 106, 112, 115, 119-20, 124, 128, 143, 162-3, 165, 168, 175
Kuestrin, Germany 153

L

Labrador, Goose Bay 88-9
Lake Como 155
Laon, France 186
Larson, Red 70
Laval, Pierre 192
Lee, General 200-201
Le Havre 117, 186-7, 193, 203, 205-6
Leipzig, Germany 98, 149, 185
Lincoln, Nebraska 215
Little Boy 15, 21, 26
Logan LDS Temple 85
Los Angeles 29, 41, 43, 69, 115, 225
Lost Horizon 207
Lovell, Ellen Radford 9
Lovell, Florence Lindsay 71
Lovell, George 25
Lovell, Harriet 72
Lovell, John Hyrum 130, 219
Lovell, Joseph H. 9
Lovell, Lois 60
Lovell, Perry 130
Lovell, Ray 71-2, 96, 227
Lovell, Rendon 25
Lovell, Velda Annie 131
Lubeck, Germany 149, 151
Luke Field 66
Ludwigshafen, Germany 74
Luftwaffe 99, 105
Lynchburg, Virginia 214

M

Major Nelander 168
Malerba, Mike 163
Manhattan Project 197
Makarov, Lieutenant 62
Manierre, Major Cyrus E. 154
Mannheim, Germany 74
Manwaring, Hyrum 22
"Many happy returns of the day." 147
Martin, Dr. Thomas L. 228-9
Mason, Sterling 23
Matheson, Rocky 101-2, 107, 110-12, 140, 149-50, 166-7, 171, 181, 189-92, 196, 198, 224
Mayfield, Lieutenant 197
McArthur, General 221
McDonald, D., Lieutenant 118
McGregor, Robert 110
Me 109 fighter plane 3, 171
Melchizedec Priesthood 23
Menzies, Lieutenant 65
Mercator charts 64
Mutual Improvement Association 17, 138
Middle Pacific (MidPac) 217
Milan, Italy 155
milk 19, 70, 88, 102, 145, 175, 189
Missouri, Battleship 225
Morgan, John "Red" 127
Mojave Desert 28, 49, 62
moles 124, 146, 148
Anaconda, Montana 28
Montgomery, General Bernard 50, 179, 183
morale charts 142, 151
Mormon 39, 67, 111-12
Moscow 176, 179, 182
Morris, Basil D. 182
Moss, Alma 224
Moss, Hyrum T. 15, 16
Moss, Jessie 223
Moss, Johnny 224
motor pool 169
movies 7, 73, 84, 91, 98, 189, 194, 201-2
MPs (military policemen) 157, 161, 166, 173-5, 178, 193
Muffoletto, Sergeant Vincent J. 5, 75, 189, 191, 193

Muller, Major Von 167
Munster, Germany 185
Murphy, Lieutenant 90
Mussolini, Benito 59, 64, 155
Mustang fighter planes 155
Mutual Improvement Association (MIA)
   17, 138

N

Nagasaki, Japan 223
Nagoya, Japan 202
navigator 1, 35, 37, 39, 75, 77-8, 81, 136
Navy 24-5, 54, 57, 71, 137, 225
Negroes 193
Neill, Sergeant Thomas 4, 75
Neuilly-sur-Seine, France 199-200
newssheet 117-18
Nicholes, Professor 228
night bombing 63
Norden bombsight 53-55, 63
Normandy 117
Normandy Base Section 200
North 1 Compound 107
Nutts Corner, North Ireland 90-1

O

Oberkommando der Wehrmacht 154
OD (Officer of the Day) 205-7
Odessa, Ukraine 161
Oder River 149
Office of Strategic Services (OSS) 154
Okinawa, Japan 213
Oklahoma 75, 77, 80, 82, 84-5, 87
Operation Gomorrah 59
Oregon Short Line Railroad 9
Ormond, Clyde 187
OSS (Office of Strategic Services) 154
oxygen masks 44, 53, 80

P

P-51 fighter plane 3, 171
Pachucos 43
Pacific 193, 195, 206, 221
Paris 142, 158, 176, 188, 192-3, 199-201
Parry, Jack 60
Patriarchal Blessing 8, 95
Patton, General George 50, 127, 191
Paul, Idaho 219
Paul's Valley 84-5, 88
Pearl Harbor 23
Peterson, Edward 28-29
Perkins 27, 39-40
Phase Training 87

Phillips, Oklahoma 82
Phoenix, Arizona 67
plane, burning 119
Planetarium, Hayden 225
Plexiglas bubble 79
Pocatello, Idaho 23, 26, 218
Poland 1, 60, 71, 138, 149, 164
Pont de Neuilly 199-200
Posen 1-3, 83, 138
Pottsdam, Germany 221
potatoes 33, 91, 97, 127, 130, 186, 208
Potato Cooperative 16
Powell, Rosie 222
Pow-Wow 117-18
POWs, liberated 168, 171, 188
Pratt, Frederick H. 2, 5-6, 75, 90, 94, 97, 166,
   169, 191, 193
Presque Isle, Maine 88
Prestwick, Scotland 90
Primary Organization 21, 67
Pringle, Frank G. 174-5, 190
Price, Dr. 11
Provisional Wing X 109, 155
Pruchten, Germany 174
Public Works Administration (PWA) 17
PX 31, 45, 188, 206, 212, 217

R

RAF (Royal Air Force) 92, 103, 188
Rainbow Center 199
Random Harvest 207
raking bombs 52
Rasmussen, W. N. 110-11
rattlesnake 15
Reading, Silvia 25-26
Recovered Allied Military Personnel 188
Rector, Fred 192
Red Army 149, 153, 155-7, 162, 173, 181
Red Cross 109, 121, 128, 130, 142, 148, 150,
   158, 161, 163, 165, 167, 184, 189-90,
   199
Reeves, Harold 56
Reimer 146-7, 162
Reims 176, 186, 189
Reserve Officer Training Corps (ROTC) 27
Rexburg, Idaho 222
Rice, Lieutenant 42, 46-7
Rich, Melvin J. 59-60, 63
Richmond, Virginia 214
Ricks College 16, 22-3, 25, 227-8
Rigby, Idaho 198, 220, 223, 226
Rigby Stake 21, 24, 198, 220
Ringer, Sergeant Harvey L. 4, 75
Ririe, Anne 14
Ririe, Clive 13, 24, 26, 57, 70, 95, 131, 134-5,
   213, 225

Ririe, David (grandfather) 9-10
Ririe, Edna 95
Ririe, James 9
Ririe, James A. 18, 26, 95, 130, 216, 218, 221
Ririe, James E. 9, 10-11, 14, 22-23, 57, 69-70, 74-75, 95, 131, 133, 135, 141, 175, 213, 218-19, 224
Ririe, James Irwin 228
Ririe, John Thomas 229
Ririe, Leah Ann Lovell 9, 20-21, 26
Ririe Garage 10
Ririe Grain Growers 16
Ririe High School 19, 227
Ririe Lions Club 16
Ririe, Idaho 10, 69
Ririe, Joseph 18, 221
Ririe, MarDean Dalley 30, 39, 85, 156, 158, 190, 217
Ririe, Marianne 229
Ririe, Max Henry 12-22, 70, 85, 131, 134-5, 213, 216
Ririe Mill and Elevator Company 10
Ririe, Parley 26
Ririe School Board 16
Ririe, Verna Fanny Perry 11, 15, 21, 69, 74, 95-96, 131, 151, 213, 218, 222
Ririe Ward 14, 19, 219
Ririe, Wayne J. 18, 26, 70, 130-31, 135, 218-19
Ritzema, William H. 174-5, 188-9, 191
Rives, Jake 44, 61
Rogers, Roy 59
Rokosoffski, Marshal 168
Roosevelt, Franklin 75, 77, 93, 130, 153, 168, 176
Rosh Hashanah 145
Rostock, Germany 3, 83, 96, 136
Roswell, New Mexico 49, 215
ROTC (Reserve Officer Training Corps) 27
Rouen, France 199
Rowan, Peggy 227
Rowan, Ruth 227
Royal Air Force (RAF) 92, 103, 188
Rugen, Germany 168
Ruhr Valley, Germany 185
Russian Army 149, 167, 176
Russian soldiers 163, 167, 174
Russell, Sergeant John M. 4, 75, 90, 189, 191, 193
Russian singers and dancers 178
Rutgers University 229
Ryder, Jack 51-5, 64-67, 78
Rzatkowski, Frank S. 164

S

sacrament 110-11, 140
Sacrament Meeting 21, 25, 60
Sacrament prayers 111
Sailors 43, 57, 206
Saint-Sylvain, France 187
Saint-Valery-en Caux, France 187
Salisbury, Bill 44
Salzburg, Carl 44
Salt Lake City, Utah 10, 26, 69-71, 74-5, 110, 186, 212, 218
Salt Lake LDS Temple 71
Sampson, Major Charles 49, 60
San Bernardino 28, 49, 59-61, 63, 228
San Diego, California 225
Santa Ana, California 25, 27-30, 40-1, 43, 47, 49-51, 60, 66, 71, 226
Sato Republic 64
SAO (Senior American Officer) 109, 118, 121, 126
SBO (Senior British officer) 118, 148, 168, 181
Scherer, Harold 62, 121
Schweinfurt, Germany 83
short-tempered instructor 51-55, 63
Scourbys, Sergeant Constantine G. 5, 75, 136, 141
Séance, The 116
secret radios, camp's 153
Segar, Elzie 124
Skousen Family 60
Senior American Officer see SAO
Shank, Sal 58
shavetail 45, 56, 91
sheep 9, 15-16, 102, 165
Shepherd Field 81
Sherman 64
Sherer, Oberst 129, 148
Shigemitsu, Mamoru 225
Shoo Shoo Baby 4
showers 90-1, 182, 191, 210, 213
Simkins, Nancy Ririe 229
Silva, Cadet 47, 64
Simmons, Lieutenant 66
simulators 58
Sixth Airborne Division 179
Smith, Francis P. 178, 193
Smitty 180-2
Snake River 11, 26, 70
Snell, Sam 46
Snyder, Jim 63
Soviet Army 157-8, 168
Spatz, General 168
Spicer, Colonel Henry Russell 120-1, 179, 192
Stalag Luft 105, 110, 118-21, 126-7, 129, 139-40, 142-3, 148-9, 155-6, 167-9, 177, 183, 194, 198, 224
Stalin, Josef 77, 176, 221
Stars and Stripes 192, 194
Stevens, Lieutenant 75, 77

Stimson. U. S. Secretary of Defense Henry 197, 202, 221
Stoke-on-Trent 91-2
Straslund, Germany 168-69
Strom, Al 110, 146-7, 164
Stone, Chief Justice Harlan F. 153
Summers, Thorland 226
Sunday School 60, 84, 110-11, 140, 171, 200, 220
Swager Motor Company 222
Swedish Red Cross 151
Swiss government 109

T

Tellez, Fernando 114
Tetonia, Idaho 227
Testimony Meeting 61
Texas State College for Women 85
The Bicycle 62
The Body 115
The Children's Friend 15
"The pain is exquisite, isn't it?" 122
Third Reich 113, 157
Tinian Island 221
Tirrell, Etta 70
Tokyo, Japan 202
Torgau, Germany 155
Transit Camp Air Force 99
Truman, Harry 10, 16-17, 21-2, 106, 153, 155, 176, 197, 202, 221, 221, 223
Tunnel Five 145-147
tunneling 123-4, 209-10
testimonies 21, 25, 61
tests 23, 35-7, 94

U

Ucon Grist Mill 10
United Nations Conference 155
University of Utah 27, 73-7, 227
U.S. 3rd Army 126
U.S. 7th Army 50, 59
U. S. 7th Airborne Corps 181
U.S. 8th Army 71, 83
Utah, Mona 28
Utah State Fair Grounds, 70-72

V

V for Victory sign 120
Valera, Henry 210
Vaslov, Andrei 181
Vichy Regime 192
Victorville Army Air Base 49-51

Victorville Branch 60
Victorville, California 56, 58-9, 63, 69, 71, 228
Virginia 207, 211, 213-14
Vistula River 149
Voice, The 209

W

Waffen-SS commandos 64
Wahlen, Gwen 61
Walker, Lieutenant 65
walking tour 173, 177, 180, 182
Wall Lake, Iowa 215
War Department 25, 95, 138, 141
Ward Teaching 20
Warnstedt, Von 129, 148, 154-6
"wasser, wasser, wasser" 102
Wehrkeise 1
Wehrmacht 192
Weir, Colonel Ginger 148, 168, 181-82
West Coast Training Command 43
West Point 207
whale 209
Wheels 157, 173
Where is my Wandering Boy Tonight? 131
Willow Creek 85
Wismar 167-8, 179
Women's Air Corps (WACs) 41, 46, 50, 211
woolen underwear 87
Wyoming, Star Valley 26

Y

Yellowstone National Park 218, 220
YMCA 109, 113-15
Yom Kippur 145
"You pull the chine." 90
"You shall return home rejoicing." 22, 95
Young, Andrew 15
Young, Brigham 228
Yvetot, France 199

Z

Zemke, Colonel Hubert "Hub" 126-7, 151, 154-8, 161, 163-4, 167-9, 173, 176, 179, 181-3, 194
Zhovanik, Colonel T. D. 157, 167, 179
Zhukov, General Georgy Konstantinovich 149, 153
Zingst 174

ABOUT THE AUTHORS

David Ririe was born and raised in Ririe, Idaho. After leaving the U.S. Army Air Corps in 1945, he obtained a B.S. degree from Brigham Young University and doctoral degree from Rutgers University. After graduation he managed the LDS Church College farm in Hamilton, New Zealand. Eight years later he became Director of the Agricultural Extension Service in Monterey County for the University of California. As a soils, irrigation, and vegetable crop production consultant, he has advised Food Machinery International and The United Nations Development Project in Hungary, Yugoslavia, Bulgaria, Iraq, Jordan, Lebanon, Israel, Egypt, Saudi Arabia, Mexico, Venezuela, and Trinidad-Tobago.

An active member of the Church of Jesus Christ of Latter-day Saints, Ririe served as bishop three times and as a counselor in a stake presidency. He and his wife Jody served a mission in Egypt, Greece, and Cyprus. He is currently patriarch in the Monterey California Stake. He and Jody have five children—Jim, John, Nancy, Marianne and David—and live in Salinas, California.

Roger W. Nielsen is the author of five books, including "Writing Content, Mastering Magazine and Online Writing," and "Big Games Handbook, Games and Activities for Large Youth Groups." He currently resides in Idaho Falls, Idaho, with his wife Carolyn.

Carolyn Ririe Nielsen is a writer, editor and David Ririe's niece (daughter of Max and MarDean Ririe). She is the former Associate Editor of *Permanent Buildings* magazine, is married to Roger W. Nielsen, and is the mother of five children.